To my [?] [?]

"Big Al"

Brel

Merry Xmas 2005

By George

~ ~ ~ ~ ~

A Memoir By
Harris "Bud" George

Edited by Clarinda Harriss

BrickHouse Books, Inc.
2005

Requests for information should be addressed to

 BrickHouse Books, Inc.
306 Suffolk Road
Baltimore, Maryland 21218 USA

ISBN-13: 978-0-932616-78-X
ISBN-10: 0-932616-78-X

Front cover photos (counterclockwise from top):
James and Tassea George
Ted, Mary, and Beulah (Boo) George
Graduation from Officer Candidate School

Back cover photo:
Sisters, Mary and Boo, with me in the middle

Book design by Carmen M. Walsh
www.walshwriting.com

Printed in the United States of America

Dedicated to my parents, James and Tassea George

Acknowledgments

I would like to thank the people who have helped make this dream into a reality:

Clarinda Harriss, a professor of English at Towson University and long-time editor and director of BrickHouse Books, Inc., the oldest continuously publishing literary press in Maryland. Clarinda encouraged me by claiming to enjoy the pieces in all their stages and making suggestions she herself insisted were "schoolmarmish" about verb tenses. Her expert editorial guidance and dogged perseverance pushed me through this project. Her suggestions were *always* on the mark—the right sentence to end a story to give it impact, the perfect title to make the story come alive.

Carmen Walsh, an independent writer, editor, and book designer. Carmen's design creativity vivified my text. And her sense of what photos should be selected and how they should be edited and arranged took my book to another level, beyond my expectations.

Michelle Horner, my secretary of 16 years (whom I hired when she graduated from high school). Michelle receives my deepest gratitude for putting up with the six million changes I made in the stories. She always remained cheerful, diligent and never complained!

Jenifer, my beautiful and talented daughter. Jenifer scrupulously read through my manuscript and offered many crucial suggestions.

Contents

By George

Introduction

What started out many years ago as notes jotted down during my naval service has grown in time to be a glimpse into my life—from a childhood in the Greek community of Baltimore, through my Navy years, and finally to the challenges of practicing law. With brief detours to the streets of Athens, the harbors of Hong Kong and Manila, and the mountains of Kythera, I've tried to capture my fondest memories of a happy life punctuated by special people and amusing predicaments in which I found myself.

This compilation puts the stories and anecdotes I've told over the years into writing so that they aren't lost. (I've disguised some names and used poetic license a few times.) The experiences reflected in the following pages have such meaning to me that I long to share them with others.

Dad and the Golden Streets

My older brother Ted had always been the family historian. According to
him, Dad had been the fourth (and last) child of the third wife of my grandfather,
Theodoros Tzortzopoulos. Although Dad had been born on an island off the
southern coast of Greece, his village, Karava, was not within view of the azure
Aegean; instead, Karava was perched high on a mountain in the northern part of
Kythera.

Kythera's coastal villages had, throughout history, been vulnerable to pirates,
who sailed the eastern Mediterranean, attacking coastal towns and carrying off
Kytherians to be auctioned as slaves in African markets. The haunting remembrance
of these marauders still lives in the lore of Kytherian mothers who to this day warn
their children to be home before dark, or "the pirates will carry you away." To
avoid the raiders, Kytherians moved inland, into small villages scattered deep in the
mountains. Thus was Karava born.

Karava's village square was at the mountain's edge, where a romanesque church,
St. Charalampos, stood—behind and alongside of which were the small houses of
the villagers and several tiny stores. Looking out from the square, one could behold
a grand view of mountains and valleys. The mountains were black and brown with
narrow slivers of green. The ancient Greeks had long ago chopped down all of the
trees to build ships, and rain and wind had eroded the mountains, exposing the dark
rock underneath. The thin slices of green had been created when the Kytherians built
rock ledges along the mountainside to trap the dirt being washed down from above
and had then planted greenery. There were also green patches in the deep valleys
between the mountains where all the erosion had settled.

In contrast to Ireland's Emerald Isle, Kythera is the Black-Brown Isle, which
seems quite appropriate since Kytherian children had always been taught that after
God had made the earth in six days, He had some rocks left over, tossed them over
His shoulder, and they had become Kythera.

When Dad was four years old, his father died, and, three years later, Dad's
mother died. Dad's older brother, Peter, who was then eighteen, became father and
mother to his two younger sisters and brother. The family was poor, but Peter held
it together by working on farms and in olive tree groves. Dad attended the village
school for several years, but, when he was ten, he left school to tend sheep and help

Peter support the family. Dad's older sisters cooked and took care of the house, and Peter and Dad worked to earn money.

When Dad was fourteen, he went to live with a relative in Athens so that he could work in a factory manufacturing roof tiles. Dad dutifully sent most of his wages to Peter to help support the family. Peter decided that, when Dad reached sixteen, he should seek opportunity in America. With fifty American dollars (partly earned in the factory but mostly borrowed) and with promise of a job in New York City with an immigrant from Kythera, Dad came to Ellis Island.

Although Dad maintained his strong ties to his Greek heritage in New York City by socializing when he could with other Greek immigrants and regularly attending the Orthodox Church, he had one consuming obsession—to become a good citizen of America, his new country. Dad insisted upon being called James George instead of Dmitri Tzortzopoulos ("opoulos" in Greek, means "son of"). Dad's employment was as a busboy at an upscale restaurant owned by a prosperous Greek family whose grandfather had emigrated from Kythera many years before. Dad soon learned that the employees of the Hellespont Restaurant were divided into two classes—the waiters and chefs were German, and the kitchen workers and busboys were Greek. The great majority of Dad's earnings he sent to Peter on Kythera.

The Hellespont's majordomo was Mr. Fritz, a tall, imperious man who spoke English with a German accent. Mr. Fritz had been an officer in the German army, and he commanded the Hellespont staff along military lines. Each morning before the restaurant opened, Mr. Fritz would line up the entire staff, starting with the maitre d' and ending with the most junior kitchen janitor. Each employee was carefully inspected to ensure that he was absolutely cleanshaven, his hair neatly trimmed, and his clothes spotless. Mr. Fritz required each employee to hold out and turn over his hands so that the cleanliness of his fingernails could be checked. Any employee who did not meet Mr. Fritz's rigorous daily standards was required to leave the restaurant that day without pay. A couple of such days, and he would leave unemployed.

Dad loved having a job, and he worked hard at learning English. As time passed, Dad was promoted to junior waiter. Dad was likable and eager to please. One day he was informed that he was being promoted to become an assistant pastry chef. Mr. Fritz formally introduced Dad to Mr. Helmut, chief pastry chef, whose German accent was even more pronounced than Mr. Fritz's.

"Jim, you vill learn how to become a goot pastry chef by vatching Mr. Helmut vhenever he makes pastries. If you have questions, ask Mr. Helmut ven he is not busy," instructed Mr. Fritz.

Dad was delighted with the opportunity to learn how to make pastries, but Mr. Helmut had other ideas. Instead of instructing Dad, Mr. Helmut would go to extraordinary lengths to keep Dad from learning anything about pastries. As he was about to create a Hellespont specialty, Mr. Helmut would turn his body, blocking Dad's view, and Mr. Helmut's hands would begin to work feverishly. When Dad would try to peer around Mr. Helmut, he would move just enough to prevent Dad from seeing what was being done. It was apparent to Dad that Mr. Helmut had no desire to share his secrets, but Dad never complained to Mr. Fritz about Mr. Helmut's actions. Dad persisted in trying to learn how to make pastries. Eventually, Mr. Helmut was won over by Dad, who was quick to learn the art and science of pastrymaking—especially how to make delicious chocolate.

Immigrants from Kythera had established communities primarily in three American cities—Buffalo, New York; Youngstown, Ohio; and Baltimore, Maryland. Although Dad was happy in New York, he yearned to own his own business, and he decided to move to Baltimore where several of his Kytherian acquaintances had settled. Dad borrowed money from several friends, and, in partnership with a cousin, Gus, Dad opened a candy store and soda fountain as the first Greek immigrant businessman to settle in Towson, Maryland. Dad's Baltimore friends strongly advised against opening a store in Towson, which was bucolic compared to Baltimore City.

"Don't you know that just eight miles south of Towson on York Road is the bustling city of Baltimore? How can your store make any money in that small town in the middle of nothing but farms and orchards?"

Gus had previously worked in a soda fountain, and Dad knew chocolates. With their combined expertise, and with Dad's insisting upon Gus' meeting Mr. Fritz's standards of cleanliness, the Candy Kitchen, Towson's very first soda fountain, flourished. It was 1912.

Dad's homemade chocolates (thanks to Mr. Helmut's secrets) were an instant success in Towson. During the Easter season, customers besieged the Candy Kitchen to purchase from the large assortment of solid chocolate bunnies. The soda fountain became the vortex of Towson's young people and their parents. A young lawyer, J. Howard Murray, destined to become one of Baltimore County's two Circuit Court judges, courted his wife there.

But troubling news was coming from Kythera. Peter was joining the Greek army. For five hundred years the Muslim Turks had ruled the Christian Balkans, and, in 1912, Christian Macedonia was still under Turkish control. Greece, Bulgaria, and Serbia were joining forces to free Macedonia from the Turks (in what was later to be called "The First Balkan War"). Patriotic zeal ignited the Greeks of Baltimore, as it did all Greek immigrant communities in the United States. Hundreds of young Greek men made hasty arrangements to depart the United States to join the Greek army and drive the Turks out of Macedonia.

Dad's arrangements were simple: Gus would stay in America to run the Candy Kitchen (sending Dad's share of the profits to Dad's family on Kythera), and Dad would fight the Turks. With hardly any military training, Dad was ushered into the Greek army, invaded (what is now) southern Albania, and returned to Towson in early 1914 to find Gus, depressed, tired of the American work ethic, and eager to return to Kythera, where he could sleep late, work for a few hours in the morning, take an afternoon siesta, and meet his friends at the coffee house in the evening. There, he could argue politics, listen to Greek music, and play cards. In America, the Candy Kitchen was open for business seven days a week from 11:00 a.m. until 10:00 p.m., and there was no time for pleasure or relaxation. Besides, the Candy Kitchen's business had not been doing well, and Gus informed Dad that America was now requiring its citizens to pay taxes on the income they earned, which Gus thought a repugnant concept.

A deal was struck: Dad purchased Gus' half of the Candy Kitchen (for one-half of the profits to be earned during the next two years), and Gus elatedly returned to Kythera. Under Dad's ownership, the Candy Kitchen again prospered, and soon, despite continuing to send substantial monies to Peter on Kythera, Dad was accumulating enough capital to contemplate buying a property in Towson to which he could move the Candy Kitchen. Dad had become thoroughly Americanized. He wanted to stop paying rent and instead use his money to pay off a mortgage. One thing that young Greek immigrants in the early 1900s had brought with them from Greece was an inveterate distrust of banks. In Greece, if you deposited money into a bank, you might never see it again; if, on the other hand, you bought land, it would always be there. Dad wanted to buy land.

The Wescott family, longtime residents of Towson, owned the property on which Dad operated the Candy Kitchen. Mr. and Mrs. Wescott, having had no children of their own, had developed a deep affection for Dad, the immaculately clean and hard-working young man from Greece. When Dad had left Towson to fight the

Turks, the Wescotts had missed him as terribly as if their own son had gone to war. Mrs. Wescott had prayed for his safe return. When Dad returned to Towson, he had brought Mrs. Wescott a colorful Greek scarf, and she erupted into tears of gratitude and welcome.

The Wescotts were devastated when Dad first told them that he had begun thinking about moving the Candy Kitchen from their property. After a sleepless night, Mrs. Wescott told Dad that she had come up with a plan: the Wescotts would sell the Candy Kitchen property to Dad, and they would ensure that Dad's mortgage payments would be low enough to accommodate his budget.

When Dad went to Towson National Bank to borrow a down payment for the Wescotts, he was gratified to learn that, although he had no collateral, the bank would lend him the money he needed. The bankers remembered Dad from his earliest days in Towson, and they knew well his work habits and the type of business he had operated. His reputation was excellent, and the Wescotts and longtime customers of the Candy Kitchen were Dad's references. The loan papers were signed, and the immigrant orphan who had come to America at sixteen with fifty dollars in his pocket had now become a property owner.

Dad's love for America had by this time become a consuming passion as he realized the opportunities he had found, only in America. Had he stayed in Kythera, he would have been a peasant or a shepherd. Athens had offered him only meager wages in a factory. In America he had learned about chocolate—a treat totally unknown to him as a child on Kythera, sampled once or twice in Athens—and Gus had taught him how to operate a soda fountain (which Gus had learned only in America).

Dad loved the people he had met in America: the Wescotts, who had treated him as if he were their own son; the strangers in the bank, who had trusted him with the bank's money; and the other immigrants operating businesses in Towson—Tony Grazziano, Towson's barber; the Levys, who owned the hardware store; the Lees, from China, who ran the laundry; and the Goldbergs, who had the clothing store. All these immigrant families lived above their stores in Towson, just as Dad did. All had come to America because it was here that they could escape the limitations of their native lands, their humble birth, and their poverty.

When the time came for Dad to pay his first income taxes to the United States government, he paid not only what was due, but an additional amount, accompanied by a handwritten note:

Sir:

I enclose a check for my income taxes plus an additional amount as sincere thanks for being in this wonderful country.

Respectfully,

James T. George

Letter to Dmitri *

Dad read a second time the letter from his brother Peter.

Dearest Dmitri,

The news from Kythera is good. With the monies you have provided from America, your sisters were given adequate dowries, and they have both now married. Your older sister Eleni married Panayiotis Diakos, a Kytherian who settled several years ago in Australia, where he owns his own restaurant. They left for Australia last month. Stavroula married Michael Vretos, who owns a farm in the valley, which he is planning to sell so that he can come to America. He has a brother who is a furrier in Youngstown, Ohio.

But your cousin Meropi, whose parents died and who I have been raising for seven years, has caused me great anguish. I had arranged that she should marry Gregory Stavros. He is a nice man who, with his brother, runs the general store in Karava. But Meropi has always been the rebellious one. She complained that Gregory Stavros was too old, and she ran off with George Mavroyioryis, barely a year older than she. They went to St. Theodore, where they were secretly married. Meropi and George will soon be leaving Kythera to join his brother who owns a flower shop in Alexandria, Egypt.

The past Sunday, all of Karava celebrated the birthday of Aunt Antonia, who, at one hundred seven, is the oldest person in the village. Vain woman, she insists that she is only one hundred five, and that the baptismal certificate at St. Charalampos is incorrect. Of course, no one is alive who can contradict her. Anyway, whether one hundred seven or one hundred five, she is a remarkable woman.

You have made us all so very proud by your accomplishments in America. Truly, God has blessed that

* This letter, written in Greek, has been translated into English.

land. An orphan boy, you went to a country of foreigners. You learned their language. You became a citizen. You established your own business. Now, you even own a piece of land of America. Here, on Kythera, we talk a lot about the countries to which our families have immigrated. We talk about Africa, Australia and America.

We talk most about America. Some say that the country is so rich that the streets are paved with gold. I find this difficult to believe, but, with what you have been able to accomplish in so short a time, I don't know.

I do know, however, that Kythera is dying. The island is all rock, no soil for farms to produce food. The vast majority of our young people are leaving the island to find opportunity elsewhere. Who can blame them? If they stay, what can they become? One need look only at our own family—you (and soon your sister Stavroula will) have settled in America. Cousin Merope will be settling in Egypt, and your sister Eleni has already left for Australia. I alone remain in Kythera.

But, let's talk about you. I believe that the time has come for you to think about getting married. You need someone by your side, to love you, work with you and give you a family.

The Souris family left Karava some years ago and have established themselves in a village called Springfield, somewhere in the province of Missouri. The father had been a seaman in the British merchant marine and had spent most of his time at sea. I was present once when his wife was talking to a visiting monk at St. Charalampos. He had asked her how many children she had, and she answered: "I have only two children." Then, sounding very embarrassed, she volunteered: "But my husband is a seaman and is not home very much."

One of the Souris children is named Anastasia. I understand that she is a lovely young lady, intelligent, hard working, and a devout Orthodox Christian. Additionally,

I understand that there is a lot of snow in Missouri. The Souris family is unhappy there and is planning to move to a warmer climate.

I have it taken upon myself to write to Mr. Souris, suggesting that you would visit the family in Missouri in order to meet his daughter and, further, that your intention is marriage. I of course wrote him what you have accomplished in your village of Towson. Recently, I received a letter from Mr. Souris, expressing approval of your forthcoming visit. He says Tassea is ready for marriage. Incidentally, you may remember Angelo Souris, who worked as a young man in the Stavros general store in Karava. Angelo is Tassea's uncle and now has his own general store in the country of Rhodesia in Africa.

I pray that this letter finds you healthy and happy. Each Sunday and Feast Day, I light a special candle for you in St. Charalampos, where our family's patriarchal chair awaits your visit.

God bless, keep and love you!

Peter

Mom's Imperatives

In my childhood in the Baltimore Greek community, almost all of my uncles and aunts owned soda fountains. All had emigrated from the island of Kythera, as had my parents, and, whether actually related or not, they were affectionately called *thee-ah* ("Aunt") or *thee-oh* ("Uncle"). As a small child, I would accompany my parents as they visited their friends, which I didn't mind because I knew that, sometime during the visit, I would be asked whether I would like to have a gigantic, hot chocolate fudge sundae, topped with fruit, nuts and whipped cream.

From my earliest recollection, Mom had inculcated me with the one immutable social imperative—a well-mannered Greek child does *not*, under *any* circumstance, accept any such offer unless and until it has been made at least three times. Accordingly, my aunt, sometime during the visit, would ask, "Buddy, how would you like a banana split with chocolate and strawberry ice cream, topped with hot fudge and nuts?"

I would dutifully answer, "No, thank you, *thee-ah*." (#1)

My aunt inevitably persisted: "Oh, come on now, Buddy, you *really would* like a chocolate nut banana split, wouldn't you?"

My tone unchanged, I would, rote-like, say "No, thank you, *thee-ah*." (#2)

Undaunted, my aunt would invariably forge ahead, "Buddy, I *know* that you love chocolate nut banana splits, and I'm going to make you one, okay?" (#3)

With the standard third request, and, trying to sound reluctant, I would say, "Well, *thee-ah*, if you insist...."

This was the social regimen for years as I was growing up in the Greek community. However, on one occasion, a certain aunt, after asking me twice, *did not repeat her request a third time*.

I was stunned! In all my years as a child, this had never before happened to me. This was not in the script. My aunt had betrayed our ethnic tradition. Since she had not asked me a third time, I could not indifferently accept. When my parents and I left my aunt's soda fountain that evening, my parents noticed that my mood was sullen. My entire Baltimore Greek community value system had collapsed. Why didn't *thee-ah* ask me a third time? Had she simply forgotten, or had she deliberately not asked me a third time? Had the word gotten around the Greek soda fountain world that I was too easy a mark? That I would always say "yes" upon the third request? Would all of my aunts in the future not ask me a third time?

My fears were calmed somewhat on my family's next visit to another aunt's soda fountain. Following the first two "No thank you" responses, I was asked a third time and apathetically accepted. My confidence in the Greek community value system became substantially restored when, during my next two visits to other aunts and uncles, I was asked a third time and unenthusiastically acquiesced.

One evening, I learned that we were once again visiting the soda fountain aunt who had asked but twice. Warily, I awaited the inevitable. It seemed hours, but, finally, my aunt asked me, "Buddy, how about a chocolate marshmallow nut sundae?"

"No, thank you, *thee-ah*", came my Pavlovian (#1) response, but my Byzantine mind was racing ahead.

"Oh, come on, Buddy, I know that you love chocolate nut sundaes."

There it was! The second request—the gauntlet! I launched my missile. "No thank you, *thee-ah* (#2), but, if you ask me one more time, I will say 'yes'."

~ ~ ~ ~ ~

When I was in high school, Mom and Dad owned a soda fountain. At fifteen, I worked regularly on weekends behind the fountain. Sometimes, Mom would pay me for helping out. One weekend, Mom had hired Paul, another teenager, to work at the fountain. Paul was not experienced, but, with my tutoring, he learned the essentials. When the shop closed, Mom paid Paul eight dollars for working at the fountain. After Paul had left, Mom said, "Bud, thank you for working hard today and for helping Paul learn."

Mom held out a five-dollar bill to me.

I said, "You paid Paul eight dollars, and you're only offering me five dollars. I don't want it."

"You don't want the five dollars?"

"No, I don't want it."

Mom took back the five dollars. I was shocked. I had really wanted eight dollars, but I would have taken five if I had realized that that is all I could get. Mom did not offer the five dollars again. I suddenly realized Mom had taught me a lesson—namely, that my choice had not been between five dollars and eight dollars; it had been between five dollars and nothing.

Many years later, in 1960, I opened my first law office in Towson in the lower level of an old three-story office building. I had been a tenant for a couple of years and then learned that my building, along with several adjacent properties, had just been purchased by a large bank, which intended to raze the old buildings in order to erect a large office building. Tenants in my building began to move out as their leases expired, and my own lease was due to end in one month.

One afternoon, a well-dressed young man came to see me, and he said, "Mr. George, I am from the bank, which realizes that your lease is due to expire. The bank wants you to know that it has no present intention to tear down this building, that there is no need for you to move out when your lease expires, and that the bank will give you at least ninety days notice of your need to move. The bank would like you to remain a tenant."

I replied, "Well, I will stay on when my lease ends, but on one condition. My present rent is one hundred forty dollars per month, and I will stay only if the bank reduces my rent to seventy dollars per month."

The surprised young man asked why I expected my rent to be reduced by fifty percent, to which I responded, "If I move out, no new tenant is going to move in, print stationery, and install telephones, since it is uncertain as to how long he will be staying. If I move out, the bank's rent for this space will be zero; on the other hand, if I stay, the bank's interim rent is seventy dollars per month. The bank's choice is not between seventy dollars and one hundred forty dollars; it's between zero and seventy dollars."

The young man, taken aback, told me that he would report my offer to the bank's board and let me know their response. Less than a week later, he reappeared in my office and informed me that the bank would accept my offer, but only on one condition—namely, that I not tell any other tenant in the building of my rent reduction.

~ ~ ~ ~ ~

Mom had made it very clear that, after high school, I was to attend Johns Hopkins University in Baltimore so that I could live at home—which meant, of course, under her control!

"After all, your brother Ted graduated from Hopkins, your two sisters graduated from Goucher College, and *all* lived at home while attending college. That is what well-brought up Greek college students are supposed to do."

But I was determined to go to college away from home, free from Mom's control. I really wanted to go to Duke, but I had not mentioned it to Mom. Since I had rejected Hopkins, I believed that Mom would reject Duke. In 1946, it was easy to get into college. No financial fee was required to accompany an application to enter college. "Early Decision" had not even been conceived, and acceptance was virtually assured. I applied to six colleges, and, from time to time, I would tell my mother the responses, knowing that she would have flunked collegiate geography.

"Mom, I've been accepted at Stanford."

"Where is that?"

"In California."

"You are not going there. You won't even get home for Christmas."

"Mom, Rice University has approved my admission."

"Where is Rice University?"

"Texas."

"No, that's much too far away."

Finally, my acceptance from Duke arrived.

"Mom, I can go to Duke University."

"Where is that?"

"It's only about three hundred miles from Baltimore."

"That's where you are going, and I don't want to hear any argument about it."

~ ~ ~ ~ ~

While attending my first year of Maryland Law School in Baltimore, I lived with my parents in their walk-up apartment in Towson. Mom was relentless in trying to get me home early from parties or dates. One night, as I was creeping up the stairs around 3:00 a.m., a step creaked, and my mother's voice pierced the silence.

"What time is it?"

Instantly, I replied, "12:30."

At that very moment, the coocoo clock sounded.

"Coo - Coo!

Coo - Coo!

Coo - Coo!"

A day or so later, a handkerchief had mysteriously suffocated the coocoo.

Ten-Story Dad

When I was about seven years old, Mom and Dad owned a small restaurant and bar where the Candy Kitchen had been, and the family lived in the apartment upstairs. Each afternoon, when the newspaper was delivered inside our apartment door, my job was to take the newspaper to Dad, who was tending bar. One afternoon, as I entered the bar clutching the newspaper, I heard a customer, sitting on a barstool, say to Dad,

"My family has been in this country for a hundred years, and we've never had anybody go to college. You weren't even born in this country, and you already have two children in college. How come?"

"Maybe it's because I'm on *this* side of the bar, and you're on *that* side."

~ ~ ~ ~ ~

Some candidate for President of the United States had proposed what he called a "guaranteed income."

Eighty-year old Dad asked me, "I hear a lot about 'guaranteed income', but I don't know what it means."

"Well, it means that the government would pay you income whether you work or not."

"Humph! I came to this country sixty years too soon."

~ ~ ~ ~ ~

Mom's death had been very sudden. Her name was Anastasia (Greek for "resurrection"), and, coincidentally, she had died on Easter eve. Mom's passing was my family's first experience in dealing with death of a close family member. Days after the funeral, my sisters, Mary and Boo, visited Mom's grave often.

Each time either got ready to go to the cemetery, she would call Dad to accompany her, and he would. One day, a week or so after the funeral, when Boo asked Dad to go with her to the cemetery, Dad said he wasn't going. Boo was shocked.

"Dad, why not?"

"Boo, she's not there!"

~ ~ ~ ~ ~

I had not spoken with Dad, who was now eighty-eight, for a couple of days, and I telephoned him. As we chatted, I was about to ask him whether he could come to dinner that evening when—suddenly—Dad emitted a loud gasp! It sounded as if he was struggling to get his breath. I asked, "Dad, Dad, what's wrong?"

Despondently, Dad sobbed, "Stephanie died!"

"Stephanie? Stephanie who?"

"Stephanie on 'As The World Turns'."

~ ~ ~ ~ ~

When Dad had reached his middle eighties, his doctor often predicted Dad's imminent demise. Once while I was conducting a deposition, my secretary interrupted, "You just received a call from the hospital. Your father's dying."

I jumped up. The opposing attorney said, "Go. We'll resume the deposition another day."

When I arrived at the hospital, Ted, Mary and Boo were already in Dad's room. Dad seemed unconscious, his eyes were closed with his head turned on his pillow, and a doctor was holding a needle over Dad's arm.

"Dad's in a coma, and the doctor is trying to get a blood sample," Ted explained.

"I can't find a vein," the doctor murmured.

Ted called out, "Dad, make a fist."

Dad's eyes flicked open. He smiled, pulled himself up slightly in bed, and—suddenly—raised both arms, flexing his muscles.

When I returned to my office, my secretary asked, "Did your father die?"

"No. He just flexed his muscles."

On another occasion, I heeded a call that Dad was close to death. In the intensive care unit, Dad had tubes protruding from seemingly every orifice in his body. The doctor turned to my siblings and me,

"I've called you to the hospital because your father has had two heart attacks in the last two hours. His kidneys have ceased functioning. He is dying of uremic poisoning. I recommend that we pull out all tubes and let your father die in peace."

A sob escaped from Boo, who asked, "Doctor, if he were *your* father, would you pull all tubes?"

"Yes, without doubt."

With quiet resignation, Dad's four children agreed, "Pull the tubes."

Two months later, emerging from my office building with a client, I said: "Do you see that white-haired man who just dashed across the intersection to beat the yellow light? He's my father, and we pulled the tubes on him two months ago."

Still another time, I was told that Dad was in the hospital dying and that the Greek Orthodox priest had already been summoned. The priest arrived, administered holy unction, and began to chant some prayers softly. About five minutes later, Ted, Boo, Mary, and I all became aware of an echo-like sound to the priest's chants. We soon realized that Dad was softly chanting the prayers along with the priest. After a time, Dad was sitting up in bed and chanting louder than the priest. Indeed, Dad continued chanting even after the priest had departed.

One day, I asked Dad's doctor: "Aren't you embarrassed at having told us so many times that my father is dying?"

"Listen," the doctor retorted, "some people, you breathe on, and they die; others, you push off of a ten-story building, and they live. Your father is obviously a ten-story type."

Big Brother

The first child born to James and Tassea George was my brother Ted. Several years later, when Ted learned that his mother was going to have a baby, he was elated—he would have a "buddy" to play with. Unfortunately for Ted, the baby turned out to be my sister Mary, who did not qualify as a "buddy." However, in a couple of years, Ted learned that his mother was again pregnant. At last, he would get his "buddy" to play with. Again it was not to be, and my sister, Beulah, would not be that buddy. Seven years later when I was born, Ted was fifteen years old, and he was no longer looking for a buddy to play with. However, he had foreordained that my nickname would be "Buddy."

Ted was the quintessential teacher. Teaching was his chosen profession, and, perhaps through his example, both of his sisters also became teachers. Ted adored books, and he had a voracious appetite for reading, tackling four or five books at the same time. He became so proficient in the Greek language that he began to conduct classes in learning to speak and write Greek. He also started teaching Greek Orthodoxy to adult classes at the Church of the Annunciation in Baltimore.

I was Ted's first pupil. When I was seven, Ted said to me: "It's time for you to start collecting stamps. Come with me. We're going to Towson's Crown 5 and 10 Cent Store to buy you your first stamp album and some stamps."

Excitedly, I followed Ted to Crown, where he looked over several stamp albums and bought one. He then handed me a thick, loose-leaf book, each page of which was headed by a country's name and had affixed to it small, transparent packets containing different assortments of stamps from that country.

Crown's stamp department had a map of the world hanging on the wall. As I flipped the pages of the loose-leaf book, Ted would point to the country on the map from which the stamps had come. I selected the stamps of Poland. Ted bought me a packet of Polish stamps, and we returned to our apartment, where Ted removed the stamps from the packet, opened the album to Poland, and found the spaces onto which I was to attach the stamps. He pulled out a small hinge and showed me how to attach the hinge to a stamp to place it over the appropriate picture in the album. To this day, I remember my thrill, as a seven-year old, of looking at Poland on the map, picking up a Polish stamp, and realizing that I was holding between my fingers something that had come from as far away as Poland. It was 1938, and I had become a stamp collector.

During the ensuing year, Ted bought me other stamps and located for me on the map the countries from which they had come, as I hinged them into my album. I also remember the day a year later when I read the *Baltimore Sun's* headline, which screamed "Germany Invades Poland." I was excited. Collecting stamps had taught me that Germany and Poland were located next to each other. I had discovered world geography through Ted.

When I was fourteen, Ted gave me a book, *The Stories of Edgar Allan Poe.* I tried to read it, but the words were too big. I got a dictionary and tried looking up the words. It was no use. Poe used too many big words. I put the book aside. A year later, I gave it another try. This time—still with the dictionary's help—I fell in love with Poe's stories. So that I would not have to look up the same word twice, I began to write difficult ones down, with a short definition. From time to time, Ted would give me a verbal vocabulary test. Ted had taught me vocabulary.

Ted then gave me *The Complete Works of Guy de Maupassant.* Compared to Poe, de Maupassant was a snap—very short stories and easy to read. As a high school junior, I walked into English class one day. On each desk was a bunch of papers, face down. The teacher announced, "When you turn the papers over, you will find three short stories and two pages of questions about the stories. Read the stories and answer the questions, after which you may leave class."

I turned the papers over and was delighted to find that all three stories were by de Maupassant. Fortunately, I remembered the stories well. I went directly to the questions, filled in the answers, rose from my desk and virtually swaggered toward the teacher, who asked, "Bud, why are you leaving so soon?"

"I have read these stories before, I've answered the questions, and I am ready to leave class."

"You've read all three of these stories before?"

I said, "I have read all of de Maupassant's stories."

The teacher was dubious.

"Tell me some other stories by de Maupassant, please."

I rattled off the names of many other stories. The teacher dismissed me, and I still remember flying out of class on wings that Ted had given me.

Ted usually gave me books every Christmas and for my birthday. When I was nineteen, he gave me the *Rubiyat of Omar Khyam* and Kahlil Gibran's *The Prophet.* Again, Ted was uncovering new worlds for me—this time, eastern philosophers. My vocabulary list grew.

I remember the summer of 1941 when Ted was drafted into the army. Mom and Dad were concerned because Hitler was rolling through Europe, and danger was lurking in Ted's future. The Japanese attack on Pearl Harbor greatly increased our anxiety, but all we could do was wait—with Mom's and Dad's daily prayers in front of their bedroom icon of the "Virgin of the Myrtles," their patron saint from Kythera. The flickering light in front of the icon was kept lit twenty-four hours each day until Ted returned five years later.

Ted told me about his war experiences—the Army had made him part of an experimental unit, the mission of which was to sit directly behind the front lines, directing the Army Air Corps to attack enemy positions confronting our troops. Ted's first campaign in the Army was in the Aleutians, on the island on which the Japanese had fought to the last man. His unit must have proved worthwhile because the Army loaned Ted on special duty to the Navy, which took Ted to battles in the Marshall Islands and the Gilbert Islands. We were so thankful, when we learned that Ted was now on rest and relaxation in Hawaii, following those two campaigns. Perhaps, we thought, Ted was finished with the war and would soon be home.

However, the Navy assigned Ted on special duty to the Marines, whom Ted accompanied to the taking of Saipan and Tinian, two more ferocious battles. At last, Ted was home, one of sixteen survivors of the eighty-four men who had originally formed his FUBAR unit—an acronym for "fouled up beyond all recognition."

When Ted's children, Jim and Tessa, were growing up, I tried to repay Ted by teaching them geography. We went laboriously over the map of the world. Ultimately, they were able to recite, from memory, such tasks as to name each country along Africa's east coast, from the Suez Canal to Capetown. I always insisted that they learn how to spell the names of the countries we discussed. I remember how proud they were when each, at a young age, was able to spell "Czechoslovakia."

One day, an excited Jim came to me: "Uncle Bud, I'll bet that you can't guess what country I'm about to spell."

I took the bet. Jim then recited a sequence of letters that made no sense to me. I said, "Jim, that is not the name of any country."

"Yes it is. I just spelled 'Czechoslovakia' backwards."

Ted would today be proud to know that, on Tessa's last visit to my home, his ten-year old grandson spelled Czechoslovakia—frontwards.

In 1962, when Annunciation Church was renovating its educational annex, Ted and his best friend, George Mesologites, happened upon a collection of boxes of discards sitting in the rain. Ted noticed a box with about eight books, and he immediately picked up the box. George and he sought out Annunciation's priest, who said, "We can't use these anymore, and I'm throwing them away."

According to George, Ted replied, "You never throw books away. Rain or no rain, I'm going to save these books." He took out each book, and with a cloth wiped them dry. He then turned to the priest and said, "We need a library here."

From that moment forward, Ted became obsessed with collecting books for Annunciation's library. Everywhere he traveled, whether in New York, Kythera, or Washington, D.C., Ted would say, "Excuse me, I'll be right back." Ted would find a bookstore and buy a few books. Soon, Ted began receiving a small appropriation from the Parish Council, and he was successful in attracting generous donors to the library. Ted's zeal for books resulted in what is officially known today as the "Theodore J. George Annunciation Library," the largest Greek Orthodox parish library in the western hemisphere.

My childhood memories of Ted:
1. Being the life of the party—playing the piano (which he learned by ear without lessons) in our apartment, as sisters Mary and Boo and all their friends gathered around to sing along;
2. Winning a tango contest with sister Mary as his partner;
3. As my hero, returning home from World War II;
4. As my mentor and teacher.

The world was a much easier place for me because Ted was my big brother!

Kampus Kops

I was thrilled to learn that, in my first year of Duke law school, I had been assigned quarters in the Duke law cabins, which were located in a deeply wooded area on campus, far removed from the rest of the dormitories and classrooms. There were four cabins, each housing eight students in four double rooms and a shower/wash room. There was a large social hall in the middle of the four cabins.

We worked hard during our first year at Duke law school—contracts, torts, criminal law, but, after class, we had one advantage over the other law students who did not live in the cabins. We could party whenever we wanted to, and we were never bothered by the beleaguered campus cops, who reportedly did not even know of the cabins' existence in this remote part of the campus.

One Saturday night, five of us had gathered in the social hall. Someone had brought a keg of beer, and, as we were chatting quietly—all of the sudden—campus cops simultaneously entered the hall from all three of its entrance doors. Drinking on Duke campus in 1951 was strictly forbidden, and, there we were, all gathered in one large room with the tell-tale keg of—it could not be denied—beer!

The leader of the campus police had a triumphant smirk on his face as he approached one of my colleagues, who was holding a mug topped with a frothy head. "All right, I'm Major Ritter, and you boys will all be reported to the law school dean. Now—you, sir," Ritter held a pen over a pad of papers—"What is your name?"

"Fletcher Versus Rylands" came the quick reply.

"You don't have to give me your middle names," Major Ritter said.

The next name was also written down—"Adam V. Lindsell", and, soon thereafter, "Lawrence V. Fox". "Hadley V. Baxendale," added the fourth student, followed by "Oliver Wendell Holmes".

We all held our breath on the last name, but no cognitive light ignited Major Ritter's eyes. All five students were placed on report. On Monday morning, during contract law class, the professor was interrupted by a knock on the door. He was handed a note, at which he stared quizzically. Scratching his head, he said: "Well, this note is from the dean. He says—and I'm not kidding—that the following students are hereby reprimanded for drinking on campus: Fletcher Versus Rylands, Lawrence V. Fox, Adam V. Lindsell, Hadley V. Baxendale and—incredibly—Oliver Wendell Holmes."

Bob

I first met Bob when I transferred from Duke law school into the second year of Maryland law school. Seated next to each other, we became good friends, shared canned briefs, and studied for exams together. Bob had a quick mind and an infectious laugh.

One of our classmates in law school was an irksome fellow. Whenever a professor asked a question of the class, Tom would wave his hand feverishly in the air. However, whenever called upon, Tom's answers were consistently wrong. One day, Bob decided that the class had suffered enough. He pulled out a piece of blank paper, drew a black spot in the middle of it, folded the paper, wrote Tom's name on the outside and passed it to his neighbor, motioning toward Tom.

The black spot was passed from student to student until it reached Tom, who unfolded the paper, saw the black spot, and gave a quizzical look in the direction from which the spot had come. Bob was looking away, but, during the next break, as Bob approached Tom, Tom asked Bob if he knew what the black spot meant.

"Have you ever read *Treasure Island*?"

"No."

"The black spot means someone wants to kill you."

"Why would anyone want to kill me?"

"Perhaps because you're always volunteering to answer questions with invariably wrong answers. Someone in the class has snapped."

Thereafter, whenever Tom gave an answer, he would glance uneasily around him, trying to discover his would-be assassin. Soon, however, with every wrong answer, Tom would get three or four black spots. Eventually, Tom wised up. He would volunteer only when he really knew the correct answer.

~ ~ ~ ~ ~

In class, Bob was an intelligent note-taker. Seated to Bob's right was a student (later to become mayor of Baltimore city) who, instead of listening to the professor, would simply copy whatever Bob wrote down. Sometimes, when Bob would turn his notebook page, this student would turn Bob's page back to finish copying what Bob had written on the previous page. One day, he copied "Compose your own notes. Stop copying mine!"

~ ~ ~ ~ ~

When Bob had entered the University of Maryland, he asked to be housed in the Hispanic dormitory—just so that he could learn Spanish. The Spanish Bob learned was not Castilian; rather, it was street Spanish. This became evident during one of Mercantile Bank's annual County Bar Association boat rides down Chesapeake Bay. After hours of drinking and card playing, when the boat docked, many county lawyers would find themselves in some exotic night club in Baltimore city.

Very, very late one night, six Towson lawyers were grouped together close to a dance floor in the 2 O'clock Club on East Baltimore Street in Baltimore city: the notorious Block. Bob had learned that the rambunctious dancer was Spanish, and he shouted something in Spanish to her. She smiled and shouted in Spanish back to Bob. The dancer began focusing her ample attributes solely upon the Towson group.

Then, Bob shouted something else in Spanish. Instantly, the dancer's smile disappeared, and, somewhat angrily, she yelled something to a hostile-looking man (the size of a mastodon) who began moving toward us. Bob said softly, "Guys, we are a long way from Towson," and, leading the county contingent, started sidling toward the front door. Once outside, we raced to our automobiles and headed north.

~ ~ ~ ~ ~

Bob's law office always exuded militarism. On his wall hung an award plaque attached to which was a bayonet. His expert marksmanship had earned him another award mounted on his wall—a rifle and bayonet. Bob's desk held a third bayonet which he used as a letter opener.

One day a lovely lady was sitting in his law office while he talked on the phone. She seemed fascinated by his military paraphernalia. She picked up his bayonet letter opener. She left her chair to touch the end of a bayonet mounted on the wall of his office. Bob finished his phone call. "I really do have a lot of weapons in here, don't I?"

"I don't think of them as weapons. To me, they are all phallic symbols."
Bob responded, "Well, beauty is in the eye of the beholder."

~ ~ ~ ~ ~

Bob and I invariably ate lunch at the Towson House, one of the specialties of which was homemade soups. Our usual lunch consisted of soup, a sandwich, and a soft drink. Friday's feature was either New England or Manhattan clam chowder. I had difficulty remembering which chowder was red or white and would sometimes ask, "Is New England clam chowder red or white?"

Finally, it came to Bob, an ultra-conservative National Guard officer during the Cold War. "Bud, you know that Manhattan is loaded with liberals, commies and reds. New England was settled by puritans. Ergo, Manhattan chowder is always red, and New England puritan chowder is always white."

I never again had to ask which chowder was red or white.

Bar Banquet

I was a third year law student when Claude "Speed" Hanley invited me to be his guest at the Baltimore county bar association annual banquet at the Greenspring Inn. The banquet's speaker was to be none other than Maryland Governor Theodore R. McKeldon, well known as a splendid orator. Excitedly, I told Mom and Dad about the invitation, and I rented a tuxedo for the evening. Speed had informed me that the cocktail hour commenced at 6:00 p.m., dinner would be served at 7:30, and Governor McKeldon would speak at 9:00 p.m.

Although I arrived at the Greenspring before 6:00 p.m., I was surprised that the parking lot was already filled almost to capacity. Inside, the bar area was stacked two-deep with men, vying vigorously for the attention of the several bartenders. I found Speed, who was apparently in the midst of telling several attorneys what had just happened to him.

"Yesterday, Judge Gontrum appointed me to represent some low-life being held in the Towson Jail. I went down to the jail this afternoon to meet my new client and learned, to my surprise, that this hoodlum had utilized 'foot bail' to get himself out."

One of the attorneys asked, "Speed, what do you mean by 'foot bail'?"

"'Foot bail' means that he used his feet to go over the wall and escape."

"Speed," another attorney interjected, "No matter what others might say, I'm sure that there is no connection between the prisoner's having learned that *you* had been appointed to represent him at trial, and his desire to escape from jail before he ever went to trial."

The group, including Speed, erupted into laughter and dispersed. Speed and I began to circulate in the bar lounge.

The noise level was already high and raucous. Pre-dinner drinks were included in the price of the banquet, but once dinner had ended, drinks had to be paid for. Accordingly, Speed explained, attorneys were compelled to drink as much as they could *before* dinner. I ordered soda water with a lime so that it would appear that I was drinking gin and tonic. Not wanting to burden Speed, I wandered about. As I finished my second lime and soda, I looked at my watch. It was 8:15 p.m., and still attorneys were drinking in the lounge, conversing even more loudly than before. In fact, the din was now so loud that one had virtually to shout in order to be heard above the commotion. Several attorneys lurched about, with slurred speech and glassy eyes. Most were smoking cigarettes, and some were clenching cigars in their teeth.

It was almost 9:00 when the lights in the lounge flicked off and on, the signal to enter the dining room. The migration of attorneys from the lounge to the dining room was captivating to behold. Some staggered, some moved haltingly, and some were guided by friends. The round dining tables seated ten, and most attorneys had reserved tables for their friends and guests. Had the attorneys been completely sober, they would have been challenged to find their appropriate table; following three hours of open bar, the task was formidable.

I found Speed's table and my chair. At the head table, I recognized the smiling face of Governor McKeldon. Speed explained that others at the head table included judges of the county bench and officers of the bar association. The noise level remained high when a distinguished-looking, older gentleman unsteadily approached the head table microphone and asked everyone to be quiet for the invocation. The unruly mob ignored his request. The speaker continued to seek quiet, but to no avail. In fact, the turmoil increased. The older gentleman, frustrated, began to look less distinguished. In a surprisingly stentorian shout, he announced that dinner would not be served until there had been an invocation. Someone began rapping a gavel loudly on the head table, others at the head table began striking their empty wine glasses with their knives, producing staccato punctuation to the tumult, all to the utter indifference of the recalcitrant assemblage. The Greenspring Inn dining room was in pandemonium.

The frustrated speaker continued to yell, and the gavel continued to pound the table, until, very slowly, the group quieted. Slowly, a man seated at the head table struggled to stand erect, wavered for a moment, and then tottered to the microphone. He stood there for a moment, listing slightly to his left, and looked around, eyes half-closed, at the bedlam before him.

"That's a Towson lawyer, Franklin Pickering. This bunch of hedonists wouldn't have become so boisterous if the Association had stuck to its schedule. But, when you give lawyers three hours of free drinks, this is what you get," Speed explained to me, apologetically.

Mr. Pickering steadied himself and garbled something about God's blessings being bestowed upon the food we were about to eat, the attorneys who were about to eat it, and so forth. With a look of profound relief, he slid back into his chair, and tuxedoed waiters began to serve the salad course. Speed, a teetotaler, was the conversational catalyst for our entire table, since, except for me, he was the only one not at least somewhat inebriated.

The entrée of filet mignon and lobster tail, along with peas and a baked potato, was served. The distinguished-looking older man stood again at the head table and announced that, the hour being late, Governor McKeldon would deliver his speech while dessert was being served. Speed leaned over, "McKeldon is one smart cookie. He learned, early on, that quintessential secret for getting elected in Maryland— namely, never make the *Baltimore Sun* your enemy because it's printing while you're sleeping. In Baltimore city and the State of Maryland, which are ninety-nine percent controlled by Democrats, this Republican maverick has gotten himself elected Mayor of Baltimore and now Governor of Maryland. Democrats tolerate him because he gets only himself elected. No other Republican ever wins anything."

Governor McKeldon rose slowly at the head table. He stood upright, shoulders back, and strode to the microphone. I had heard the governor on the radio. He was eloquent. When Governor McKeldon spoke his first words, I realized that either he had had nothing alcoholic to drink, or he could hold his liquor miraculously well. In carefully measured and perfect diction, the governor proclaimed that, in ancient days, society had been ruled by the law of the jungle, with the strong dominating the weak, but that the legal profession had become the champion of the weak and the bulwark against injustice. Enunciating precisely each syllable of every word, the governor began virtually to sing his speech.

For a brief moment, the dining room had quieted. However, as the Governor's speech continued, the room grew noisier. Governor McKeldon paid no heed. He simply raised his voice one octave. All around the dining room, men began to mill about, visiting other tables, talking and laughing loudly. Unperturbed, the governor continued his soliloquy. At a table in front of me, I noticed a white-haired gentleman stagger to his feet. Very deliberately, he leaned over his table, selected a small roll of bread, and, to my dismay, suddenly heaved it at Governor McKeldon. Riotous laughter erupted at the thrower's table, and, soon, another man at the same table casually tossed a roll at the governor. Governor McKeldon, unfazed, continued his mellifluous oration, seemingly gaining strength from his ordeal.

I noticed that a number of peas were now lofting their way toward the governor. Attorneys were using spoons to catapult peas in his direction. At a table to my right, a young man, with massive shoulders, stood. Carefully, he picked up a roll, brought it up to his eye level, aiming at McKeldon, and, with a leg kick and full arm extension, he winged the roll at the Governor. With the missile rocketing toward his head, Governor McKeldon, at precisely the appropriate moment, deftly shifted his body ever so slightly to the left—never missing a syllable, and the roll sailed harmlessly past him.

I was impressed! No wonder this Republican champion has dominated Democratic Maryland. Finally, with the flourish of an exaggerated Scottish brogue, McKeldon finished his speech and sat down. Every man in the dining room stood, clapping loudly with sincere admiration for the survivor who had successfully passed the annual crucible of being guest speaker at the Baltimore county bar association annual banquet.

Naval Intelligence

I had recently passed the bar exam—I was now an attorney at law! Still, I sat with eight other graduates of college or professional schools, waiting to take a physical examination to determine whether I could be admitted to the U.S. Naval officers candidate school ("OCS") in Newport, Rhode Island.

It was extremely difficult to become a naval officer in 1953. Military conscription was in effect, and, ever since the Korean War had begun, college graduates and professionals had flooded into the Navy just to keep from being drafted into the Army. The Navy had become highly selective about the quality of men getting into the Navy judge advocate general. Only those attorneys who had successfully passed officer candidate school could qualify for such commissions.

But it was supremely difficult to get into OCS. I had been forewarned: even one cavity in your teeth would disqualify you from entering OCS. Accordingly, I had spent the previous two weeks at my dentist's office. My teeth were absolutely cavity-free. We sat there, the nine of us, just waiting. We had been instructed to report promptly at 0900 for physical exams. It was now almost 1100, and no one had started the process yet. I glanced at a bulletin board, and a small poster proclaimed

Lawyers!
Apply for Naval Intelligence.

At last, the door opened, and our physical exams began. Each was thorough, lasting more than an hour. I was ushered back into the same reception room in which the nine of us had waited. Only this time, I was alone. Where were the other eight?

Chief Petty Officer Warren entered the room.

"Congratulations, Mr. George, you have passed the physical. In fact, you are the *only* one of the nine applicants who passed."

"Wow," I said, "what knocked them out?"

"Well, four of them had cavities. One was overweight, one had curvature of the spine and I can't remember what flunked the others. Anyway, Mr. George, you passed and can enter OCS. What would you like to do in the Navy?" asked Chief Warren.

"Well, I see that poster on the board over there. I'm a lawyer, and I guess I should apply for naval intelligence."

"Oh, you can't get into naval intelligence," Warren shot back.

"Why not?" I asked.

"Because you're physically fit."

"Wait a minute! I *can't* get into naval intelligence because I *am* physically fit?"

"That's right. You *are* physically fit, and therefore you *must* be an unrestricted line officer."

"Do you mean that those guys who flunked their physical examinations today might get into naval intelligence, if they applied, because they are *not* physically fit?"

"Well....Yes, I guess," was Warren's reply.

Still a civilian, I said, "Now I understand why we never guessed that the Chinese Reds would pour across the Yalu River by the hundreds of thousands."

"Why is that?" Warren asked.

"Our naval intelligence is composed of the halt, the lame, and the blind!"

A Sweep of the Broom

Upon my arrival at officer candidate school in Newport, Rhode Island, it was my good fortune to befriend Matt Ford, who, I learned, had graduated from a military prep school before attending Tulane. Matt was quickly appointed a section leader, and I was assigned to his section. Each recruit was assigned a daily duty by his section leader. Some of these duties were bad, like scrubbing urinals, other duties were better, such as sweeping the deck. Matt assigned me to sweep down one-quarter of the barracks deck.

My sweep-down duty was considered posh, but it did have one irksome feature. In my area, there was a large radiator which sat so low to the deck that the head of my wide broom would not fit under the radiator. I had been given a small hand brush and dust pan, and I had to put my broom aside, get down on my knees and brush the dust under the radiator into the pan. I had been warned by Chief Betz that I must—every day—remove all the dust under the radiator. It was important for every recruit to perform all of his duties well. For infractions of the rules, recruits were given demerits. Fifty demerits meant that a recruit would be dismissed from officer candidate school, and he would have to finish out his Navy time as a seaman.

For the first week, I was punctilious in the performance of my sweep-down. Dutifully, I got down on my knees each day and swept any dust into my dust pan. Some days there didn't seem to be any dust, but I hand-brushed under the radiator anyway. One day I thought, it's ridiculous for me to get down on my knees every day. There's hardly any dust there. I decided to brush under the radiator every other day. This was taking a chance, because, each morning following the performance of recruits' duties, the barracks were inspected by Chief Betz, and I was not the chief's favorite recruit. Nevertheless, I started brushing under the radiator on alternate days. Following morning classes, I would rush back to my barracks to see if Chief Betz had noticed any dust.

Hah, I thought, I got away with it. No demerits. However, one day, as my broom approached the radiator, a sense of recklessness overcame me. I wonder if I could get away with brushing under the radiator every third day. Once again, I did not brush under the radiator, and, exactly as before, my omission was not noticed at inspection. A dangerous thought began to career inside my brain: I bet they don't inspect at all. Inspection is a big bluff to intimidate Navy officer candidates into blind obedience to orders.

I stopped sweeping under the radiator altogether. Each day, upon my return to barracks, I checked the bulletin board to see if I had been given demerits, and, each day, I became even more confident that there was, in fact, no inspection.

One day, I saw, neatly written in the thick layer of dust which had accumulated under the radiator,

George,

5 DEMERITS!

Betz

Reveille

It was disgusting. Every morning we were awakened at reveille by Chief Betz, screaming at the very top of his voice—over an electronically amplified loudspeaker system—"Reveille! Reveille! Get your asses out of the sack *now*. Right now, you no good SOB's" etc. Chief Betz's verbal abuse was gross and vividly descriptive. He had informed us that he was now chief of our universe, and he proudly displayed five gold hash marks on his sleeve for his twenty-year exemplary service in the U.S. Navy. He seemed to have an undisguised contempt for the ninety-day wonders at the officers candidate school in Newport, Rhode Island.

Chief Betz's job was to make U.S. Naval officers out of those recent college graduates in his charge. Plainly, he enjoyed watching the young officer candidates struggling from their bunks at 0500 each morning after having had their slumber pierced by his stentorian, vulgar blast. "Reveille, reveille, get your asses on the deck—pronto!"

One night, just before taps, Betz came to my bunk and said, "I've noticed that you are the last to get out of your sack every day. I have a great surprise for you tomorrow morning, George, but don't let it worry you out of getting your usual great night's sleep."

I wondered what sadistic plan he had crafted, but I soon fell off to sleep. It seemed like only five minutes later when I was being roughly shaken. Betz whispered, "George, get your ass out of that bunk *now*—and I mean *now*." I struggled out of my bunk, still half-asleep. Betz was grinning maniacally. I looked at the clock on the bulkhead. It was 0458.

"George," Betz whispered, "today, *you* are going to sound reveille, but George, *you* are not going to do it my way; you are going to do it in an educated way, and, in fact, George, if your reveille is not educated enough, you will get five hours extra rifle drill."

Roughly, he pushed me toward the loudspeaker. It was exactly 0500. "*Now* George. Right *now*. Sound reveille—but remember, do it in an educated way." Betz shoved the microphone into my hand. I took the microphone,

"Awake!
For morning in the bowl of night
Has flung the stone
That sent the stars to flight...."

For an instant, Chief Betz stood paralyzed, staring at me. Then with one hand, he snatched the microphone from me, while the other hand pushed me away, saying, "You crazy bastard."

"Reveille, reveille, get your asses out of the sack *now*," he yelled into the microphone.

I got five hours extra rifle drill anyway.

First Few Days Aboard Ship

Following graduation from officer candidates school and attendance at the school of naval justice in Newport, Rhode Island, I received orders to report to Commanding Officer, U.S.S. *Midway* (CVA-41) in Norfolk, Virginia.

On my third day aboard ship, dressed in a sport shirt and slacks, I was waiting for shore leave on a rather hot day, when up sauntered a short man, similarly dressed, who stuck out his hand, saying hesitantly, "Sokoloff is my name."

I smiled, clasped the newcomer's hand, and asked, "Well, what's your first name? I can't call you Sokoloff all the time."

"Norman" was the answer.

I said, "Okay, I'll call you Norm."

The next day, at morning quarters, although startled, I recovered in time to say, "Good morning, Commander Sokoloff," while rendering a snappy salute.

My First Impressions at Sea

The 45000 ton *Midway* a paradox—at times, seemingly a helpless steel hulk, rolling impotently in the midst of angry waves whipped into a frothy frenzy by a desperate wind; at other times, an intrepid giant steaming forward while relentless and monstrous waves were smashing ineffectually against the tremendous hull. An orange sun setting in a pink-purple sky. Small fish lunging free from the sea for a moment and swiftly disappearing again beneath the surface. Jet planes sitting serenely on the forward flight deck, then suddenly thrust ahead as if kicked by an invisible giant.

Walking along the hangar deck during darken ship drills, the only light an eerie florescent red. Seeing the gaunt planes, wings half-folded, looming in semi-darkness, like terrifying specters in a horrible nightmare.

Racing out to sea to avoid a hurricane roaring up from Florida. All over the ship, loose gear being secured and battened down. The sea getting rougher, and blobs of gray-black clouds beginning to cover the sky. The hurricane passing, and, in its aftermath, enormous swells rocking the ship incessantly.

Taking a motorboat on a moonlit night, the moonbeam continually reflecting from water to your eyes as the boat glides along the surface. Everywhere else, darkness.

Planes taking off from nearby carriers like bees leaving the hive and swarming. Sharp-nosed jets racing overhead.

The bosun's mate of the watch passing the word, "Testing, the 1MC: 1..., 2..., 3..., 4..., 5..., 5..., 4..., 2..., ...uh, 5..., 4..., 3..., 1..., uh... test complete." (1MC: electronically amplified loudspeaker system throughout the ship.)

Commander Davis

The executive department aboard the U.S.S. *Midway*, composed of nine officers and ninety-nine enlisted men, was charged with general administration of the ship—morale, discipline, personnel records, legal matters, mail, central files, training, public information, religion, the band, and even the well-stocked athletic gear locker. The department was headed by the executive officer, at least theoretically, but the exec's duties on the bridge and as second in command of the ship left little time to administer the executive department with all of its responsibilities.

The real power of the executive department resided in the administrative officer, LCDR Davis, a mustang (an officer who had originated his naval service as an enlisted man but who had worked his way up to being an officer). LCDR Davis had made the Navy his career, and he was determined to exact sixty seconds worth of distance-run for every minute in the life of any boot ensign reporting for duty aboard the U.S.S. *Midway*.

When I first reported aboard the *Midway*, I was interviewed by LCDR Davis. I still remember that, although the interview lasted twenty-five minutes, Davis never once smiled. He reminded me, on two occasions, that I was the executive department's boot ensign—the department's most junior officer.

My orders read that I had been assigned as the *Midway*'s assistant legal officer. I was informed that LTJG Conyers, the *Midway*'s current legal officer, had been assigned to shore duty. I was to have a short break-in period, following which I was to become the *Midway*'s legal officer.

I sensed that I was not going to be one of Davis' favorite junior officers, and I really didn't know why. Later I learned that Conyers was shifting from Navy Reserve to regular Navy, which had endeared him to Davis and facilitated Conyers' transfer from sea duty to shore duty.

"Mahogany Row" was the name given to the corridor along which were lined all of the offices of the executive department—the administrative office, the personnel office, the chaplain's office, the public information office, and the legal office. After my interview with Commander Davis, I met Conyers in the legal office, and we chatted for some time. I told Conyers that I had sensed that Davis did not take to me, and Conyers explained that perhaps Davis was concerned that, when Conyers left, the responsibility of the legal office aboard ship would fall to a boot ensign.

In my next several days, I met the other officers of the executive department, and we chatted amiably from time to time during the working day. Often, Commander Davis seemed to enter the legal office solely to see if I was busy working. If I was not at that precise moment occupied in some legal task, he would intone, in front of my enlisted staff, "Mr. George, since you have so much free time available, I will have to find some collateral duties to keep you fully occupied."

The large coffee urn of the executive department had always resided in Davis' office—because Davis drank coffee incessantly. It was quite a surprise when, one day, his yeomen carried his coffee urn into the legal office and placed it on a table behind my desk. I wondered why Davis would be separating himself from his beloved coffee. His motive soon became clear. His coming into the legal office, ostensibly to obtain a cup of coffee, was a pretext to see how busy I was keeping myself during the working day. One day, clutching an empty coffee cup, Davis entered the legal office, saw me perusing a magazine, and proclaimed, "Ensign George, you obviously have available free time from your duties as legal officer. Accordingly, I am assigning you collateral duty as the *Midway*'s movie officer."

In quick succession, I was appointed assistant information and education officer, boat officer, band officer and library officer. Commander Davis obviously considered it his divine commission to keep me fully occupied, both during and after the working day. When the *Midway* was in port, however, Davis often found that his handiwork had become his undoing. When he would ask legal office personnel, "Where is Ensign George?," my yeomen would answer variously; "In his capacity as movie officer, Ensign George is at the base movie station, trying to swap some of the movies we've already seen for ones we haven't," or "As band officer, Ensign George is over at the U.S.S. *Coral Sea*, trying to swap one of our two trombones for a clarinet."

One evening, I was summoned to Commander Davis' office at 1900. When I arrived, LT. Chris Warren, a gunnery officer, was already there. Davis spoke: "George, LT. Warren has just received emergency orders, and he will be flown off at dawn tomorrow. LT. Warren is custodian of the *Midway*'s welfare and recreation fund. I am appointing you as his replacement. Please sign these papers, assuming responsibility as custodian."

I looked at the papers which Davis handed me. One of them stated that I, as custodian, assumed responsibility for five thousand one hundred forty-six dollars worth of itemized athletic and recreational equipment. I scanned the list of equipment, looked at LT. Warren, and asked, "Where is the boxing ring?"

Warren answered, "I don't know."

I continued. "I've been onboard for six months, and I haven't seen any boxing ring. So far as I know, the *Midway* has two footballs and two basketballs. This inventory shows eight footballs and seven basketballs. LT. Warren, where is all of this gear?"

Staring straight ahead, Warren answered, "I don't know."

Looking directly at Davis, I said,

"Commander, I cannot assume responsibility for five thousand one hundred forty-six dollars worth of equipment and gear until we have a current inventory to determine precisely what is onboard and what is not onboard. If LT. Warren were going to be aboard for a few days, he and I could review this list and ascertain what's here, but I cannot sign this paper at this time stating that I am responsible for all of the equipment and gear on this inventory."

Commander Davis, glowering at me, bristled, but he realized that he could not order me to sign the papers. The next morning two things happened:

1. LT. Warren departed the *Midway*; and
2. the *Midway*'s supply officer and I formed an ad-hoc committee to locate the equipment and gear listed on the inventory of the U.S.S. *Midway* welfare and recreation fund.

The boxing ring was located at the bottom of the elevator shaft which transported planes from the hangar deck to the flight deck. Having been pummeled many times by the descending elevator, the crushed ring was useless, and it was deleted from the inventory. Similarly, eight footballs became two, and seven basketballs became three. In fact, the value of the assets of the welfare and recreation fund shrank from five thousand one hundred forty-six dollars to two thousand one hundred fourteen dollars. With an eyeballed inventory list of athletic equipment and gear, I dutifully signed the papers, accepting responsibility as custodian of the Halfway welfare and recreation fund three days after LT. Warren's departure from ship.

In the 1950s, junior officers were never permitted to see their performance reports which were composed by their department heads. I suspected that Commander Davis delighted in writing my report, but I wondered what he could truthfully say about me that was bad. I knew that I wasn't his favorite junior officer, but I believed he was an honest man.

One day, McDaniel, my leading petty officer, handed me a sealed envelope. He explained that Commander Davis' leading petty officer, Turner, had asked McDaniel, who painted oils in his spare time aboard ship, to teach him how to do oil paintings.

McDaniel had said that he would, but the price would be a copy of Harris George's last performance report. I ripped open the envelope and read my report which could be characterized by one sentence: *Ensign George is a bright officer, but his attitude epitomizes that of a reserve officer who is not committed, long-term, to doing things the regular Navy-way.*

During a bright, beautiful visitor's day, while the *Midway* was docked in Norfolk, in my capacity as the *Midway*'s assistant information and education officer, the ship's photographer and I were walking through the crowd of civilians. I noticed Commander Davis animatedly talking with a voluptuous young woman in very tight attire. I asked ship's photographer to take a picture of Commander Davis, who at the time was totally distracted. The next day, the picture showed Commander Davis staring lasciviously at the young lady's chest. I held that picture in my hands and fantasized his wife's reaction to it. Then I tore it in half and dumped it into the trash.

Bunkroom #9 Game Night

When I first reported aboard the U.S.S. *Midway*, I was assigned quarters in junior officers' bunkroom #9, which consisted of two large connecting spaces, in one of which were three double-decked bunks—the "sack space." The adjoining space had six desks arranged around the perimeter, leaving a large empty space in the middle. Although the accommodations were for six, only four ensigns were assigned to bunkroom #9. I met Don Bull, Willie Haynes, and Tim Tebo, my bunkroom mates.

Soon after my arrival, the *Midway* departed for a week's flight operations. That first cruise made me realize that my bunkroom 9 friends and I would have a lot of free time while the *Midway* was at sea. I also knew that in several months the *Midway* would be departing on its six-month cruise. When we returned to Norfolk, I busied myself accumulating various game paraphernalia. I bought a dartboard, two monopoly games, four decks of cards, poker chips, two electric football games, and a cribbage board.

The next time the *Midway* left port, I established my at-sea routine. I was in the legal office until 1600 and consistently chose the early wardroom dinner seating at 1700, which allowed me to attend the first officers' movie from 1800 to 2000.

Immediately upon the movie's conclusion, I sponsored and promoted—each night at sea—"bunkroom #9 game night," which featured a different tournament to be held in the center of the desked space—the "game room." For example, at the dart tournament, six officers each put up a ten dollar stake or entrance fee. The winner of the dart tournament would win a first place prize of sixty dollars.

On some nights, monopoly tournaments were held, in which four or eight officers put up, say, twenty dollars each. A round robin didn't end until there was only one winner, even if it required more than one night. The monopoly procedure also governed the electric football tournament. Other nights featured card game tournaments of poker, hearts, gin rummy, cribbage or casino. There was never a shortage of officers seeking to participate in the different nightly tournaments. Each Monday morning, I posted a list of the upcoming weekly tournaments in the legal office. Bunkroom #9 became the social epicenter of officers' country when the *Midway* was at sea.

Seaman Montemuro

Seaman Montemuro was a carefree comedian whose chief talent was impersonating people. While the ship was at sea, he discovered that he had already seen the movie scheduled for that evening. He called the movie booth, and, pretending that he was the command duty officer, told the movie booth personnel to submit a list of movies available to the officer of the deck. He then called the officer of the deck, said that he was the captain, and told the OOD to select a good movie for the evening.

On another occasion, he found himself standing in a long chow line. He noticed that he was in blues, whereas everyone in line ahead of him was in dungarees. So he went to a phone, called the quarterdeck, said he was the captain, and ordered the bosun to pass the word that only those in uniform of the day would be served chow. He then scurried back to the chow line and waited. Sure enough, the word was passed, and the line dissolved in all directions, amid much grumbling. Seaman Montemuro then swaggered to chow, the first to be served.

Montemuro found himself alone at the ship's tailor shop, where he saw the captain's uniform. He decided to see how he would look in it, put on the jacket and looked at himself in the mirror. Then he decided to see how it would feel to be saluted. Montemuro wrapped the uniform in a white sheet and carried it to an empty locker. He dropped by to see a friend of his who worked in the ship's laundry and there picked up an officer's shirt and tie. He returned to the locker where he put on the shirt, tie and uniform. He climbed the ladder and strutted up the hangar deck at dusk.

The eyes of most sailors go no farther than the four half-inch gold stripes on his sleeve, and Montemuro returned two salutes. However, the third sailor was a squared-away bosun's mate, who also happened to be a master-at-arms. The next place Montemuro found himself was behind bars in the ship's brig, wearing only his skivvies.

Montemuro appeared at Captain's mast where he received ten hours extra duty as punishment. The *Midway* had recently received a shipment of one hundred sixteen books for its newly-established ship's library. The books had been stacked in small piles on the deck of the library space. Montemuro's orders were simple—report to the library space at 2100, take the books from the deck and place them in the library shelves, alphabetically, by subject, from arithmetic to zoology. I went to the library space the next morning. All books had been removed from the deck and were now in the shelves. Unfortunately, *Advanced Geometry* was in the "A" section, *Basic Psychology* was in the "B" section, etc.

LTJG Tyler Jamison

Handsome Tyler Jamison always seemed to have his way with attractive women. "My engaging charm is the key that unlocks the bedroom door" was how LTJG Jamison modestly explained his consistent conquests. If there was one attractive female in a room full of naval officers, somehow the evening ended with her leaving with Jamison.

While at sea, Jamison ate gluttonous portions of the good food served in officers' wardroom, and he faithfully exercised in the gym room every day. He regularly participated in bunkroom 9 game night, and he slept soundly each night. Jamison delighted in regaling his fellow officers in exquisite detail with the suave tactics by which he captivated the many gorgeous women who had happened into his path.

One of his buddies, Phil Rankin, had had enough. As the *Midway* began a two-week cruise, Rankin arranged through a friend a bogus telegram to LTJG Jamison: Missed period. Worried. Contact me ASAP. Mary.

Jamison stared at the telegram. It had come from Norfolk. Jamison's brows furrowed. In 1954, there was no way for Jamison to contact Mary. In the ensuing days, friends began to notice that Jamison's voracious appetite had slackened. He participated no longer in bunkroom 9's game night. For the first time, he attended religious services aboard ship. Jamison also began to spend much more time in his stateroom. Rankin began to worry. Jamison had lost his *joie de vivre*. He seemed severely depressed. What if Jamison, now so distracted, screwed up while acting as officer of the deck? What if Jamison committed suicide?

Rankin knocked on Jamison's stateroom door. A bleary-eyed Jamison appeared, and Rankin entered. Once the door was closed, Rankin confessed that he had faked Mary's telegram. Jamison, furious, launched a punch, but Rankin, anticipating it, dodged and locked Jamison in a tight hold, repeatedly saying how sorry he was to have played such a horrendous trick on a good friend. A relieved Tyler Jamison finally stopped struggling, and, heeding Rankin's incessant stream of apology, smiled. The two friends shook hands. Thereafter, Jamison became much more reserved in his comments concerning his amorous adventures to his friends aboard ship.

Kowalski

Three yeomen were assigned to the legal office of the U.S.S. *Midway* when I first reported aboard in 1954. McDaniel was the leading petty officer, having served ten years in the Navy. Fox and Kowalski, who were both from Brooklyn, New York, completed the office staff, and, although they had not known each other prior to reporting aboard the *Midway*, they were remarkably similar. They were always comparing stories about their pre-Navy days, when they hung out on Brooklyn street corners with a group of their friends. Neither had graduated from high school, and each spoke quickly and in Brooklynese: "Dose papers are ready" and "Dese pencils are mine." Their reading material consisted solely of girlie magazines, and they looked only at the pictures. Most annoyingly, every other word out of their mouths was the four-letter "F" or "S" word. Nevertheless, Fox and Kowalski had high IQs, which is why they had been assigned as yeomen to the legal office.

LTJG Conyers, whom I was to replace, didn't mind the foul language or the bad English of Fox and Kowalski. He was totally focused on shortly leaving the *Midway* for shore duty. On the day after Conyers departed, I called my first office meeting. Pleasantly but firmly, I proclaimed new guidelines for the legal office:

1. There would be no more use of four-letter expletives.
2. "Dese," "dose," and "dems" would be replaced with "these," "those," and "they."

In the succeeding days, I learned that my new guidelines were being ignored. Foul language and "dese," "dose," and "dems" continued in rampant use in the *Midway* legal office.

I called a second office meeting and decreed that henceforth:

1. Anyone using a four-letter expletive would immediately pay a fifty cent fine.
2. Anyone using "dese," "dose," or "dems" would pay a twenty-five cent fine.
3. The monies would go into a magazine fund to pay for the legal office to subscribe to *Reader's Digest*.
4. To replace the language now banned, I would select a "word of the day," which would be posted—with definition and commentary—in the office. Each yeoman would be required to use that word in a sentence at least twice that day.

5. Fox and Kowalski should sign up for the Navy GED Program, which
   would allow them, while in the Navy, to earn the equivalent of a high
   school diploma. (I acknowledged that I could not compel them to do so,
   but, if they did, I would reward them with special privileges, such as extra
   liberty when the *Midway* was in a foreign port.)

At the conclusion of the meeting, I posted my first word of the day.
Persist: to continue stubbornly toward a positive result,
sometimes even despite initial failure.
If you want to be successful, you must persist. If at first you
don't succeed, try, try again.

All three yeomen came over to look at the posting. Kowalski seemed to linger longest.

The next day my second posting appeared:
Positive: confident of a successful result; self-assured.
A positive attitude does not guarantee that you will always
succeed, but, without it, you will more likely fail.

From the *Midway*'s library, I borrowed *Cyrano de Bergerac*, which I kept in the office. From time to time, I would read a passage aloud. Fox and Kowalski listened intently to each reading. They noticed that plays had relatively few words on each page. One day, Kowalski came to my desk and whispered that he would appreciate my telling him when I would be taking *Cyrano* back to the library. He would like to take it out, but he asked that I not tell Fox.

When our first *Reader's Digest* arrived, I used its word power section as the source for each word of the day. Fox and Kowalski, being bright young men, had no difficulty in mastering the word of the day game. I decided to make the game more challenging by selecting similar but confusing words—principal/principle, it's/its, prey/pray, commend/command. Fox and Kowalski enjoyed vying with each other in contriving unique sentences using the word of the day. Kowalski came up with "The principal of my high school could not command commendable principles," but Fox got the biggest laugh when he wrote, "It's said that Ensign George surprised Chaplain O'Toole when he told the good Chaplain that lawyers prey often."

After a month or so, they asked me to give them a vocabulary test. I did so, even though I had learned that they had bet as to who would achieve the higher score. At their insistence, I gave them tests every two weeks. No longer were expletives or "dese," "dems," and "dose" heard in the legal office. In time, Fox and Kowalski each passed the Navy's high school equivalency program. They took turns in borrowing the *Reader's Digest* to read some of the articles. Kowalski began to save some of them.

In the 1950s, a stenomask machine was used to make a record for court martials aboard ship. The yeoman, who would act as the court reporter, would repeat into the mask what was said or done at the court martial. What he spoke would be recorded and later would be typed by the yeoman. One day, a new stenomask machine arrived at the legal office. Fox and Kowalski were as excited as children on Christmas morning. Fox held the mask close to his mouth. "Testing, 1, 2, 3, 4, testing."

Kowalski grabbed the mask. "Hello, Joe, what do you know?" Kowalski handed me the mask. "Mr. George, please, sir, say something."

> "The moving finger writes and, having writ, moves on.
> Nor all your piety nor wit
> shall lure it back to cancel out half a line.
> Nor all your tears wash out a single word of it."

Kowalski asked, "Mr. George, can you give us more?"

> "If she love me, this believe,
> I would die ere she shall grieve.
> But, if she slight me when I woo,
> I can scorn and let her go.
> For if she be not for me,
> What care I for whom she be?"

That night I was walking by the legal office at 2300 and noticed that a light was on in the office. I opened the door and saw Kowalski sitting at his desk, playing back (and typing) what I had recited into the stenomask. He was embarrassed and stopped typing.

"Go for it, Kowalski," I said.

"Please, sir, don't tell Fox, " he said.

Thereafter, I brought books of poetry to the legal office, and, from time to time, I would read something aloud. Kowalski began to copy parts of poems he liked into a special notebook. One day in the legal office, Kowalski complained that, although he had tried, he simply could not do one of the tasks I had assigned to him. I asked,

"Is this the creature God made to have dominion over land and sea? How will the future reckon with this man?"

Without a word, Kowalski plunged anew into his task.

Years after I had left the Navy, I opened a formal-looking envelope with a Florida postmark and found an invitation to a graduation ceremony at Stetson University. Accompanying the invitation was a note:

> *Mr. George,*
>
> > *"A man's reach must exceed his grasp.*
> > *Else, what's a Heaven for?"*
>
> *I know that you will not be able to attend my graduation from Stetson University. Had our paths not crossed, I would probably be back on dat Brooklyn corner in front of da candy store.*
>
> *Following graduation, I will marry my college sweetheart, Helen Tate, a beauty of a gal (both outside and inside), who was Stetson's homecoming queen. I think Helen fell for me when I first said to her*
> > *"Is this the face that launched a thousand ships,*
> > *And burned the topless towers of Ilium?*
> > *Sweet Helen,*
> > *Make me immortal with a kiss."*
>
> *I owe to you—and to the U.S. Navy—my University degree and my clear shot at the brightest future a poor high school drop-out could ever have.*
>
> *Many, many thanks!*
> > *Kowalski*

The Last Night on Shore

It was the night before we were to leave Norfolk, Virginia, to begin our six-month cruise. At 2200 quarters, everyone was noisy and restless, and some were sad. Some tried to bolster themselves by false laughter, but almost everyone seemed ill at ease. Liberty expired at 2200, and I had the midwatch. Anyone returning during my watch was UA (an unauthorized absentee). I had the unpleasant task of having all such men escorted down to the master at-arms shack for booking.

There seemed to be almost an embarrassed excitement aboard the ship—of tension temporarily subdued, but threatening to explode any moment. The faces of last minute transfers from the ship were ecstatic with the thought of leaving, and, almost cheerfully, they requested permission to leave the ship. The new men reporting aboard tonight were awed by the size of the *Midway*, and some seemed thrilled at the prospect of a world cruise well beyond their civilian means.

The bulk of the crew—those who had previously sailed on the *Midway*—were neither cheerful nor awed. Most felt a profound emptiness within themselves, and their view of the world cruise was not pleasant, since most left wives, families and sweethearts ashore. The *Midway* seemed to have a shroud of sadness hanging above it, threatening to fall momentarily.

Mayport, Florida

The *Midway* pulled into Mayport, Florida to pick up its air group. The huge pier was filled with planes with their wings folded. During the next twenty-four hours, planes and equipment were loaded aboard, and flight personnel came aboard. Soon it was time to depart.

I was junior officer of the watch, and I was watching the birdmen saying goodbye to their wives and sweethearts. Right by the quarterdeck accommodation ladder, there was an intense mutual clutching. A flyboy ensign was kissing his wife/sweetheart goodbye for six months. They were holding each other so tightly that soon many sailors on the starboard side of the ship began to call out. The ensign and his wife/girlfriend swayed ever so slightly, and the white hats really began to howl. The 1MC blared, "All personnel must be back on the ship by 1200."

I was checking the clinch through my binoculars. It's only when they separated that I realized that the ensign's wife/girlfriend was especially attractive. She had dark hair, pulled back in a ponytail, big, moist, blue eyes, and a beautiful face. But when she started to walk back to her car, the sailors really let go. She was buxom yet narrow-waisted in a maroon jersey outfit, and her very tight skirt, made of some clingy material, hugged her hips so snugly that her slow walk seemed sensuous, sending the sailors into a raucous frenzy. My quartermaster, his binoculars focusing on her every move, announced solemnly, "If I had to leave her for six months, I'd go right now and throw myself off the fantail."

A Normal Day at Sea

In 1955, when the bridge received word that a man had fallen overboard, Navy protocol required the bridge:

1. to throw a float over the side of the ship which would immediately begin to emit smoke upon contact with water;
2. the bosun's mate of the watch would pass the word "man overboard" over the shipwide 1MC;
3. the 1JV talker (an enlisted man on the bridge who had a direct line to the fantail) would call the fantail watch to look for the man overboard and throw its own smoke float into the sea;
4. the junior officer of the watch on the bridge would race to the fantail where he would board a small boat launched by the fantail watch to rescue the man overboard.

I was junior officer of the watch when someone shouted "man overboard." The response on the bridge went by the book. The smoke float was tossed over the side of the ship from the bridge, the bosun's mate announced "man overboard" over the 1MC, and the 1JV talker notified the fantail. I was on my way to the fantail to jump into the boat.

However, the bridge's smoke float did not ignite. Back on the fantail, a poorly trained seaman watched the dummy float by, but he did not throw his smoke float into the sea. Instead, he called the bridge with "Request permission to throw over the smoke float." The 1JV talker on the bridge told the fantail "Wait one" and asked the officer of the deck for permission to throw the fantail smoke float into the sea. The officer of the deck shrieked, "Of course, throw off the damn smoke float." By the time the fantail seaman got the word and threw his smoke float over the side, the dummy was two miles aft of the ship.

Later that same day, while taking on ammunition from the U.S.S. *Fireduke*, five rounds of 20 mm ammunition went off. Everyone scurried for cover, figuring that the whole load of ammo was about to explode. Upon investigation, it turned out that an air group enlisted man, while de-arming one of the *Midway*'s planes, an AD Skyraider, had accidentally fired five rounds from the Skyraider's outboard cannon. No one was hurt, but there were now four holes in the smokestack of the U.S.S. *Midway*.

Equator Day

Whenever a U.S. Navy ship first crosses the equator, the ship's crew confronts "Equator Day." Shellbacks have crossed before, but Pollywogs have not. For three days prior to the ship's arrival at the equator, Neptunus Rex attempted to frazzle the nerves of the Pollywogs over the *Midway*'s 1MC: "Pollywogs are repugnant baggage, composed of bowery bums, drifters, vagrants and hobos, who have been pretending to be able seamen and mariners aboard the good ship *Midway*."

At last, the *Midway* reached latitude zero, and Equator Day commenced, the sun scorchingly hot directly overhead. Two thousand eight hundred thirteen Pollywogs— from commander down to seaman apprentice—clothed in undershirts and swimsuits, were confronted by three hundred fifty-one Shellbacks, led by Neptunus Rex and his royal party, most of whom were garbed in pirate costumes.

The ceremony began with the Pollywogs begging for mercy from Neptunus Rex, king of the raging main. Being refused mercy, the Pollywogs were pushed toward one of four Royal Babies, obese sailors whose huge bare bellies were smeared with a two-inch coat of black grease. The Pollywog's face was pushed hard into the black grease coating on the Royal Baby's belly. The Royal Dentist then splattered flour over the Pollywog's greased face, following which the Dentist squirted a combination of foul-tasting meat sauce and vinegar into each forcibly-opened Pollywog mouth.

As I waited in Pollywog line for my face to be rubbed into the Royal Baby's belly, I conceived a plan for getting even with Royal Baby. As my head was being shoved into the grease-laden belly, I suddenly put my hand in front of my face, filling my fingers with grease. Then, as my face was being forced into the greased belly, I rubbed and rotated my grease-filled fingers all over the Royal Baby's face. He sputtered and yelled, "Get this guy. He's a special case."

The next thing I knew I was grabbed by many hands and forced into a wrist and neck stock (a wooden yoke that loosely encircled your neck and locked your wrists at neck level). Then a repulsive liquid was again squirted into my mouth, and I, with both wrists still locked into the neck stock, was made to run a gauntlet of what seemed to be a hundred swatting paddles.

Just as I was running toward the water tank, I saw a burly Shellback wind up with his paddle, his face ecstatic at the prospect of clobbering me. I deliberately ran right into him, stock and all, and knocked him to the deck. I was grabbed and pushed up onto a platform, my buttocks still smarting. Here I found a fellow stock prisoner.

I released the latch on his stock, and he undid mine. With much bravado, we tossed our stocks over the side and into the Atlantic. I was forced into a chair, which turned over backwards into a hastily contrived pool. Actually, this turned out to be the only refreshing part of the ceremony. But the pleasantness was short-lived. As I scurried out of the pool, I saw that I had yet to run another long gauntlet, which I did in record time.

All during the ceremony, the blazing sun beat down relentlessly. It had been a miserable day, but at last I was a Shellback.

Capetown

On January 15, 1955, the *Midway* secured its lines to Duncan's Dock, Capetown, Union of South Africa. It had taken eighteen days for the *Midway* to sail the six thousand two hundred miles from Mayport to Capetown. The most striking feature as one entered Capetown's harbor was the sight of Table Mountain and its flanking peaks. Capetown being in the southern hemisphere made January 15 summertime.

The Grand Hotel was the center of all activities in the heart of the four-block long business district. On the second deck was an outdoor bar, above which was the restaurant. All the waiters seemed to be Indian—bright-eyed and intelligent-looking, garbed in white coats and black trousers. While in the bar of the Grand Hotel, I heard a short-pantsed, mustached Britisher with a Scottish accent say to a U.S. sailor: "Wherever there's trouble, there you'll find an Englishman."

The *Midway* had arrived on a Saturday, and I decided to try to locate a Greek Orthodox church, which I did, with the help of the Grand Hotel's concierge. The next morning, attired in my dress blues, I took a cab to the Greek church, which was small but pleasantly decorated. The church was extremely old-fashioned—men sat on the right, and women were seated on the left.

Since there had been so much advance publicity about the arrival of the *Midway*, following church services I was welcomed by several parishioners. Everyone wanted to know from what part of Greece my parents had come. Unfortunately, none of the parishioners had come from Kythera.

Two parishioners invited me to accompany them to their homes for lunch. I chose the one who had a young lady standing next to him. Her name was Sophia. Following lunch, I asked if anyone would like to visit the *Midway*. Both parents politely declined, but Sophia offered to accompany me. Sophia's automobile was a convertible, and you can imagine the reaction of my *Midway* friends when I introduced them to the attractive young lady whose convertible had brought me back to the ship.

The days were very hot in Capetown at that time of year, although sitting on the cocktail patio of the Grand Hotel proved cool enough. On Sunday, no liquor or beer was sold, and I had to content myself with a pleasant-tasting native drink called a Wade Special. Ice was scarce, but the waiter, after a three shilling coax, brought me a small bucket of ice. In the evening, powerful winds raced down from Table Mountain, kicking up dust, papers, and cinders.

Hundreds of people attended visitors day aboard the *Midway*. The after-brow was mobbed. When visiting hours were over, the Capetowners filed quietly off the ship. Still, many did not leave the dock, where they stood, and, seemingly for hours, just watched the normal activity on the ship. This incited some sailors standing on the starboard catwalks to call out and wave to some girl on the dock. Even after midnight, one could still hear the sailors calling out to the girls, and, some of the time, you would hear the girls call back. I overheard two sailors who were leaning on the rail of the catwalk: "Look how they just stand there and stare at you." The other sailor replied, "Yeah, but when they start tossing peanuts, that's when I'll begin to worry."

And so we left the city of Capetown, nestled between Table Mountain and Table Bay, the meeting place of the Atlantic and Indian Oceans. (Capetowners claimed that the Indian Ocean was warmer.) The whole Cape area was tremendously windy. Even on warm summer days, there were fifty-knot winds across the flight deck. All planes had to be secured with hurricane tie-downs. The white-capped sea was whipped incessantly by the ever-pressing wind.

As the *Midway* rounded the Cape of Good Hope, I was filled with it—good hope that what lay in store for me in the far east would be exciting, exotic and fun. At last we left the Atlantic behind and now plunged into the Indian Ocean.

Harold David Durkin *

Durkin, Harold David

3716104, Seaman, U.S.N.

Age: 22

Home - New York city

Unmarried

Religion - Protestant

Reported to the U.S.S. *Midway*, 23 November, 1954

Attended Virginia Polytechnic Institute

Civilian Employer - General Electric

On this date, 19 January, 1955, died on board of a heart attack.

---

* From the *Midway*'s log.

Colombo, Ceylon

As the *Midway* approached Colombo, small boats with multicolored triangular sails came to greet us. Since the *Midway* was too big to enter Colombo harbor, we anchored some distance outside the harbor. Tebo, a camera in hand, and I took a boat ride into fleet landing. Colombo harbor was teeming with little native boats, on which one man stood and flicked two oars with his wrists. Native oars and paddles were crudely made—a long sturdy pole, at the end of which a round metal disk is attached to push the water.

Tebo and I hopped a rickshaw to the Galleface Hotel, outside of which a snake charmer asked Tebo to take a picture of him. Tebo obliged and then started to walk away, whereupon the snake charmer began to yell, demanding one dollar for services rendered. Tebo again obliged, complaining that he had been conned. Sitting on the veranda of the Galleface Hotel, we looked out at the emerald green Indian Ocean and, facing it, the yellow Parliament House.

The hostess was an attractive Indian woman. Her white sari was trimmed in green, and was becomingly wrapped around her. Her eyebrows were arched, and her tan skin emphasized the white of her large brown eyes. Her long hair fell to the middle of her back. She wore white shell earrings, and her hair was pulled back tight behind her ears. When her red lips parted in a smile, they revealed straight white teeth. On her wrist, she wore an Indian bracelet and a modern wristwatch.

We found (or were found by) two educated Ceylonese who worked together. One had a small car, and the other acted as guide. They drove Tebo and me to a Buddhist temple. There, all the priests had shaved heads and wore golden robes. A priest, who spoke perfect English, guided us, barefoot, through the temple, which had one main room with a giant statue of a seated Buddha. The walls were decorated with paintings of adoring, bald disciples. A circular hall surrounded this room. Everywhere were statues of Buddha—reclining, on a mountain, in front of a lake, as well as scenes from Buddha's life. The striking thing about my visit there was my discovering the similarity between Buddha's life (born 600 B.C.) and Christ's: scenes depicted Buddha's temptation and his ascension. I understood that Buddhists believe in reincarnation, and that they worship the statue of Buddha, believing that Buddha is reincarnated there. It was permitted to take pictures of the statue of Buddha, but it was forbidden to have a person stand before the statue to have his picture taken.

Native goods sold were primarily wooden figures—elephants, lions, alligators, all made of ebony, rosewood, satin wood and coconut wood. Everyone reporting back to the *Midway*, whether enlisted or officer, had two or three elephants or tigers tucked under his arm. I was one of those officers.

The Raffles Hotel

Norfolk, Virginia in the early 1950s was not what one would call a wild town. The State limited the public sale of alcoholic beverages, and mixed drinks were not served in bars or restaurants. Indeed, one of the few places to get a mixed drink legally in the Norfolk area was at an officers' club.

Capital Airlines was the only airline which originated commercial flights out of the Norfolk metropolitan area. A number of its stewardesses were home-based in the Norfolk area. It was inevitable that the bachelor naval officers based in Norfolk would meet and date the Capital stewardesses living in Norfolk. The officers appreciated attractive, unmarried young women, and the stewardesses wanted access to the only social game in town—the officers' club! As stewardesses regularly flew out of Norfolk on their assigned flights, it was customary for Capital stewardesses based in other cities to stay overnight at the apartment of the stewardesses who had flown out of Norfolk that day. Similarly, as U.S. Navy ships left Norfolk on cruises, those ships were replaced by other U.S. Navy ships, each with a new complement of bachelor naval officers.

I had been dating one stewardess for about four months. One evening, she told me, "Bud, I won't be able to see you any more after Saturday." Utterly surprised, I asked why.

"Because the U.S.S. Missouri is coming into port on Sunday, and I'm engaged to marry the navigator. But I want you to meet Gail Dexter, a good stewardess friend of mine. She's really nice, and she's just been selected 'Miss Norfolk Destroyer Fleet'."

I was shocked but flexible. Gail and I began dating.

Since I had been stationed aboard the *Midway* for a number of months, I had accumulated the names and phone numbers of a number of stewardesses who were based in Norfolk. I also had recorded the same information about Capital stewardesses who, although based in Charleston, Charlotte and Philadelphia, overnighted from time to time in Norfolk.

News broke that the *Midway* had just received sailing orders to depart from Norfolk on a six-month cruise heading to the Pacific to join the Seventh Fleet. I was excited to be going to the Far East, but I also realized that I would be leaving what had been a very active social life in Norfolk. When the news reached my officer friends, I got several phone calls asking for my "little black book". After all, they reasoned, when the *Midway* completed its cruise to the Orient, it would be based on the West Coast. "Your Norfolk - East Coast book will be useless to you because everyone in the Navy knows that, once you join the western Pacific fleet, you *never* leave the western Pacific fleet."

At a particularly raucous gathering at Breezy Point officers' club in Norfolk, where it was customary for my group of friends to gather each Saturday night, I was offered fifty dollars for my book. Succeeding bids quickly raised the ante to eighty dollars, but I announced that I did not feel right selling my book. It seemed too crassly commercial to sell something which was very personal to me. Then Frank Pierce spoke up. He was a Navy flier attached to an air group stationed aboard the U.S.S. *Oriskany.* "Bud, I offer you a trade—something of equal value."

The group hushed.

"My air group has heard that the *Midway* is scheduled to operate out of Singapore for a couple of weeks—in joint exercises with the British. The *Oriskany* was there last year."

"So?"

"When the *Oriskany* arrived in Singapore harbor, it was the inaugural of the Singapore Sea Fair. Ships from many countries arrived for the First Singapore Sea Fair. The streets, shops and hotels were all festooned with colorful decorations, and there were all sorts of social events specially set up."

"So what?"

"Bud, the highlight event of the Sea Fair was a beauty contest to select Miss Singapore Sea Fair, and the bachelor officers from the *Oriskany* and the *Coral Sea* served as escorts for the beauty contestants. Half of the contestants were Quantas airline stewardesses based in Singapore. That's what gives me the idea. We spent our entire stay in Singapore partying with them at the Raffles Hotel, and I have tons of pictures of our great time. Bud, what I'm offering for your Norfolk book is my own book of the names and phone numbers of the beauty contestants—PLUS pictures of the beauties. Imagine what that book will be worth to you and your *Midway* buddies for the two weeks you spend in Singapore!"

Frank and I met the next day for Sunday brunch at the Oceana officers' club. Frank showed me his book of names and phone numbers. He also showed me corroborating pictures. Some of the pictures were of the bathing suit competition, and others were casual shots at an officers' party aboard the *Oriskany* (dress whites for the officers and good looking young women in sleek, short cocktail dresses). Other shots showed them in their trim Quantas uniforms. Frank also let me read several postcards he had received since the *Oriskany* had left Singapore. One of the writers was bemoaning the fact that, since the *Oriskany* had left, things had been very dull, socially, in Singapore. The deal was struck! My Norfolk book for Frank's book—and pictures!

The first port of call on the *Midway*'s cruise to the Orient had been Capetown, South Africa, where the *Midway* stayed three days. Our next stop was Columbo, Ceylon—interesting, but my friends and I were looking forward to our next destination—Singapore!

I had sent a long wire to one of the Singapore contestants whose picture I had most admired. She had quickly wired back that she had set up a welcoming party at the Raffles Hotel to be held on the evening of the *Midway*'s arrival. She would bring eight of her friends (stewardesses and contestants), and I promised nine bachelor officers. Although the *Midway* had stayed in Columbo harbor only three days, the wait seemed endless. My buddies and I were eagerly anticipating our Singapore fling at the Raffles Hotel.

Finally the *Midway* departed Columbo. We talked excitedly about the upcoming party. The pictures were scrutinized so often that they had become dog-eared. Elaborate plans were made for continuing the party for the entire four-day period when the *Midway* would be docked, awaiting the arrival of the British ships for the exercise. The U.S.S. *Midway* entered the Straits of Malacca between the Malay Peninsula and the island of Sumatra—Singapore was one day and one night ahead!

Suddenly, the captain's voice boomed on the ship's 1MC speaker: "I have just received word that the Chinese Reds are believed to be preparing to attack the Nationalist Chinese Tachen Islands of Quemoy and Matsu, and we have been ordered to proceed at flank speed to those islands to participate in their defense, along with other elements of the Seventh Fleet. We shall, of course, by-pass Singapore."

We learned that the *Midway* would steam past Singapore on Saturday at 2135. At precisely 2130, with sincere solemnity, nine bachelor naval officers assembled on the *Midway* flight deck, looking longingly at Singapore's bright lights in the distance off our port beam. We were certain that some of those lights emanated from the Raffles Hotel.

The Other Singapore Story

While the *Midway* was anchored in Colombo, a Communist Colombo paper reported the *Midway*'s change of orders, bypassing Singapore and steaming directly for Formosa. Aboard the *Midway*, opinion was divided, some saying that it was just a Communist attempt to upset the crew, others claiming that the Communists had somehow learned about the *Midway*'s mission. The *Midway* weighed anchor and set course for Singapore.

A couple of days out of Colombo, I had the eighteen to twenty watch, and ominously I heard the navigator order main control to cut four additional boilers on the line. I wandered back to the chart house and saw five commanders, the captain, and the executive officer conferring. This seemed to verify that big (bad?) news was about to break. About thirty minutes later, the officer of the deck received a call from the executive officer saying that the captain would speak to all hands at 1945.

At precisely 1945, the 1MC blared forth: "This is the captain speaking. While in Colombo, I read in a local paper that the *Midway* was to skip Singapore and head directly for the Formosan Straits. This was news to me. I asked the American ambassador if he knew anything about it. He confessed that he knew nothing. At any rate, this convinced me that the newspaper, which was reputedly a Communist paper, was just trying to shake up the crew of the *Midway*. Upon leaving Colombo, however, we received a top secret dispatch, directing us to proceed directly to the operating area of the Seventh Fleet, and to bypass Singapore. We are needed, and we shall endeavor to fulfill that need in true *Midway* fashion. That is all."

The *Midway* steamed into the Malacca Straits. Ahead of us was a sea of uncertainty and mystery. Who knew into what we steamed? It was certain that we were to participate in a task force to evacuate Chinese civilians and Nationalist solders from the Tachen Islands. But what did that involve? Would it be a peaceful affair, with small boats shuttling back and forth, ferrying hordes of people beneath a peaceful sunlit sky, or would it be a new Dunkirk?

We crept through the Malacca Straits, which were narrow. It was a rainy night, and visibility was poor. The captain, executive officer, navigator, officer of the deck, and junior officer of the watch were all on the bridge. The *Midway* was sounding its whistle every two minutes. These Straits were where, in World War II, the Japanese had surprised the U.S.S. *Houston* and the U.S.S. *Marblehead*, and the *Houston* was now somewhere beneath us. We edged along the coast of Malaya, following scrupulously the lights dotting the not too distant land—Malaya to port, Sumatra to starboard. Visibility became somewhat better. Danger could really have come from the many small, unlighted fishing vessels. During morning quarters on the flight deck, we saw the rocky coast of Sumatra, with jagged mountains looming on the horizon, while on the port side we could see the closer Malayan shore, behind which was the jungle.

We steamed northeast and into the blue Pacific, leaving the emerald green Indian Ocean behind us. China lay ahead, but not the exotic China of spices and silk sought by Columbus and Marco Polo, but the China of Chou en Lai and Mau Tse Tung. On 1 February 1955, while traversing the South China Sea, I noticed the sun reflecting off of something metallic ahead of us in the water off of our starboard bow. I was junior officer of the watch, and I alerted the officer of the deck to some glistening object in the water as the *Midway* drew near. The *Midway* steamed closer to the shining object, and, at last, with the help of my binoculars, I identified the object in the water—one Budweiser beer can.

The *Midway* was commencing another gunnery exercise. As junior officer of the watch on the bridge, I could see very clearly. Aerology released a balloon. I watched it drift up lazily. The three-inch guns opened up. Their aim was remarkably bad, not even close to a hit. When the five-inch guns boomed, they were on in bearing but short in range. The gunnery exercise concluded with no hits and no near misses. I wondered: if the *Midway* can't hit a balloon floating in the sky, how were we going to stop a six hundred knot mig fighter?

On 6 February 1955, the *Midway* joined up with the Seventh Fleet off of northern Formosa. Awaiting us were the carriers *Wasp, Yorktown, Essex*, and *Kearsage*, in company with a screen of six destroyers on circle six (six thousand yards). We were now part of Task Force 77. The moon was full, and, although an occasional cloud drifted by, the sky was generally clear.

The air department was in Air Condition II (planes ready to take off in five minutes). Pilots were sitting around in their flying suits. Planes were spotted for quick takeoffs. Two Banshees (all-weather, night fighters) sat on the catapults. Two more Banshees were lined up on the port side of the flight deck. Just abreast of the island were two rows of three Cougars. The Banshees were on five-minute call. The Cougars were on twenty-minute call (Air Condition III).

Every hour or so the *Midway* steamed into the vicinity of a fishing boat. It hardly seemed coincidental that these fishing boats were strung all along the *Midway*'s course. Although some boats had trawling lines out, we suspected that some were serving as intelligence outposts for the Chinese Reds. These boats were pitifully small, with a freeboard of less than ten feet. Yet they found the *Midway* one hundred twenty-five to one hundred fifty miles from shore.

While walking through hangar bay two, I heard the word passed on the 1MC, "All personnel stand clear of the starboard side aft." Upon reaching hangar bay four, I stepped out on the sponson deck and saw the muzzle of a five-inch gun pointed at my face. Suddenly, there was a loud scratching sound of metal rubbing hard on metal, and a jolt shook me. The fleet transport, the U.S.S. *Hoover*, which was replenishing the *Midway*, had wandered off course and had collided with us. The two ships backed apart and surveyed the damage. The transport had lost its anchor and had sustained a mangled gangway. Our damage consisted of a mashed-in storage space. Investigating, it turned out to be the void housing all the beer for the ship's parties overseas. Two hundred fifty cases were hastily removed to safer storage.

The next day, while being transferred from the U.S.S. *Hoover*, a baby atomic bomb, weighing in excess of two thousand pounds, had fallen into the Pacific Ocean. Fortunately, someone had had the foresight to make the bomb watertight and buoyant, and, when it dropped, it floated. A small boat was lowered. Its crew took the bomb in tow and had it hoisted aboard the *Midway* by means of the flight deck crane.

It seemed apparent that the lieutenant commander, who was captain of the *Hoover*, would never make commander. In the space of two days, his ship had collided with the *Midway* and had dropped an atomic bomb into the Pacific.

Lost at Sea

Once again, completely overcast skies covered Task Force 77, but a bit of drama developed: two Banshees on routine patrol got lost, reporting that they were both low on fuel. One was ninety miles away, and the other eighty miles. Both would try to make the task force. Ready Deck was set. Plane guards were standing by, and helicopters were hovering off the starboard beam. Suddenly, a Banshee was spotted. It was going slowly, low in the sky. It wheeled around and made its approach on the *Midway*. Everyone waited, and the captain was visibly apprehensive, as the Banshee's fuel could have given out momentarily. But the Banshee came in safely, and everyone breathed a sigh of relief. It was fifty-three minutes overdue—one more Banshee to go.

Report from combat: contact had been made with the stray Banshee at a distance of forty miles. His fuel was low. Our eyes strained against the clouded horizon. The wings of the bridge were jammed with birdmen, among whom worry about the stray Banshee had spread rapidly. At last a lookout reported on the 1MC: "Banshee sighted, zero, nine, zero degrees." This Banshee too was low on the horizon. All eyes watched while the Banshee made the arc and approached the *Midway*. Finally, the Banshee eased in and taxied up to its spot. The captain rushed off for the bridge. The duty photographer was standing by in flight deck control.

Out of the cockpit climbed a very tired looking young ensign. Eager hands helped him to the flight deck. The captain strode up to him and gave him a hearty handshake. The ensign, although managing a smile, still showed anxiety on his face. Flashbulbs clicked while the captain pumped the ensign's hand. You could see genuine relief radiate from the captain's face. Later, it was learned that the ensign had had enough fuel to remain aloft for only seven more minutes.

Another pilot got lost the next day. Eventually he found the ship. I was not on watch at the time, but I heard that, once he landed on the *Midway*, his Banshee didn't have enough fuel left to taxi to the forward end of the flight deck.

Light the Ship

Steaming in fast carrier formation forty miles off Formosa during the Tachen evacuation, the 1MC blared out at sunset, "Darken ship, darken ship, submit darken ship reports to damage control central." An hour later, we received word that the evacuation had finally been completed. Anti-aircraft Condition III was secured. Condition IV (peace time cruising) was set. The armada dispersed throughout the Pacific—the *Yorktown* and five destroyers headed toward Yokusuka, the *Pittsburgh* and two destroyers sailed for Hong Kong, and the *Midway* and three destroyers steamed for Manila.

Dramatically, the officer of the deck turned to me, the junior officer of the watch, and said, "Mr. George, light the ship." I turned slowly, faced the bosun's mate of the watch, and said, quite solemnly, "Boats, pass the word 'lighten ship'." (After all, I figured, if you say "darken ship," why can't you say "lighten ship"?) The bosun, dutifully obeying my order, passed the word "lighten ship" over the *Midway*'s 1MC.

A moment later, the bridge phone rang. I, as JOOW, picked up the receiver and heard, "Would you prefer that we jettison personnel or gear in lightening the ship?"

Manila City

My bunkroom mate, Don Bull, and I hopped the admiral's barge and made a high speed run to Manila. One didn't often make high speed runs in Manila Bay in 1955 because the bay area had a considerable number of wrecks protruding above the surface. Some of the wrecks in Manila Bay were reputed to date back to the Spanish-American War. Obviously, the admiral had carefully picked the coxswain who was helmsman of the admiral's barge.

We docked at embassy landing and went immediately to the army-navy club, a magnificent building exuding plushness. The overheads were very high and paneled in mahogany. The furnishings were posh: a running pool gurgled through the main lobby. Open patios were everywhere, all tastefully decorated.

We walked to the Manila Hotel, another magnificent building famed for its jungle bar. The jungle bar was just that—a bar set in a jungle. It was absolutely black inside, with trees and vines hanging everywhere and a few dim lights around a crashing waterfall right next to the bar. In rapid succession, we checked out the Top Hat, reputedly the hangout of Manila's White Russians, and the Yellow Bar, in front of which we saw a shore patrol officer sitting at the door. "Strictly white hat," he explained. "An undisguised cat house with eighty girls, and fights every ten minutes. I definitely wouldn't recommend officers in there."

A high log fence prevented us from seeing what Cafe Andrews looked like. We held the swinging doors open and stood there for a moment. We saw a little darkened courtyard with candlelit tables. As we looked into the club itself, we saw a dimly lit dance floor, and we heard a soft Philippine melody wafting throughout. Don and I entered the club and saw a number of young Philippine girls standing around, every one of whom seemed to be attractive. Don and I sat at the bar, and two girls approached, but, receiving no encouragement, they left us alone.

The next night, Don and I headed for Minamotos, a restaurant specializing in Japanese dishes. As we entered the front door, we saw an open courtyard. We did not enter this courtyard, but went into a modern bar where we placed our orders and waited. There, we saw the *Midway*'s Chaplain, Father O'Toole, and LT. Denny Fogarty, a gunnery officer. Don, Father O'Toole, Denny and I ordered sukiyaki. Three martinis later, we were invited to the courtyard, which had grass in the center and two large rooms on each side of the grass. Before we could enter a room, we had to take off your shoes. (I later discovered that, while we ate, our shoes were shined.)

Sukiyaki is an unpleasant-looking dish, but I was determined not only to like it but to eat it with chopsticks. After a few failures, I discovered the knack and found myself enthusiastically shoveling down mouthfuls of sukiyaki, which had been prepared by a girl in a corner of the room. The Japanese custom, of course, was to sit on the floor. Yet the proprietor of Minamotos had been smart enough to realize that, while it's a charming custom, no American would be comfortable eating that way. Accordingly, a pit had been dug in the center of the room, and a table placed in the pit. Although you sat on the floor (on a cushion), you for all practical purposes were eating in the normal western position. After the sukuyaki, we ordered brandy.

Afterward, the four of us adjourned to the bar of Minamotos, where a Philippine string combo was playing. We ended up singing with the combo, which played (at our request) the fabled "Princess Papooli has Plenty Papaya."

We then headed for Hai Lai, which was in a tall building. We entered and took an elevator to the top deck which was a sophisticated night club, with a good band and intimate tables. We wandered out on the very long balcony to watch the hai lai matches below. After watching a match, Don and I decided to place a bet. We each chipped in two bucks and bet on number one, who had been recommended by our tout—our waiter. (Waiters suggested players. If you won, you gave them part of your winnings. If you lost, you lost.) Unfortunately for us, we lost consistently and decided to return to the ship.

Two Sailors on Liberty

Commander Davis had summoned me to his office. "Mr. George, these two men have to go ashore to see the Philippine police. I want you to go with them." I looked at the two sailors standing at attention beside Davis' desk and said, "Come with me." On the way, Seaman Doyle, by way of explanation for our rendezvous with the authorities, told me of his earlier trouble. Doyle had been looking for his Philippine girlfriend who had left the bar in which he had just met her. Doyle had ordered a beer, and, bottle in hand, he had set out in search of his girlfriend. He had inadvertently walked into the backyard of one Jose, who ordered him off his property. As Doyle started to leave, Jose swatted him with the flat side of a board. Doyle, whose previous beers had made him somewhat reckless, was not about to take this, and he bounced the bottle off of Jose's head. Doyle was later apprehended by the local police.

Seaman Fraser had a girl-related story too. He said that he was in a bar when a girl asked him to sleep with her "for love." Fraser had quickly accepted the offer. He followed her to her room, which contained a bed and nothing else (not even sheets). She told him to disrobe and hop into bed. He obliged, and she followed suit. However, she suddenly demanded five pesos (two dollars fifty cents). Fraser had at first argued, but the girl refused to perform. Fraser got out of bed, got his wallet, and found that all he had was a ten dollar bill. He gave her the ten dollars only after she had promised to return with change. She slipped on a housecoat, and, before she left to get change, she "playfully" pulled off Fraser's ring.

When the girl returned, she said that she had no change. When Fraser demanded his ring, she refused. Fraser dressed quickly and went to get a shore patrolman. He couldn't find one and therefore returned to try to get the ring. The girl had local police arrest Fraser for creating a disturbance. This made Fraser late for liberty, and he had become an unauthorized absentee from the *Midway*.

After hearing of the ruckus Doyle and Fraser had caused in Manila, I asked Doyle to dig up all the money he could before leaving the ship. Doyle came up with forty dollars (eighty pesos). We went to the local shore patrol office where I met the Navy's Philippine hatchet man, affectionately (but inaccurately) called "Judge." Doyle's alleged victim, Jose, was a slight man, whose head was bundled in a huge bandage. Judge talked with Jose in Tagalog, expressing regard for his injury and a desire to settle amicably. Jose demanded one hundred pesos. Judge said that Doyle could only scrape together forty pesos. They bickered for a time in Tagalog. Finally,

Judge said that, if Jose would accept fifty pesos, Ensign George would contribute the extra five dollars. Jose, who until this time had been afraid that he'd receive only forty pesos, beamed and quickly accepted Judge's offer.

While Judge typed out the release, the chief of police sent out one of his men to locate the girl in Fraser's case. When she appeared, I was shocked at her repulsiveness. She was skinny, about four and a half feet tall, and her hair hung in oily black clumps. Her lipstick was smeared from her nose to her chin. She displayed several gold teeth when she smiled. The girl had the ring with her, but she claimed that it is hers, Seaman Fraser having given it to her for services rendered. He, of course, denied this and claimed that she had taken it from him, despite the fact that he outweighed her by probably eighty pounds. However, Seaman Fraser struck everyone as such a hayseed that it wasn't hard to imagine him letting her take the ring off his finger. Of course, she denied taking a ten dollar bill from Fraser.

Quite a scene developed, with the police chief questioning the girl in Tagalog. I had an interpreter translating for me. Finally, to stop the bickering, I told the chief that we would pay her two pesos to get the ring back. She refused, saying that her services were worth more than that. The chief interjected that, if she wanted pay for her services, she was admitting that she was a prostitute, and he would have to jail her. The two pesos were only for the ring. He also warned that she had better sell the ring for the two pesos because he was going to take it from her anyway. The prostitute took the two pesos, Fraser put the ring on his finger, and we quickly departed police headquarters.

The Gun Boss

Captain Vaughn and Commander Allen, the "Gun Boss," were talking softly at one end of the open bridge as the *Midway* steamed off the Philippines, three days out of Cavite Naval Base, Manila. I was junior officer of the watch, and Lieutenant John Taylor was officer of the deck. John and I were also on the open bridge. All four of us were watching the flight deck, where an aerologist, who had been holding a balloon, released it. The balloon drifted up slowly but soon lost its roundness and became a solitary white dot in blue vastness. It looked like a star.

"Commence firing" was the word passed on all circuits. Suddenly there was tremendous noise and concussion, immediately following which was the sound of metal hurtling through space. Then all was quiet. About seven seconds later, a little burst of black appeared very near the star. Soon other bursts bracketed the first burst. When the balloon had drifted out of the range of the 3-inch guns, the 5-inch batteries opened up. After a few more bursts, the balloon was hit and slowly made a plumb line for the water, miles from the *Midway*.

Commander Allen had now left the captain and was headed toward John and me. I had never dealt with the gun boss and didn't know what to expect of him. I supposed that he must be a mental giant, the officer-in-charge of all shipboard gunnery, whose superb and finely-tuned mental acuteness directed the awesome firepower of the mighty U.S.S. *Midway*.

Commander Allen's first words told me much about him. He spoke as if it pained him to emit words. His drawling manner of speech left you in suspense as to whether he would ever reach the end of his sentence.

After we had exchanged greetings, Commander Allen said to John Taylor, "John, what is the phone number of that infernal 3-inch gun shop?" Taylor, who was in charge of the 3-inch gun shop, replied, "three, four, five, commander." The gun boss stuck his head inside the pilot house and said to the bosun's mate, "Say there, son, how's about dialing three, four, five and handing me the phone?" Holding the phone to his ear, Commander Allen said, "Hello, 3-inch gun shop? Let me speak to Mr. Taylor."

John and I looked at each other for a second. Then John spoke up. "Commander, are you looking for me?"

"Oh, there you are, John. Never mind, 3-inch gun shop, I've found Lieutenant Taylor."

The Corregidor-Bataan Cruise

At 0830 on 21 February 1955, I hustled to the deck edge elevator where the Margaret, a sixty-five foot yacht of ComNavPhil awaited me (Commandant, Navy, Philippines) and forty-four other officers. The sky was sunlit and the day brisk, as the Margaret headed for Corregidor. We tied up at the landing and walked past rusted ammo into a village of huts in the center of which was a chapel, with statues of Christ and the Virgin Mary guarding the entrance. We hopped into trucks for a tour of the island. Dense growth stifled all travel except on the winding dirt roads. Along both sides of the roads were bombed-out bunkers and pill boxes. Large pieces of metal and gun barrels lay in disarray all over the island.

The first stop of our truck tour was the headquarters of a mortar battalion consisting of a deep ravine between two hills. The ravine was paved and its bottom flattened. Four giant twelve-inch mortars were mounted. The hills had been hollowed in order to store the ammo used by the mortars. Apparently, the Japanese had strafed the area, because the paving was pocked with hundreds of small holes. Even the barrels of the mortars were dented and pocked. Two holes in the center of the ravine were evidence of bomb hits. The steel doors to the ammo magazines were torn and damaged by nearby shell bursts.

All over the island you could see craters of various sizes. Now the dense tropical greenery obscured them, and, in the past ten years, there had been a lot of such growth. Still further up went the truck, past a large two gun emplacement, one gun of which had been blasted by a direct hit. We passed General McArthur's headquarters, the skeleton of a large three-story edifice which had been completely bombed out.

Our truck then took us back to the Margaret for Bataan, now a tropical paradise. At the foot of a large mountain was a small beach, the sand powderized and volcanic. The white beach was flanked by palm trees and jungle greenery. The steep rock of the mountains served as a background. The water was a light blue, and the sandy bottom was clearly visible. We exited our trucks and unloaded beer and sandwiches. While we swam, laughed, and partied, we were all struck by the very short distance separating Bataan from Corregidor.

Frank A. Sullivan *

Sullivan, Frank Albert

681644, Lieutenant, U.S.N.

Age: 26

Home: Cleveland, Ohio

Unmarried

Religion: Catholic

Reported to the U.S.S. *Midway*, December 27, 1954

Graduated Ohio State University

On this date, March 4, 1955, at 1241, AD5-172346, piloted by Lt. Sullivan of Air Group 12, crashed into the water off the starboard beam at latitude 23-50N, longitude 128-16E in 100 fathoms of water. Debris floated to surface, retrieved by small boats. At 1622, search discontinued. Results: Debris included what turned out to be a human scalp. Lt. Frank A. Sullivan presumed dead.

* From the *Midway*'s log.

Benny Boys

The *Midway* pulled into Manila for one day, and I was assigned to be shore patrol officer. SHOPAT headquarters was in the Cavite City police station. Meadows, BM1 (Bosun Mate, 1ˢᵗ Class), was briefing the shore patrol on what we were to crack down on: fights, off-limit houses, and the Benny Boys, who were Philippine transvestites who let their hair grow long, shaved the hair on their legs and face, and dressed as women. They hosted lavish parties, but, as homosexuals, U.S. Navy personnel were to be kept away from them.

The shore patrol dispatched jeeps all over Cavite City. Each had a helmeted enlisted driver, a naval officer, and a civilian policeman with a pistol. (A week ago a civilian policeman had been shot six times by an unknown assailant. Since that time, the Philippine checkpoints throughout the city were armed with submachine guns.) I witnessed the changing of police guard at one of these checkpoints. With submachine guns changing hands, it was like a wartime army maneuver. The police station had a large map of Cavite City on which were marked all of the Benny Boy houses and houses of prostitution. Benny Boy houses were strictly out of bounds for naval personnel.

On a routine jeep check, I went along as officer-in-charge. We drove rapidly through the narrow streets, teeming in darkness with sinister-looking Philippinos hanging together in small groups. Suddenly we stopped in front of a house that looked like all the rest. With flashlights, we probed the dark. Steps led up to the house, but, on ground level, there was a row of doors. Meadows pushed open these doors. Inside our flashlights revealed a small, dirty room with nothing in it but a bed. There were no windows, no table, no chairs, no pictures. The bed was old and dilapidated, and a tattered, flattened straw mattress with a filthy torn blanket was thrown on top of it.

We got back into the jeep, and again we raced along dark streets, screeching to a stop in front of a house, in front of which we spotted a sailor. We jumped out of the jeep, and Meadows, who was the first to reach the sailor, asked him what he was doing. The sailor, who was quite drunk, answered that he was waiting for a buddy who was inside. Immediately, the civilian policeman and Meadows, after telling the sailor to wait, raced into the dark yard. I followed. Doors were pushed open, but all they revealed to the probing flashlights were empty beds. While running across a yard, Meadows was almost decapitated in the darkness by a low hanging wire clothesline. Apparently, the sailor inside had been warned, for we found nothing.

Returning outside, we saw our drunken sailor surrounded by hideous women, all screeching at him that he was lying and that there was no sailor inside. The sailor, who was off of the U.S.S. *Essex*, was so drunk that all he could do was smile affably. We took the sailor with us and hopped into the jeep.

"Well, sir," Meadows asked, "What did you think of our Benny Boys?"

"Benny Boys?" I said, surprised. "You mean they weren't women."

"That's right, sir."

Later, while at the police station, we got a call from one of the Benny Boy houses that sailors had entered another Benny Boy house. A flying patrol was sent out to round up the sailors. When I expressed surprise that the Benny Boys would squeal on each other, I was told that Benny Boys were intensely jealous of one another. And when one attracted sailors, the others promptly reported that house to the shore patrol.

The Greeks of Manila

I finally got together with Nick Poulos, a Greek-American officer off a destroyer based at Cavite. We went into Manila. He had met some Greeks in the city, and, since my Navy future seems destined only for the western Pacific, I was eager to meet these people. Nick and I took a cab to Adamson University. During the ride, I asked Nick why all Manila movie theaters had signs posted: No Firearms Allowed. Nick explained that sometimes, when the theaters showed American cowboy movies, Philippinos, during exciting scenes, pulled pistols out and started firing into the ceiling, causing chunks of concrete to fall into the audience.

The cab arrived in front of a large building which looked like a monastery, outside of which a Greek flag was flying. We entered and walked into a large administrative office where we were asked to be seated by a secretary. After a moment we were ushered into a large air-conditioned office by a fifty-five year old man who looked obviously Greek. His name was George Adamson, and he turned out to be ardently proud of his Greek roots. Adamson recounted how he had traveled from Greece to Africa, to Australia, to the United States, and finally he had settled in the Philippines. He had founded the Adamson School of Industrial Chemistry, and the school had grown until it was now a fully accredited university.

Adamson went on to say that he had been editor of a Greek newspaper and that he had furnished his native village in Greece with electricity. During World War II, the Japanese had destroyed his university, but, after the war, he had returned to the Philippines, where he had bought an abandoned monastery. Now the school seemed to be doing quite well and had received from the Philippine government the only NROTC program in Manila. Unfortunately, Mr. Adamson was committed for the evening, but he invited us back in the morning.

Nick and I went to see a friend of Nick's named Serge Fatsios. Serge was half Greek and half Swiss. The Greek, I was to learn later, was decidedly predominant. We arrived at Serge's address, but Serge was not home. His maid let us in. Nick penned him a note. The apartment was quite large and comfortable, a perfect setting for a bachelor operation. Nick and I left and killed an hour or so wandering into nearby shops. When we returned, Serge let us in, and we also met four girls and another young man. Serge was short and stocky. He spoke with a continental accent. The young man turned out to be Serge's roommate, a Swiss, who was already reeling drunk. As to the girls, two were around thirty, and the two others were about nineteen. We learned that the girls' names were Olga, Helen, Lolita and Lilly.

It seemed that Serge's roommate, Meier, had had a date with Olga, who, with large brown eyes and long jet black hair, was quite attractive, high heels and short skirt nicely setting off her shapely legs. But, prior to his date, Meier had gone to a nearby bar, and, in the process of getting drunk, had become entangled with Lolita, a hostess, whom he had brought to the apartment. Meanwhile, Serge, assuming that Meier would pick up Olga at her home, had stopped by there. Helen had had a date with someone named Dick, who had driven up to her home and honked the horn, but, when she came out, had driven off. Serge, Lilly, Helen and Olga had gotten into a car to catch Dick, but they did not succeed. Since Meier was late, they decided to go to the apartment where they assumed that Meier was asleep. They had found Meier asleep, of course, but with Lolita. Still, everyone seemed quite nonchalant about the tangled situation. Meier and Lolita had dressed and come out for a drink with Serge, Olga, Lilly and Helen. However, at this point, Serge's date for the evening, one Mary Lou, rang the doorbell, and, seeing all the women, became angry and stomped out. At this point, Nick and I had entered.

The next thing that happened was that Meier virtually collapsed. We put him to bed. Lolita left. Olga, Helen and Lilly remained with Serge, Nick and me—three Philippine girls and three Greeks. Serge was no fool. He pursued Olga. Respecting our host, Nick and I settled for Lilly and Helen. Lilly was a dentist who had studied at Georgetown University and had traveled widely throughout the United States. Her underarm still bore a long scar where a Japanese bayonet had struck her.

Outside a vendor shouted, "VA-LUTE," and I went out to buy one. Helen had promised to eat it, and I had never seen one. A volute was an unhatched chicken, and it was considered by some Philippinos to be a delicacy. We gathered around as Helen carefully picked away the upper part of the eggshell. First, she drank all of the egg juice. Then she broke the rest of the shell and exposed the oval solid mass of the unhatched chicken. Helen gently pulled apart this solid oval and showed us the beak and eyes of the bird. Then, she ate it. Lilly and Olga refused to eat any.

Nick announced, "Lips that touch volute will never touch mine."

Great Expectations

Don Bull and I in our dress navy blues went ashore in Cavite Naval Base. As we left the main gate, I saw several sailors, obviously half drunk, leaning against the fence. Suddenly I heard, "Mr. George, Mr. George." As we got closer, I recognized Fox and McDaniel, my legal yeomen; Greco, from the pastry shop (who on some mornings surprised me with freshly baked pastries); and Burk, my INE (Information and Education) yeoman. They swarmed around me, asking to let them buy me a drink. I said, "Okay, we'll join you for *one* drink," believing that we would get that drink in one of the nearby bars.

But my enlisted friends insisted that we go to the American Bar, which had been their "real find." McDaniel pulled a handbill out of his pocket, which proclaimed: Gorgeous Women and Beer at Half Price from 1600 - 1900. I reluctantly agreed to join them, and we all crowded into a large cab. We must have driven for twenty minutes, over dirt roads, through a field, and finally we pulled up in front of a rambling, barn-like building.

As Don and I got out of the cab, we heard, "Hey, sirs, let me talk to you for a minute, please." Although we knew what was coming, we said, "Okay."

"Would you like a nice blonde Polish girl?"

I lied and said, "Thank you, but I'm married, and my wife wouldn't like that." Don just said, "No." The short Philippino figured that Don was his better bet, but maybe he just didn't care for blondes. He looked at Don, "How about a nice dark haired Russian girl?"

Don again said, "No."

"How about a nice girl just out of the convent?"

Don responded, "No thanks, I'm not Catholic."

The Philippino man was stymied temporarily but said, "Wait one minute, please, sirs." He then conferred with one of his cohorts. Amused, Don and I waited. Finally the Philippino turned to Don and asked, "How about a nice young boy?" Don and I broke out laughing. (Don and I later mused that the blonde Polish girl, dark haired Russian girl, and girl just out of the convent might all have been the same girl, clutching different wigs, pocket language books, and/or a catechism.)

There were two doors to the American Bar. Over one hung a sign, "No Unescorted Ladies Allowed." As we entered, the first thing I noticed was a skinny dog languishing in the center of what turned out to be the dance floor. A sign, hanging on a post in the middle of the dance floor (supporting a sagging ceiling), announced, Dancing Forbidden by Order of the Police Commissioner. The next thing I noticed was the many young women around the bar. Don left me to begin talking to an attractive young woman with big brown eyes.

I saw Burk talking to the proprietor. He looked my way, nodded, and then disappeared. I sat down and ordered a bottled beer. Suddenly the proprietor was behind me. He pushed up a chair, and a Philippine girl sat down. The boss leaned over and whispered in my ear, "Nice girl, sir."

I looked at her and, in truth, she had vivacious eyes and a toothpaste smile. She invited me upstairs, but I declined saying, "My wife wouldn't like that." She immediately grabbed my left hand to see if I was wearing a wedding ring. Fortunately, my Duke ring had what appeared to be a gold band around it. She smiled and said, "What your wife no know never hurt her." I said, "Thanks, you are very pretty, but no thanks." She promptly left my table, and Don Bull joined me.

I saw Fox, my legal yeoman, in the corner with a petite, cute girl. In twenty minutes, he sauntered up to me, smirking. He said, "She really gave me a workout." I asked, "Did you use a contraceptive?" His answer was negative. Don then suggested that he buy a glass of liquor, take it into the lavatory, and wash himself. Ten minutes later, everyone in the American Bar heard a deafening bellow of pain emanating from the lavatory.

The music in the American bar was very good, and I had yet to see a Philippine girl who could not dance instinctively to Latin music. A besotted Greco sat at our table and said, "You know, for officers, you are genuinely good joes." The girl who had earlier sat at my table again approached me. "Changed your mind?" she asked, as she started to sit again. Don spoke up, "Listen, why are you wasting time with us when that big sailor over there is Bill Motors?"

Don nodded toward a fat sailor, semi-catatonic with drink. She glanced in the sailor's direction, made an unpleasant face, and asked, "Who's Bill Motors?"

"Well, I'm sure you've heard of his father—General Motors."

She looked again at the large sailor, but this time her look had a hunger about it. She left our table without another word. In several moments, she was pulling the dazed sailor up the staircase, with one of her girlfriends pushing him from the back.

Subic Bay

Into the Philippines' exotic Subic Bay steamed the good ship *Midway*. Subic Bay (in Navy parlance, sometimes called "Pubic Bay") was the most picturesque place visited yet. The water, unlike Manila's, was so clear that you could see the bottom from way out. The whole bay area was protected by high, densely green hills, and in the distance there were high mountains. Surely, this seemed like a tropical paradise.

I tried to contact Bill Raptor and Tom Chaste, friends of mine from OCS, who were stationed at Subic, but I was informed that both were on TAD (temporary additional duty), due to return the following day. Don Bull and I were pleased to find that the officers' club was nearby. The O club didn't look luxurious from the outside, but inside it was comfortable indeed, with deep cushion seats placed so as to take good advantage of the beautiful vista outside. At the O club, we joined Tim Tebo, downed a martini, and headed into the small town of Olangapo.

Olangapo had one main street, which was unpaved, and bars adjoined each other for at least a mile in each direction. Every one of the bars was packed with sailors and attractive Philippine girls. We headed for the Grandilla Club, reputed to be the nicest bar in Olangapo. We entered the club, which was dark, and I saw Barnes, the personnel yeoman, dancing with a slender Philippine girl. The club had several cute girls, but one in particular caught everyone's attention. She was called "Virgin."

Virgin came to our table, and Don asked her how she got her name.

"Because I am the only virgin in Olangapo" was her answer.

Hello Dolly

The next day, Bill Raptor, Tom Chaste and I met at the officers club. Tom was sullen.

"I was shanghaied! When we were at officer candidate school, we were given a choice, shore duty or sea duty. The Navy said, if you choose shore duty, just list your three top preferences for duty stations. I picked shore duty. I listed Copenhagen, Paris and Rome. How the hell did I get stuck in sucking Subic Bay Naval Base in the God-forsaken Philippines?"

Bill chimed in. "Tom, I was shanghaied too. My choices were San Diego, Honolulu and San Francisco, and here we've been in Subic for almost a year. Bud, you were the lucky one in OCS, picking sea duty. You've spent your year cruising the Caribbean—and now the Pacific—and, Bud, how especially kind and thoughtful of you to send us cards from your cruises to Florida, the Caribbean, and those other resorts."

I tried to sound sincere. "Well, one thing the *Midway* doesn't have is this posh officers club, with an eighteen-hole golf course, swimming pools, and billiard room."

At that moment, a young woman, unescorted, entered the lounge and sat at a distant table.

She was slender, her blonde hair tied casually in a pony tail, and she crossed long, nicely proportioned legs beneath her shortish skirt.

I was entranced and burbled: "Wow, who is that?"

"Her name is Dolly Pringle. She graduated from college two years ago and has been at Subic for a week visiting her dad. He is a captain and Subic's communications' officer, and she has rebuffed *every* attempt by *any* officer on this base to get to know her."

Tom interrupted.

"Bud George, you are the *Midway*'s ambassador to Subic Bay. Approach her, show the flag, and sail that beauty back to our table."

Bill, his eyes never straying from Dolly's legs, also challenged me, "Go ahead, Bud, I'll bet you don't have the guts. Besides, what do you have to lose? The worst she can do is turn you down, and tomorrow night the *Midway* leaves Subic anyway."

"What a transparent twosome you guys are. You want to sit here, watching me make a clumsy fool of myself, attempting to meet that curvaceous pair of legs, and, when she turns me down, you gutless goons will howl in laughter. No thanks!"

With one last, longing, lustful, lingering, lascivious leer, we all gulped our martinis and ordered another round. I excused myself and left the lounge. Seeing two public telephone booths in the lobby, I quickly jotted down the telephone number of one of the phones and sidled into the adjacent booth. I dialed the phone number of the first. The phone rang three or four times before it was answered by one of the club's stewards. I dropped my voice an octave and spoke slowly:

"This is Captain Pringle. Would you please page my daughter?"

"Aye, aye, sir. Please wait one minute."

The club's loudspeaker announced, "Telephone call for Miss Pringle."

I closed my booth door, saw Dolly Pringle pass, and heard the door to the next booth close.

"Hello?"

"Miss Pringle, my name is Bud George, and I am an ensign aboard the U.S.S. *Midway*, which just arrived at Subic two days ago. I've been sitting at a table in the lounge with two of my fellow officers, who were trying to get me to come to your table, introduce myself and make a clumsy attempt to get you to join our table—to your embarrassment and mine."

"Why are you calling me, Ensign George?"

"I wonder if you would be a good sport and gracious enough to walk into the lounge with me, arm in arm? I'd like to teach my friends a lesson."

There was a pause.

"Where are you calling from?"

"I'm in the next booth."

We both emerged simultaneously.

Dolly was smiling. She offered me her arm. Together, Dolly and I, arms joined, entered the lounge and headed for my table. Tom looked up and gaped.

Bill followed Tom's stupefied gaze and murmured, "Let that SOB out of your sight *one minute* and BINGO!"

Both ensigns stood erect as Dolly and I approached their table.

I asked, "Gentlemen, may I present Ms. Dolly Pringle?"

Starboard Catapult Scare

The *Midway*'s starboard catapult had been out of commission for almost seven days. The sole purpose of our going to Subic Bay in the first place was to put the starboard cat back in commission. While at Subic, the cat always had men tinkering with it, and cranes working on it. Finally, the catapult was deemed operational.

The *Midway* departed Subic to conduct air operations. With the first launch on the starboard catapult, a Banshee failed to get sufficient power and plunged into the water. The Banshee hit with such momentum that it became nothing but debris in less than one minute. Fortunately, the pilot did not lose consciousness at impact. He scrambled out of the cockpit and was immediately picked up by the helicopter.

The Banshee debris sank in less than four minutes.

Hong Kong

As the *Midway* approached Hong Kong, we found that the harbor was so shallow the *Midway* had to anchor far out. Don Bull and I took the captain's gig into fleet landing. During the long ride, we had ample time to observe Hong Kong harbor, which was filled with junks of all sizes. (Junks are Chinese sailing ships characterized by high forecastles and sterns and square matting sails.) Most were small, with one person paddling and another steer-paddling. They jumped various sizes until you came to huge junks. We in the States tended to scoff at the prospect of a 1955 invasion of Nationalist Formosa by junks. To Americans, the junk seemed a flimsy boat, crudely constructed and of clumsy appearance. Actually, the junk was an extremely seaworthy vessel. Its hull was twelve to sixteen inches of solid wood which gave it excellent buoyancy.

U.S. Naval experts, trying to decide the best defense against the junk, had concluded that anything less than a direct hit by a five-inch shell would be useless. It would have taken numerous hits by a three-inch shell to cause enough damage to sink a junk. Except for wounding the crew, it would do no good to strafe a junk, as twenty millimeter shells would merely bury themselves ineffectually in the thick hull. Some of the junks had poured concrete deep in the hull for ballast and balance. Junks were, however, vulnerable to napalm or incendiary attack.

What kind of armament did the junks have? Some of the larger ones actually had sixty-five millimeter howitzers mounted in the forecastle. Others carried all sorts of mortars. Naval experts had concluded that in any attack upon Formosa, unless the United States intervened with its full potential might, four out of five junks would land on the island. As our little boat puttered along in Hong Kong Harbor, I noted the various sizes of the junks, right down to the three-man variety with bamboo slat sails and paddles. A noteworthy thing to me was that women, and sometimes even elderly ones, did the paddling. The men steer-paddled or stood on the fantail with long poles acting as rudders and paddles. Women manned the long paddles amidships. To the Chinese, the junk was not merely a boat. It was their home. Inside the crude, Quonset-like shelter, we saw children and the elderly. Cooking took place atop a square of concrete. There was laundry hanging to dry.

A short walk from the landing brought us into downtown Hong Kong. "Hong Kong" means "fragrant island." But Hong Kong was people. The streets, flanked by a multitude of signs with Chinese characters, teemed with pushing, jostling, hurrying people. You didn't actually walk in Hong Kong; instead, you were carried along by the current of moving humanity. Although vehicles moved slowly along main streets, the side streets had few vehicles and were mobbed with people walking fast in different directions.

Hong Kong offered the *Midway* a striking new feature compared to the foreign ports we had already visited—the slit skirt. Almost all of the women wore dresses with a high mandarin collar topping a straight sheath of dress, which slimmed at the waist, snuggly grabbed the hips, and ended just below the knees. But one side of the dress was slit to about one-half of the thigh. So, as *Midway* personnel walked along the street in Hong Kong, their eyes were constantly being distracted by legs and thighs flashing everywhere.

Hong Kong was the paradox of east meeting west—two men chatting, one wearing a western, single-breasted suit, the other attired in a long black Chinese robe with a stiff collar; or two women walking together, one pushing a baby carriage, the other with her baby tied to her back, papoose-style. The young women were often products of that paradox. Exotic combinations of Caucasian-Chinese abounded, their faces oval, their skin pale, their short black hair stylishly cut, their eyes slightly slanted, and the ubiquitous slit skirt revealing well-formed legs.

Just after World War II, Hong Kong had had a population of six hundred thousand, but, with the advent of red power in mainland China, Hong Kong's population had swelled in 1955 to two and a half million. Don and I walked through what must have been the financial district of Hong Kong. Here all the banks, finance companies and moneychangers were grouped together. Each establishment had its own guard, usually a Sikh with a turban, but otherwise dressed like anyone else. In his arms he cradled an elephant gun, and he trained his eyes on anyone who seemed to linger a second too long in front of the establishment he was protecting. The gun he fondled looked powerful enough to cut a man in two.

We passed a large construction job, and I was appalled to see women standing in a line with small sacks on their backs. As you watched, the line ended at a large pile of rocks. Each woman paused in front of the pile where another woman picked up a rock and placed it into the sack on the woman's back. You could actually see their brows knit, as the burden was heavy. Once the rock had been placed into the sack, the woman slowly trudged out to the street where a man was waiting to take the rock out of the sack and throw it into the back of a truck.

As we continued on our way, we passed a three-story structure that was being painted. The scaffolding was nothing more than a patchwork of tied-together bamboo poles, which were not implanted into the ground. The poles were merely resting on the sidewalk, the scaffolding being held to the building by two bamboo poles reaching out from the roof. About twelve feet up on the bamboo scaffolding were two Chinese painters.

Don and I decided to go to Kowloon, the mainland part of Hong Kong. ("Kowloon" means "nine dragons.") We boarded the Star ferry boat and, in ten minutes, stepped ashore on mainland China. Since Don wanted to buy a Hong Kong suit, we stopped by Singh's Hong Kong Suits, which had been recommended by the Navy Exchange. Here we encountered the omnipresent Indian merchants, with black hair and intelligent eyes, and Don walked off with a salesman. I strolled around the shop, peeking into corners, and I came to a place where several pictures of many-armed women (with halos) were collected. In front of these pictures stood a vase of fresh flowers. In another room I saw the merchants' wives. They were not dressed western-style, as were their husbands, but wore saris, bangled jewelry and had dots painted on their foreheads. Don appeared, announced that he had bought his suit, and we left.

We came upon Tachenko's Restaurant, where we decided to have a drink. We found Russian music, played by a cossack quartet and wild dancers in boots and fur caps. The dancers continually drank vodkas as they danced, and the dance became more frenzied. Tachenko's bar soon was virtually bedlam, as inebriated, boisterous Russians slapped each other on the back after downing still another vodka. We left Tachenko's and headed back to the *Midway*. During the boat ride, Don said he wanted me to see him in his new Hong Kong suit. I responded, "Let's don't waste Hong Kong time trying on suits. Wait till we're on the cruise when there's nothing else to do."

The next evening, Don and I arrived at the Cafe Wiseman, which swarmed with young women, each obviously trying to outdo the other in sex appeal. Makeup was very carefully applied, and stocking seams were unerringly straight. As the music played, the girls put everything they had into the dance.

It was dark now. Don and I entered the Bamboo Cafe, which was crowded with exotically beautiful young women. The cafe consisted of a dance floor surrounded by tables. With lights seductively low, we watched the young women glide along the dance floor to soft music, their slit skirts flashing what seemed to be the most beautifully proportioned legs in the world. At a bar in the corner, appealing hostesses perched provocatively on barstools, giggling among themselves, awaiting an invitation to dance and have a drink.

I asked one to dance. "My name is Blue Moon," she tittered. "Please do not judge me because you have found me here at the Bamboo Cafe. Actually, I am the daughter of a Manchurian warlord who was killed by the Japanese. I fled for my life, walked across China and found myself here in Hong Kong. My family had lost its wealth, and I have been reduced to becoming a dance hall girl here at the Bamboo Cafe."

We chatted amiably until the dance ended. I walked Blue Moon back to her bar stool, ordered her a drink, and returned to our table. A short time later, I asked another hostess to dance. "My name is Kitty Kat. Please do not judge me by having found me working as a dance hall girl here in Hong Kong. Actually, I am the daughter of a Manchurian warlord who was killed by the Japanese. I had to flee for my life. I walked all the way across China to Hong Kong, and I had to become a dance hall girl to make a living."

I responded, "Then you must know Blue Moon over there. She too is the daughter of a Manchurian warlord."

A look of contemptuous disdain crossed Kitty Kat's face, as she sneered, "Blue Moon is a colossal liar."

Sunrise and Singh's Suits

The *Midway* had left Hong Kong and was steaming toward Japan. I was junior officer of the watch. It was a moonless, clear night. Venus hung low in the horizon. The light it reflected was so bright that it cast a beam on the water, just as the moon often does. It was now a half hour before sunrise. A section of sky was beginning to glow a glorious orange-blue. At 0545 we commenced air operations. We were on course zero nine zero degrees, and we were heading directly into the sunrise. As the jets were catapulted into the orange-blue vastness, their black fuselage gradually disappeared, and one could see only the glow of the jet flow against the background of an orange sunrise. It was a spectacular sight.

When my watch ended, I walked into bunkroom #9, where Don Bull said, "We're at sea, and it's time for you to see my new Hong Kong blue suit." I agreed and sank into an easy chair. Don took his suit jacket off of its hanger and stuck his right arm into the jacket's right sleeve. As he did so, the right sleeve immediately separated from the jacket, except for several long loose white threads. The top of the sleeve was now at Don's right bicep.

Don smiled, and, after a moment, said, "Now I understand how Singh's suits can sell at such bargain prices."

Japan

As the U.S.S. *Midway* approached Japan, the captain had distributed a directive to all *Midway* personnel. The directive, which was nine pages long and single-spaced, included the following information about Japan:

1. *Yokosuka*: Nightclubs and cabarets abound. Prostitution and venereal disease in Yokosuka exist on a scale exceeded by few other cities in the Far East. Control of venereal disease is a major problem of the Navy in the Far East. Prostitution is legal in Japan. It is estimated that in Yokosuka alone there are approximately one thousand prostitutes registered with the authorities from the officially recognized houses and over seven thousand "free lancers."

2. *Food*: vegetables in Japan are commonly grown with the use of human feces as fertilizer ("night soil"). Therefore, naval personnel must avoid salads and other dishes containing raw vegetables. Raw fish should not be eaten due to intestinal parasites. All milk is unsafe except that which is served in military facilities. The same is true for ice cream, cheese, and other dairy products. Naval personnel must not be misled into a false sense of security because the local inhabitants eat these unsafe foods without ill effects.

3. *Water*: normally safe in some larger cities but may be dangerous elsewhere in Japan. Be wise. When in doubt as to the safety of the water, drink bottled beer.

Into Tokyo Bay steamed the *Midway*. I went ashore with Tim Tebo, and we hailed a cab into downtown Yokosuka, which was the largest naval base in Japan. We noticed that, as sailors left the gate at the naval station, hordes of girls descended upon them. Terms were quickly arranged, and, after several moments, they paired off.

As Tebo and I walked along, girls came up to us on the street and tried to initiate contact. We had been warned that officers' uniforms smelled of money. The shops exhibited curios typical of every port of call. *Midway* men went wild, buying inexpensive wallets, silk smoking jackets, and silk water colors displaying Japanese scenes and samurai on horseback.

Tebo and I headed for a bar called the Trade Winds. Sailors in all sorts of foreign uniforms abounded. As we walked in, we came to a large oblong bar. To the right was a dance floor, with tables and chairs crowded around. There were, of course, a large number of girls available to join us for a drink or to dance.

Two girls attracted everyone's attention: the first one danced the mambo displaying fabulous hip control. She was dressed in a Chinese-style straight black sheath with a red dragon crawling over protruding parts of her anatomy. The skirt was slit, but conservatively by Hong Kong standards. As the mambo band got wilder in its tempo, this girl kept time gyrating her hips. Within the tight confines of her dress, her body moved sensuously. As she danced, everyone around her began clearing space, and soon she was an exhibition solo.

The other girl had a pretty face and short stylish hair. Her features blended into a lovely complexion. Her lips were full and well-formed. Her eyes were slightly slanted, adding exotic enchantment, and they seemed to smolder. She too was an excellent dancer, and, while her movements were not as exaggerated as those of her competitor, they invited just as much scrutiny.

The next day, Don Bull and I arranged to meet Willy Hanes at the Yokosuka officers' club. This was my first chance to look over the club, and it turned out to be not one club, but a number of clubs. There were seven separate bars (some for commanders and above), and lots of little rooms, comfortably furnished, Japanese in decoration and taste. While sipping our first round, Willy mentioned that he had heard that there was a floorshow at the Trade Winds, due to end at 1900. In three seconds, we had downed our drinks and were out the door.

We arrived at the Trade Winds and a sign greeted us: Stag Show in Progress. In we went to see a stripper gyrating to "Temptation." The show was not subtle. The stripper danced off the stage and into a cluster of tables, where she targeted a sailor. She undulated in his direction, sat on his lap, and attempted to touch his face with various parts of her upper body. She then returned to the stage, removed most of her garments and performed an exotic dance. Immediately following the strip, there was a jam session. The band played American favorites, although its arrangements were not original. The band simply mimicked the arrangement which had made the number famous, but the music was nostalgic and enjoyable.

Once the jam session had ended, the Trade Winds swarmed with hostesses. A customer could dance with a hostess for one hundred yen per dance. (Three hundred sixty yen equaled one dollar.) A dance at a time was the sailor's usual choice. However, if one preferred, he could invite the hostess to his table, agreeing to pay her six hundred yen per hour.

Tebo, Willy and I hopped a cab and said, "Clover Club." The cab raced along dark, narrow little streets and through a poor section of town, ending up in front of an unimpressive little house with a sign reading: Clover Club, Officers Only. We exited the cab and entered a small courtyard. We came to two steps on which there were several pairs of slippers, and we were greeted by a Japanese woman who took our shoes and puts slippers on our feet. We entered a low-ceilinged room decorated in Japanese style with a cherry tree in one corner. Little green and yellow lights were everywhere, and we finally came into a bar with a small dance floor surrounded by couches, behind which were curtains. We sat down on a couch and ordered our drinks. The waiter asked us if we wanted hostesses, and, despite Don's protests, Willie and I said, "Not yet."

We were facing a couch across the room on which some officers were having a drink. To our surprise, arms slowly emerged from behind the curtains and gracefully encircled the neck of each drinker. The officers gently pulled the arms and out come several attractive girls. They were soon on the small dance floor, swaying seductively. And, soon everyone began disappearing from the room. Naive Billy Haynes asked me where everyone had gone, and I answered, "Guess."

"What are you talking about?" was his response, and we mildly argued as to what the Clover Club was. However, in the midst of our conversation, we heard the sound of slippers scuffing behind us. We parted the curtains and saw a cute Japanese girl, about twenty-one, clad in a transparent housecoat and panties. Billy looked at me, and, almost sullenly, said, "You win."

We left the Clover Club and grabbed a cab for the Cross Roads, which was a small eight-barstool bar with a small dance floor. A quartet played good dance music. There we spotted Kyoko, who was obviously the number one girl of the Cross Roads. She was buxom for a Japanese girl, and she wore a low cut dress to display her cleavage. She had a lovely face, long black hair, and pale skin. Her eyes seemed just a shade lighter than jet-black, and red lips seemed to be in a perpetual pout. She was beautiful.

Kyoko told us that she averaged three thousand yen nightly (almost nine dollars) in a country in which the average pay was thirty dollars monthly. She slept until noon and spent the afternoon fixing her clothes, working on her hair, and shopping. As she talked, her eyes flashed incessantly, and her lips frequently parted into a smile. She was a cuddly kitten, oozing sex appeal. But Willie and I decided that it was time to return to the *Midway*, and Don reluctantly agreed to accompany us.

The next morning, I got a call from Dick Rover. His ship, the *Estes*, had just pulled into Yokosuka. Japan is old stuff to Rover, who had been based in Japan for eight months. Don and I made plans to meet Rover at the train station to catch the 1315 train for Kamakura. Don and I left the *Midway* at 1305. I asked the cabbie how long it would take to get to the station. He said ten minutes. I said, "Please try to make it eight." The cab raced through the streets, the cabbie leaning on the horn the whole way. People jumped out of the way constantly. We pulled up in front of the station at 1312, where Rover was waiting for us. He had had the foresight to buy three tickets. We ran to the station. A bell was ringing. We all knew that, when the bell stopped, the train would pull out. We jumped onto the train, relieved that we had made it.

I felt a slight tug on my arm and turned to find a small Japanese man bowing as he held out two cigars to me. The man looked up, said something in Japanese and dashed off the train. Rover shouted "dom arigato" ("thank you") and explained that the cigars had dropped from my shirt pocket as I had been running to the train. The Japanese man had retrieved them, followed me to the train to give them back to me, and rushed off of the first class section in which we were seated because his ticket was for the second class section, which he had to get to before the bell stopped ringing. "The Japanese are unbelievably polite," Rover observed.

The ride was picturesque, passing little thatched huts amid oceans of blossoming cherry trees. We exited at the second stop and took a cab to the Green Hotel, where Rover was an old friend. He introduced us to the owner, Katie-san. The Green Hotel had been the mansion of Katie-san's family, which had been quite wealthy. As the cab pulled up to the sign saying Green Hotel, we couldn't see any buildings. All we could see were steps leading up the side of small hill with thick greenery on both sides. At the top of the hill we could see a low rambling house that reeked of comfort, with a magnificently flowering garden and lawn in back. All of the many windows were open. Outside the house, we came to two steps where we deposited our shoes and put on slippers. Here we met Katie-san, who led us to a small club cellar-like bar where we had a round of drinks.

After a time, we left to visit the sitting Buddha of Kamakura. I understood that one becomes a Buddhist merely by living the good life exemplified by Gautama Buddha, "enlightened one."

The next day I went into Tokyo by train with Daring Don. We took a short walk from the station to the Emperor's Palace. Although not allowed on the grounds, we walked up to the moat, where we could see three-foot long carp biting at bread being thrown into the moat by Japanese visitors. The palace was surrounded by a high stone wall, and all we could see was the peculiarly slanted roofs which exemplified Japanese architecture. We could also see the bridge connecting the inner and outer palaces.

We decided to get a sukiyaki dinner at a good restaurant. We entered a modern building and took the elevator to the seventh floor, where we removed our shoes and walked down a short passageway to our private room. Here there were three mama-sans who fussed over us, spread pillows for us to sit on, and, once we were seated, gave us hot towels to wipe our hands. We ordered steak and sukiyaki, which, of course, was prepared within the room. The raw meat was cooked and placed on white rice. Soy sauce was poured over the meat, to which some onion-like greens were added. We drank cold beer during the meal and hot saki immediately afterwards. It was a superlative meal.

After a while Don and I left and took the train for Yokosuka in order to attend a wetting down party for *Midway* lieutenants who had just made lieutenant commander. Drinks flowed, and the food was excellent.

The next morning, with a horrendous headache, I learned that I had legal duties ashore. A sailor had been walking along thieves' alley, where he had been approached by a pimp who asked him if he wanted an attractive girl. When the sailor answered in the negative, the pimp became aggressive and grabbed the white hat's arm. The pimp called friends, and the sailor, in fighting, hit the pimp, causing a cut on his face. Now the white hat was being asked by the Japanese police to pay fifteen hundred yen to the pimp to settle the matter. Additionally, a chief petty officer had picked up a prostitute, gone to her apartment, paid her, and spent the night. He had been quite drunk during the night, and, when morning arrived, he dressed and started to leave when the girl screamed that he'd taken nineteen hundred yen from her purse.

I hustled both the sailor and the chief into downtown Yokosuka where the sailor paid fifteen hundred and the chief nineteen hundred yen. I was not sorry about the chief because I actually believed that he could have taken the girl's money, his story being full of inconsistencies. I was disturbed about the white hat, inasmuch as he had been a victim in the fight. Still, it had been wise to settle.

I learned that Burke, my INE yeoman, after a few too many beers, had brought an electric guitar without knowing a note of music. He had been assured that he could learn to play in ten easy lessons. Upon sobering up back on the ship, Burke opened the instruction book and found it written in Japanese.

We lifted anchor and headed out of Tokyo Bay, bound for Manila. Heading south, the skies were heavily overcast, and the seas were thrashing relentlessly. Once again, the *Midway* became a warship. I had time to think about my visit to Japan. The Japanese people were extremely polite. They bowed and were scrupulous not to offend. Merchants and madams dealing with Americans smiled and were cheerful but shrewd. The Japanese were an industrious people. They were rightly called "the Prussians of the Orient."

The Japanese had converted their 1955 economy into an economy of luxury. For me, Japan seemed geared toward the comfort and convenience of American servicemen. The best hotels were used for R and R (rest and recreation), and the industry turned out smoking jackets, trinkets, china, and watercolors, all for the American dollar. The Japanese population increased at the rate of one million per year. There were eighty-five million people crowded into the Japanese islands, which are a smaller, area-wise, than the state of California. Hence, overpopulation was the ever-present problem, and in 1955 normal migration to Formosa, Korea and China was blocked. The problem promised only to increase, especially with American science promising greater life expectancy for the Japanese people.

The Japanese people, who were not blessed with the material well-being of Americans, had nonetheless fashioned themselves with a way of life which was leisurely, yet efficient; picturesque, yet workable. In homes, doors, for instance, were not heavy and wooden, and no doorknobs existed. The doors were made of light wood (like balsa), and they slid easily on runners. It was almost impossible for them to jam, and, from time to time, the Japanese simply ran a bar of soap over the runners, which helped the door slide.

Traditional Japanese shoes were called *getas*, consisting of a flat piece of wood, supported by two short wooden stilts, all very light. Hence when, after rain, people had to walk over puddles, they could do so without getting their feet wet, since the stilts kept their feet above the puddle. When Japanese wished to carry something like a package, they didn't do so in the fold of their arm, as Americans did. They merely wrapped it in a silk handkerchief and carried it easily in their hand.

I remembered the day that a group of wives of influential Japanese men had come aboard ship for lunch. I had sat next to one, and we chatted throughout the meal. She may have been overly polite, or she may have been trying to make me feel good, but she informed me that Americanization has in some ways benefited the Japanese. She claimed that Japanese children were demanding more and more that they be allowed to sit on chairs and eat at higher tables, rather than squat on the floor and eat from a low table. The result had been that Japanese children were growing taller than their predecessors. She also said that Japanese mothers had been using more baby carriages, and there had been less of the old fashioned, papoose-style of carrying babies. In the papoose-style, the child, which was carried even when it was quite large by America's standards, wrapped its legs around the mother. Doing less papoose-style carrying, she informed me, had apparently resulted in fewer bowed legs among Japanese children.

Emergency Leave

The *Midway* was steaming out of Yokosuka when I received a telegram:

> Your mother has suffered a heart attack. Your family
> has requested emergency leave, which is granted: ten
> days commencing arrival continental USA.

But I was custodian of the *Midway*'s welfare and recreation fund, and I needed to be relieved as custodian before I could begin my emergency leave. In one day, I conducted an inventory of general property and the hobby shop, and I had the books of the recreation fund audited. I reported to the administrative officer, who said, "You leave tomorrow at 1100 by helicopter to the *Yorktown*, then by Skyraider aircraft to Okinawa." At 0800, I was taking a shower when a lieutenant rushed in and said, "Your helo leaves at 0815." I jumped aboard the helicopter, was strapped into a lifejacket, then secured into my seat, and up we went. It was a unique thrill going straight up and down.

We landed on the *Yorktown* at 0915. My Skyraider was scheduled to depart at 1530. I located the wardroom and was surprised by its plushness. I wandered aimlessly around the aircraft carrier and into its ship store, which had large display cases, just like a civilian store. I noticed an escalator, which traversed two decks. Compared to the *Midway*, the mighty *Yorktown* was a luxury hotel, the closest thing to shore duty in the fleet.

My AD Skyraider came in. I got into the rear cockpit, but not until I had been fitted with a Mae West (an inflatable vest-like life preserver) and instructed about the fundamentals of operating a parachute. I was jammed into the cockpit. My pulse began to race. Slowly, the AD taxied into position, its wings unfolding to their full span. Then the propeller raced, and the AD started toward the bow, picking up momentum. In an instant, we were airborne. Time 1645, 18 May 1955.

Two ADs made the flight toward Okinawa. They kept close together in formation, and it was a stirring sight to behold the task force below as we circled for Okinawa. We passed over the *Yorktown* and the *Midway*, and we could see the destroyers plowing through heavy seas. At exactly 1800 on 18 May, the ADs landed at Naha Air Force Base, Okinawa. Here, my orders were scrutinized, and I was directed to a station wagon headed for Kadena Air Force Base from which all flights for Japan departed.

I checked with the operations officer of Kadena airbase and learned that there were no passenger flights scheduled for Tokyo departure, although a cargo plane was to head there in about thirty minutes. There were several passenger seats available on the cargo plane. After a short wait, I was about to board the cargo plane when I was stopped by an Air Force sergeant. "Sir, passengers flying cargo planes are required to wear a Mae West, and a parachute. If you will step this way, I will assist you in putting them on."

The sergeant pulled out a yellow life jacket with two flaps. He guided my arms through the flaps, and then buckled the straps to my body. There were two yellow lines hanging from the front of the Mae West. Next, the sergeant placed a parachute on my back on top of the Mae West, and he proceeded to strap the parachute to my body. There were two brown lines hanging from the front of the parachute.

"Sir, if you are required to jump from the plane, be sure to pull *only* the longer brown line after you have fallen about one hundred feet, which will unfurl your parachute. When you hit the water, pull shorter brown line, which will release the parachute automatically from your back. Then, pull the longer yellow line, and it will inflate the life jacket, which will allow you to float in the ocean until you are rescued. Sir, above all else, be careful not to pull the shorter brown line or either yellow line when you first leap from the plane, because, if you do, you will foul your parachute and drop straight down."

"Sergeant, I'm not going to jump from this plane under any circumstance. I will simply go down with the plane."

"Sir, you're not the first to say that, but, if the time comes, believe me, you will jump."

With my Mae West covered by my parachute, I leaned back on the bench in the cargo plane and tried to get some sleep. At 1300 our C46 touched ground at Nagoya Air Force Base, Japan, where we remained until 1500, at which time we were to head for Haneda, which was Tokyo International Airport and from which all flights to the States depart. However, once in flight, the pilot received instructions that, in view of the overcrowding at Haneda, he was being switched to Tachikawa Air Force Base, some forty miles west of Tokyo. At 1800, 19 May, we touched ground at Tachikawa AFB. I hustled to Operations to find out how to get to Tokyo. I was told that there was no transportation whatever to Tokyo. Upset, I tried to learn of any means of getting to Tokyo when, suddenly, I heard the PA blurt out: "Anyone desiring transportation to Tokyo, check at Air Force liaison."

I raced to the liaison desk and was pleasantly surprised to learn that a general had just driven to Tachikowa from Tokyo, and his staff car was heading back to the city. I jubilantly loaded my bag into the trunk of the staff car, my Japanese chauffeur took his seat behind the wheel, and off we went. I politely asked the driver if he would take me directly to Haneda instead of Tokyo; in Tokyo I would have to get yen and somehow obtain transportation to Haneda. The driver, however, was adamant and insisted that he could only go to Tokyo. Glad to get a ride at least, I settled back and lit up a cigar.

What phenomenal luck, I realized. Here I was, a lowly ensign with one measly stripe on my sleeve, and I was being chauffeured in a general's staff car with a two-star flag fluttering prominently from the right fender. The road from Tachikowa Air Force Base to Tokyo traveled through some small villages, the streets of which were so narrow that the staff car barely fit in the roadway. The driver had to proceed very slowly, but I was in no hurry. I was reveling in my chauffeured opulence.

As we made our way through the towns, the villagers, both young and old, curious when they saw the limousine approaching, gathered on both sides of the road and bowed politely as my limousine passed. I thought, these villagers don't suspect that a mere Navy ensign is being chauffeured in the limousine of a two-star general. They undoubtedly thought that I was that general, and they probably wondered how a guy so young could have risen so quickly to become a two-star general. I puffed contentedly on my cigar.

Although it was evening now, the fields teemed with workers. I could see that virtually no ground went unused in Japan. In the small towns, houses pushed right up to the edge of the narrow road. In the country, the patches of wheat and greenery virtually smothered each other. There seemed to be no such thing as a vacant lot in Japan.

I had practically ignored the driver (since a large sign read: please do not talk to driver while car is in motion), when, suddenly, the car came to a stop. The driver turned, gave me a huge smile and, nodding his head, repeated "Haneda, we go to Haneda."

Pleasantly shocked, I repeated "dom arigato" several times, as the driver whisked off the main drag onto a shortcut. We arrived at the main gate of Haneda, located the base terminal, and off loaded my baggage. I gladly pressed ten dollars into the driver's hand and soon learned that a flight to Hawaii was leaving in four hours. I went to Navy liaison, and, on the basis of emergency leave priority, I bumped someone who was slated to leave on the 2100 flight. I chowed down heartily.

What a break, I thought, a civilian flight. Perhaps they would have stewardesses or attractive female passengers. I was a bachelor, and it was a long way from Tokyo across the broad Pacific to San Francisco. Boarding the giant C97, my fantasies were quickly dashed. There are no stewardesses, nor were there any attractive female passengers. The plane was packed with matrons and children, and the din from squalling babies, squabbling children, and rambunctious adolescents was deafening.

At 2100, I heard the engines revving up, and down the runway we raced. But one engine conked out. The pilot immediately put reverse pitch on the props and brought the plane to a stop.

Everyone filed out, and it was later determined that the plane was unfit to make the journey. We were all relieved that the faulty engine had been discovered before the plane got aloft. The next plane was to leave at 2400. Once again, everyone emplaned. Just as the door was secured, a woman passenger called out, "Stop, let me off." It seemed that the previous experience had shaken her, and, with her two children, off they got. Three servicemen immediately filled the vacancies she had created.

At last, the plane took off, Midway Island being our first destination. It was a long flight, and I had nothing to do other than study my fellow passengers. What an incredibly dull-looking lot: some, innocuous looking old timers, but mostly complaining, hyperactive youngsters. I drifted off to sleep several times, and, when I awakened, we were almost at Midway Island. The time of the trip from Tokyo to Midway was nine hours plus four hours difference in time. The plane was flying at nineteen thousand feet, high above the clouds. At 1415, 20 May, the C97 glided to a stop at desolate, forgotten Midway Island. I spotted servicemen stationed on this purgatory eagerly lined up, probably hoping to glimpse some attractive female.

As soon as the plane landed , all passengers were ushered into a large waiting room while the plane was refueled. Suddenly, the loudspeaker announced: "Ensign George, report to the security office at once." I left the waiting room and was directed to the security office, where I was told: "Ensign George, you are the junior officer aboard the flight, and you have been designated courier to carry top secret documents which are located in this security pouch. These documents you are to deliver to Base Operations Officer in San Francisco immediately upon your arrival there. The pouch containing these documents will be handcuffed to your wrist."

Courier! How could there possibly be top secret documents originating on Midway Island (of all places) needing to get immediately to San Francisco? And why did they have to be couriered by *me*? Nevertheless, the pouch was handcuffed to my wrist, and I left the security office. When I returned to the waiting room, I found some of the passengers outside, staring at a strange, grotesquely ugly bird called the gooney bird, which had a long, narrow curved beak, a duck's head, and a mass of ugly down. At 1530, 20 May, we departed Midway.

I tried to read a magazine, but the bulky pouch got in the way. How naive, I thought, anyway, for the military to send top-secret stuff so openly. In the first place, every one of the passengers was in the waiting room and heard me being summoned to the *security office*. I came out of the security office with a huge green pouch suddenly handcuffed to my wrist. Wouldn't anyone of even sub-normal intelligence have asked: What could have been so important that the security office would handcuff it to his wrist? Must be top secret stuff. Need to chop off his hand.

As I looked around the plane, the same passengers who had previously seemed so harmlessly average-American had now taken on suspicious, sinister appearances. Some seemed to be directing furtive glances in my direction. Others simply stared at the green pouch, clasped clumsily to my right wrist. Some of the older kids seemed to have matured rapidly since Midway and were gazing, glassy-eyed, at the pouch.

I thought, Communist spies must have known that Midway would be sending top secret documents to San Francisco through a lowly ensign. All they had to do was get on the plane, act like an average American until the courier appeared with top secret stuff in the obvious green pouch, and then—POW.

We crossed the International Date Line, which meant that it was again 19 May. We lost an hour's time on route to Hawaii. Flying at nineteen thousand feet I observed an unusual sight. We were flying over a thick bank of clouds, and, as the evening progressed, the sun seemed to set beneath the clouds, leaving the sky above varied hues of red, orange, purple, and finally darkness.

At 2130, 19 May, the plane touched ground at Hickam Field, Hawaii. It was anticipated that the plane would depart Hawaii at 0335, but an engine defect put our C97 out of commission. I was not actually to leave until 20 May at 1845. I called home and learned that Mother had survived the coronary, was resting well, and there was no need to rush. Thank God!

I took the order not to rush very seriously. My leave did not commence until my arrival continental United States. I checked in overnight at transient officer's quarters and, early the next morning, went to see the island of Oahu. The most distinctive feature of Oahu was that everywhere there seemed the be the aroma of flowers.

I hopped a cab and headed into Honolulu. On the way, I noted a range of mountains, the hills being basically green but containing blotches of crimson and yellow (where wild flowers grew). A thick cloud bank crowned these hills. The climate in Hawaii was apparently always moderate—sunny with balmy breezes, the temperature ranging from sixty to eighty.

I got out of the cab on the main drag and was struck by the variety of people who lived in Hawaii. Most looked like native stock, with round, Polynesian faces, wide brown eyes and black hair. But there seemed to be an abundance of Japanese and Chinese also, along with a large Caucasian group. Intermarriage had produced some exquisitely beautiful people. One in particular caught my attention: a lanky figure, her jet black hair tied into a ponytail and her pale blue eyes containing only the slightest suggestion of Asia.

I went to Waikiki Beach and stopped in at the luxurious Royal Hawaiian Hotel, a pink stucco palace overlooking the emerald Pacific. The lobby of the Royal Hawaiian contained many exotic plants and trees, all vying for attention by reason of their starkly strange beauty. They were so colorful that they actually appeared artificial. I was not disappointed at the narrowness of the beach, as I had been forewarned. I was surprised, however, to note that the beach was not crowded. Back to the terminal, and off we went at 1845. Next stop: stateside. At last, I saw the green hills of California. At 0741 21 May, our wheels touched the runway at Travis Air Force Base.

~ ~ ~ ~ ~

Leave was now over, and I was approaching the San Francisco Naval liaison office. Gosh, the *Midway* would be in Japan only for another two weeks before it would leave for San Francisco, which is where I was now. Why should the Navy send me all the way across the Pacific to enjoy two more weeks in Japan when all the Navy had to do was station me here in San Francisco until the *Midway* arrived? Flying me to Japan would be a waste of taxpayers' money.

I desperately wanted to return to Japan. I had had a good time there. I enjoyed the countryside and cities, as well as the exotic culture and food. I still had other site-seeing I wanted to do and other Japanese goods I wanted to buy. I wanted to top off my visit to the Orient in a spectacular, celebratory way. Besides, when the *Midway* arrived in San Francisco, it would be stationed here for two weeks. That was plenty of time for me to get to know San Francisco. I had to figure out a way to get the Navy to send me back to Japan for a fabulous two-week fling.

But how could I refute the Navy's logic when I was told, "Ensign George, we're not going to ship you all the way across the Pacific only to have your ship leave in two weeks. You'll have to stay here in San Francisco until your ship arrives."

I entered the Naval liaison office and saw a craggy-faced Lieutenant Commander sitting behind the desk. He looked at my orders and snapped, "Ensign, I know what you want. You want me to station you here in San Francisco until your ship arrives, but I've got news for you. I'm sending you across the Pacific *pronto*."

Sayonara

The morning after I was flown aboard the *Midway* we had special atomic drills. Damage control parties went about the shop, washing down hot areas. It was hot, stuffy, and uncomfortable. An atomic hit anywhere within a four thousand yard radius of the ship would probably be fatal. It seemed unlikely that a bomber could miss us by that large a margin. Later, we set anti-aircraft condition Readiness III, which meant that I spent eight hours per day on the bridge. At 1300, the U.S.S. *Twining* commenced making an approach on our starboard side for refueling. The *Twining* was directly astern of us, but, for some reason, it did not come right. It was within twenty feet of our fantail when our captain suddenly shouted, "Right ten degree rudder." The officer of the deck immediately repeated the order to the helmsman, "Right ten degree rudder." The captain said, "Right twenty degree rudder," and, again, that order was repeated to the helmsman.

The orders seemed wrong to me. The *Twining* was approaching our starboard side. Yet the captain ordered right rudder, seemingly a collision course. Suddenly, I understood. The *Twining* had already been almost on our fantail. By ordering "right rudder," the captain had swung our own fantail away from the *Twining*. Had the captain ordered "left rudder," our fantail would probably have collided with the *Twining*. (It was easy to see why he was wearing the eagle, and I was wearing a solitary bar.)

Word was that we were to rendezvous with a large task force off of Okinawa, where we were to carry out atomic drills. The bridge was crowded with the captain, executive officer, the navigator, the officer of the deck, the junior officer of the deck, and me, the junior officer of the watch. At 0600, fleet formations were to converge on one rendezvous point. Our formation is one carrier and four destroyers, and another comprised the carriers *Kearsage, Yorktown,* and *Essex* and eight destroyers. A third formation was the replenishment force of supply ships. All formations were to join together, with Rear Admiral Rugle on the *Midway* taking command of the whole task force.

The task force was tremendously impressive. The *Midway* was at the flagship center of a huge formation. All around were carriers, cruisers, destroyers, and the replenishing force of tankers, oilers and freighters.

The weather had been consistently dismal at sea—every day was overcast, the seas were rough, and the sun had yet to shine. It reminded me of the old sailor's lament: You're not alive, you're not dead, you're just at sea.

The *Midway* was completing its stay in Japan, the culmination of its six-month world cruise. We were to sail at break of day for Hawaii and ultimately San Francisco. But, oh, that last night on shore. Officers, vowing to make it a night to remember the rest of their lives, attended a marathon party, commencing at 1600, replete with geishas, drink, kabuki dancers, drink, more geishas, endless arrays of sukiyaki, drink, still more geishas, etc. The officers' party formally ended at 2300 in order to allow enough time to return to the *Midway* prior to the expiration of shore leave at 2345. Dutifully, my officer cohorts and I reported to the ship at 2340. Exhausted and slightly tipsy, I collapsed into my bunk and was soon in deep sleep, confident that I would awaken on my way to Hawaii. My slumber was pierced with what seemed to be loud, repetitive pounding in my head. Half awake, I realized that the pounding was on my door.

"Yes?" I called out.

"Sir, I am the captain's orderly. The captain wishes to see you—as *he* put it, sir—RIGHT NOW."

"Right now?", I repeated, incredulously.

"Sir, they were the captain's exact words."

I quickly pulled on my uniform, tied my tie, opened my door and began following the captain's orderly, who was sprinting ahead of me. We arrived at the captain's cabin. The orderly knocked, announcing, "Mr. George, sir."

"Come in," an angry tone came through the door.

I looked at my watch. It was 0350. I entered the captain's cabin. Captain Vaughn was obviously incensed. "George, the U.S.S. *Midway* cannot get underway. This ship will be the laughing stock of the Navy."

"Cannot get underway?"

"Yes, George, the U.S.S. *Midway* cannot get underway. Fully twenty per cent of our crew has chosen not to return to the ship. WE CANNOT GET UNDERWAY."

Still not comprehending, I asked,

"Sir, what do you want *me* to do?"

"Dammit, George, *you* are the legal officer. *You* know where they are."

My mind still somewhat befogged, I repeated,

"Where they are?"

"Dammit, George, get moving! Twenty percent of my crew is on that dammed street in Yokosuka lined with bars and geisha houses. You're standing here, and the *Midway* is not weighing anchor. Mobilize the shore patrol and our marine detachment and get my crew back—and I mean—PRONTO!"

"Aye aye, sir."

Thirty minutes later, I met with LT. Spalding, duty officer of the Yokosuka shore patrol and Captain Ferrus of the *Midway*'s marine detachment.

LT. Spalding spoke. "Gentlemen, we will comb the buildings on both sides of Babysan Street. There are alleys in back of the buildings on both sides of the street. Captain Ferrus, you post some of your marines along one alley to cut off escape from the back of the buildings. I will put my shore patrol along the other alley across the street to do likewise. I'll bring shore patrol wagons outside the houses on both ends of the street. The marines will go into the bars and upstairs rooms at one end of the street, and the shore patrol will do the same at the other end. As we check ID's on every sailor, we'll run all *Midway* personnel into the wagons, and when the first wagon is filled, it will return personnel to the ship while we fill up the second wagon."

Babysan Street was the name given by U.S. military personnel in Yokosuka to a street lined on both sides by two and three story buildings. The first floor was a bar, crowded with vivacious and attractive hostesses, who were dance and drink partners (the hostess was always served plain tea in cocktail glasses, for which military personnel are charged liquor drink prices). On the second and third floors were rooms where the hostesses stayed.

The plan was executed. Small groups of marines and shore patrolmen entered each bar and began systematically to check the ID of all military personnel. When all sailors and marines in the bar had been checked (those with *Midway* IDs were escorted into the waiting paddy wagons), the groups proceeded up the stairs to check all rooms on the floors above. Some sailors tried to leave by the rear fire escapes, but they were collared by the alley sentries, and, again, *Midway* personnel were delivered to the wagons.

I was standing on the sidewalk as the mission neared its end. I will never forget the scene of a hulking marine emerging from a bar, carrying a slender sailor over his shoulder toward a wagon. A petite hostess was running behind the marine, hitting his back with a small purse, crying, "Let Joe go. Let Joe go."

The sailor, impassive at first, suddenly stretched skyward and shouted—with a fist raised high, "Better the brig in Japan than freedom in the United States." Then he collapsed in an alcoholic stupor until tossed into the back of the wagon.

The U.S.S. *Midway* weighed anchor for Hawaii twelve hours late, saying sayonara to Japan.

Blackjack Goes to a Carrier

Visitors' day was clear and balmy. The *Midway* was tied up in San Francisco, and the ship and dock had been crowded all afternoon with throngs of civilians who wished to board this large ship, which so recently had returned from a round-the-world cruise. The command duty officer was on post on the quarterdeck, and the officer of the deck was busy greeting the visitors who gushed, unendingly, from the two gangways. It was the command duty officer who first noticed two messcooks, clutching a large garbage can, pushing their way through the crowd on the aftergangway. Quietly, he informed the officer of the deck that he wanted to halt the dumping of all trash and garbage until after the visiting condition had secured. Dutifully, the officer of the deck informed the bosun's mate of the watch to pass the appropriate word.

Blackjack, who had only recently come aboard the *Midway* on TAD (Temporary Additional Duty) from a destroyer escort, had never seen this many people before. He approached the 1MC shipwide loudspeaker, brimming with the responsibility of his commission. Carefully, he depressed the button. "Now knock off the dumping of shitcans on the pier" was the word passed on all the electronically amplified circuits.

For a moment, both officers were stunned. Then each moved quickly toward Blackjack and began castigating him verbally. How dare he use such foul language when the ship was overflowing with hundreds of civilian visitors? Exuding disgust, they turned and walked away from Blackjack. Slowly, dejectedly, Blackjack approached the speaker and again depressed the button:

"Now, belay that last word about shitcans."

The Ship from Hell

The keel of the U.S.S. *Forrestal* (CVA-59) was laid in July 1952, and the ship was launched in December 1954. The ceremony officially commissioning the *Forrestal* as part of the U.S. Navy was held on October 1, 1955, at the Foremost Shipyard, Norfolk, Virginia. During the first nine months of 1955, U.S. Navy officers and men on ships and stations around the world had received orders to report to the *Forrestal* pre-commissioning command in Norfolk, Virginia. I received my orders to report as the *Forrestal*'s legal officer.

The *Forrestal* was to be the largest ship in the world—the first of a class to be known as supercarriers. She was to have an overall length of one thousand one hundred one feet, to displace sixty-five thousand tons, and to have a complement (including air group) of five thousand men. The *Forrestal*'s flight deck area was to comprise four and one-half acres.

Navy tradition dictated that each member of the initial crew of any newly-commissioned U.S. Navy ship was awarded a certificate that he was a plank owner, stating that he was entitled to "free and clear title to a single plank in the deck of the ship, final selection to be made in order of seniority."

October 1, 1955 dawned, and, promptly at 1000, the commissioning ceremony commenced. The entire ship's complement, officers and men, in dress whites, stood at attention in the huge hangar deck which thronged with hundreds of family and friends of the crew, as well as notable dignitaries. First, the *Forrestal* was officially delivered to the Navy by the Foremost Shipbuilding Company, and then the ship was accepted by the commandant, fifth naval district, on behalf of the U.S. Navy. Following an invocation by one of the *Forrestal*'s chaplains, the commandant read the commissioning directive and ordered that the *Forrestal* be placed in commission. The Stars Spangled Banner was played while the American flag and other military pennants were hoisted. The commanding officer read his orders, assumed command and set the *Forrestal*'s first watch.

Finally a message from the chief of naval operations was read to those assembled:

> You are plank owners of the most powerful warship
> ever built. Your ship is a symbol that the United
> States intends to maintain the most effective combat
> service in the world.

You are the men who will give this ship her character.
She was a cold mass of steel until this moment. You
will give her life, energy and power.

Fair winds and smooth sailing!

The moment that that message ended, the 1MC loudspeaker system was used for the first time aboard the mighty supercarrier, U.S.S. *Forrestal*: "Will the legal officer please call six one two? "

I broke ranks and went to a nearby telephone. "This is the legal officer."

A voice responded: "Sir, there's been a stabbing in the mess deck."

I looked at my watch. It was precisely 1026—the *Forrestal* had only moments before been commissioned a part of the U.S. Navy, and, already, a major crime of violence had occurred on board. Fourteen months aboard the U.S.S. *Midway*, and no stabbings. Twenty-six minutes aboard the *Forrestal*—a stabbing!

Over the next hour, the story unfolded:

1. Two mess cooks, preparing chow for the crew's first day aboard ship, had gotten into an argument.
2. The blade of a knife had found itself inside the abdomen of one of the cooks.
3. When the stabbee was taken to sick bay, Commander Rood, the *Forrestal*'s surgeon, after examining the wound, had removed the stabbee's appendix before suturing the cut.

I was dumbfounded. "The surgeon did what?"

"Sir, when the surgeon examined the wound, he noticed that the incision provided a canal directly to the appendix. He decided not to waste the opportunity, so he removed the appendix."

"Did the surgeon at least obtain the consent of the stabbee?"

"No sir, he did not!"

Thus began the career of LTJG Harris George, plank owner legal officer of the U.S.S. *Forrestal*. The next two weeks were a nightmare: fights broke out among the crew; two masked sailors held up a poker game aboard ship and walked away with one thousand three hundred dollars; forty-two men were scheduled for captain's mast disciplinary action the very first week following commissioning.

The captain's orderly appeared at my doorway. "Lt. George, the captain would like to see you *now*!" I hustled behind the orderly to the captain's cabin.

"George, you have to come up with a plan for ridding this ship of the cutthroats, thieves and felons comprising this crew."

I gulped "Plan, sir?"

"George, do you have any idea where the United States Navy gets the crew for a newly-commissioned ship?"

"No, sir. I don't."

"The chief of naval personnel sends out requisitions to ships and naval stations around the world. Send the *Forrestal* three seamen, four firemen, two airmen, etc. Now, George, if you are the personnel officer of a ship which receives that order, which seamen and firemen do you send? Do you send your best and brightest? Of course not! Accordingly, George, the *Forrestal*'s celebrated plank owner crew is the horrendous conglomeration of the Navy's heaviest bottom dregs—the whale dung of Navy personnel. That's the Navy way of furnishing the initial complement of any ship. But, once we get rid of this whale dung, the Navy will fill any individual vacancies with decent young men from boot camp.

"Sir, I'm not sure what you mean by 'get rid of'."

"Understand, George, the *Forrestal* is a 'Ship from Hell', and it is going on a shake-down cruise in two months. I cannot allow this present crew of hooligans to go ashore in a friendly foreign port, particularly because, with the *Forrestal*'s notoriety as the first of the supercarriers, there will be extensive press coverage of our every visit to foreign shores."

"Sir, my *Midway* experience gives me an idea for a plan. You, as the *Forrestal*'s captain, can convene two special court-martial boards. One will be composed of the ninety-day wonders, like myself, college graduates who survived officer candidate school or NROTC. They invariably give the lightest possible sentence, if any. However, the second board should be totally mustangs—career officers who joined the Navy, usually as teenagers, and served honorably as enlisted men before they became officers. They know all the tricks, excuses, screw-ups and screw-offs imaginable. They have the perspective to decide between what is a harmless shenanigan and what is a serious offense committed by a really bad actor. As the *Forrestal*'s legal officer, when a sailor is placed on report, I will check his personnel record. If his record is clean, he will be assigned to the ninety-day wonders.

"And the mustangs get him if his record isn't clean?" the captain asked.

"Captain, when my review of a personnel record shows that the sailor has spent most of his Navy time in the brig, he will go before the mustangs, who will do the American taxpayer a favor and make that bad actor a civilian."

Thereafter, naval justice was swift and focused, and the results were predictable—most bad actors were shipped off the *Forrestal*, whereas the good guys received punishments of five-day restriction to ship while the *Forrestal* was on a seven-day cruise. As time passed, a lot of cut-throats, thieves and felons left the *Forrestal*. Within a relatively short time, the Ship from Hell was resurrected, and the *Forrestal* at last enjoyed "fair winds and smooth sailing."

The Dope Fiend

A rumor reached the legal office that a mess steward had smuggled explosives aboard ship, and I decided to launch a raid on the mess decks. With precision, at exactly 2100 on a Saturday, the *Forrestal*'s marine detachment blocked all passages to the mess decks, and the ship's masters-at-arms systematically searched each locker, seizing contraband consisting of several switchblade knives, partially empty bottles of a variety of liquors, a pistol, and a sawed off shotgun. No explosives were found, but the door to the legal office flew open, and Horsham, bosun's mate second class—acting master-at-arms—excitedly rushed in, "Mr. George, Mr. George, we've got a dope fiend on board."

Horsham clutched aloft a large hypodermic needle, which he cradled in a small paper towel. Now, the crew of any U.S. Navy ship in the mid-1950s got into a smorgasbord of trouble, but drugs were not a problem at all. In fact, during that period, dangerous substances were not even called "drugs;" they were referred to, generically, as "dope," used only by big band drummers, who were notoriously called "dope fiends."

"Where did you find that needle?"

"In the locker of Seaman Raoul Sagan, sir! We've placed him under arrest."

"Bring him up right away," and, turning to my yeoman first class Carter, I said, "Carter, get ready to take a statement."

Several minutes later, two marines stood in the doorway of the legal office, and in between them was Seaman Sagan. Carter donned his stenomask, and I motioned Sagan to a chair next to him. The marines remained in the doorway, and I addressed Sagan quite solemnly.

"You are Seaman Raoul Sagan."

"Yes, sir!"

"I am LTJG George, legal officer of the *Forrestal*, and I represent the captain in this very serious matter."

"Yes, sir," he said meekly.

"Do you wish me to appoint defense counsel to advise you before I proceed with this interview?"

"No, sir. I don't need defense counsel."

"Seaman Sagan, does this needle belong to you?"

"Yes, sir."

"And would you tell me what you use it for?"

Carter was repeating the conversation into his recording stenomask machine.

"Mr. George, sir, it's part of my detective kit."

"Your what?"

"My detective kit. When I leave the Navy in six months, I am studying to become a private detective."

Incredulously, I asked, "and what use would a private detective make of this hypodermic needle?"

Almost patronizingly, Sagan explained, "Sir, when a private detective comes across a dead body bearing no identification, the fingers are often too shriveled to take fingerprints."

"So?"

Speaking slowly to ensure that I could understand, Sagan said, "Well, sir, the private detective simply fills the needle with water and injects it into each of the fingers, blowing them up fully, following which he would be able to take the corpse's fingerprints."

"So you have a kit which contains this needle?"

"Yes, sir."

"How about going with the marines to get it and bring it back here?"

"I'd be happy to, sir."

Seaman Sagan, clutching an oblong box, returned ten minutes later, escorted by the marines. Warily, I lifted the lid of the box. It was full of all sorts of detective paraphernalia, each held in place by cardboard fittings. In the disguise section, there was an unrealistic black wig, a thin mustache and dark glasses. The necessary items section contained a magnifying glass, held in place by elastic snaps, and a pair of handcuffs looped together.

"Sagan, where does the needle fit into this kit?"

Sagan pointed to two empty cardboard brackets in the necessary items section, "The needle sets in there, and here is the plastic needle guard that fits over the head to prevent you from sticking yourself accidentally. And here, sir, is the instruction booklet, where it tells you how a detective is supposed to use the needle."

I read the several sentences, which verified what Sagan had claimed.

The big dope fiend scare aboard the *Forrestal* evaporated, but I took custody of the needle, promising Seaman Sagan that, if ever he came upon a corpse with shriveled fingers, the *Forrestal* legal office would lend the needle to him.

Little Bud

Tassea, James, and little Ted George

Standing: Mary, Ted, and Boo, surrounding Bud

In Officer Candidate School (1954)

Commissioned (1954)

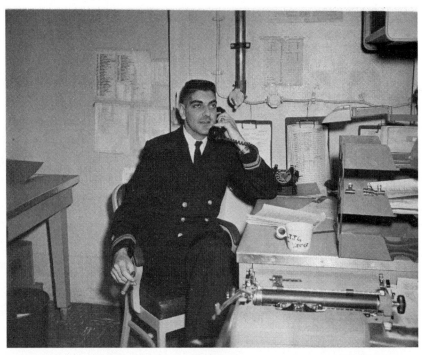

Legal officer aboard the U.S.S. *Forrestal*. (Official photograph U.S. Navy)

U.S.S. *Midway* (CVA-41) steaming off the coast of Cuba, 3 Nov. 1954.
(Official photograph U.S. Navy)

U.S.S. *Forrestal* (CVA-59). (Official photograph U.S. Navy)

Section K-5, Officer Candidate School, Newport, Rhode Island (Class of February 1954)

What the guys on the deck below thought of Section K-5 ("Those guys topside")

Legal Eagle

Being legal officer aboard the largest warship in the U.S. Navy was, without doubt, one of the poshest jobs in the fleet. Keep in mind that whoever serves as captain of a large aircraft carrier in the Navy is, following his tour of duty as captain, almost assured of being promoted to rear admiral—*unless* he screws up by

1. his ship running aground.
2. his ship colliding with another ship.
3. his incurring the disfavor of some higher authority—an admiral, Congress, the court of military appeals, etc.

Any newly-appointed captain of an aircraft carrier quickly summoned his legal officer (whom he invariably called his "legal eagle") and made the same speech: "George, you are the *Forrestal*'s 'legal eagle.' If you keep me out of trouble, you will enjoy the best duty in the Navy. If you screw up, you'll be the sorriest LTJG in the Navy."

In 1955, the captain of any navy ship received a multitude of letters addressed to "commanding officer". Most were routine, but one caused any captain instant anxiety—a thick batch of papers, stapled together, including endorsements from CINCLANT (commander-in-chief, Atlantic fleet), Congress and the bureau of naval personnel. Examination of the documents revealed that the first letter was usually from a Norfolk merchant (for example, ABC Cleaners) to his congressman, complaining that Frank Flanigan, seaman apprentice attached to the *Forrestal*, owed ABC Cleaners a bill of six dollars, which Flanigan had failed or refused to pay. The congressman, wishing to show positive response to the concerns of his constituent, promptly sent a letter asking for immediate attention to ABC's request to the Navy liaison officer to Congress, attaching ABC's letter.

The Navy liaison officer, after adding his own endorsement, forwarded ABC's letter and the congressman's letter to the chief of naval personnel, asking that ABC's correspondence be forwarded to seaman Flanigan's current duty station. The chief of naval personnel, after adding his own endorsement, forwarded all four documents to commander in chief, Atlantic fleet, which, after appending CINCLANT's endorsement, sent all five papers to the admiral under whose command seaman Flanigan's ship had been assigned. That admiral, after adding his own cover endorsement, forwarded all six documents to commanding officer, U.S.S. *Forrestal*.

This intimidatingly huge accumulation of endorsements atop ABC's letter would ultimately be delivered to commanding officer, U.S.S. *Forrestal*, who would flip a few pages; see endorsements from Congress, chief of naval personnel and several Admirals; and then scribble his inevitable comment—George, make this go away!

As the *Forrestal*'s legal eagle, I interviewed seaman apprentice Flanigan, who usually complained that ABC had ruined his dress white uniform, and he had therefore refused to pay ABC's bill. Thereafter, my duty as a U.S. Navy legal eagle was clear. Following written directives of the bureau of naval personnel, I wrote the following letter to ABC Cleaners:

> *Your letter concerning the alleged bill owed by seaman apprentice Flanigan has been forwarded to me for action. Seaman apprentice Flanigan, when interviewed, denied liability for your bill.*
>
> *In accordance with bureau of naval personnel directives, you are hereby advised that your remedy, if any, lies in the civil courts.*
>
> Harris George, LTJG
Legal Officer
U.S.S. Forrestal (CVA-59)
By Direction of Commanding Officer

This letter from the *Forrestal*'s legal officer was never sent directly to ABC Cleaners; instead, it was required to revisit every stop along the chain of command which had conveyed the letter in the first instance (each again adding its return endorsement)—namely;

1. from commanding officer, *Forrestal* to the admiral, Norfolk squadron;
2. from admiral, Norfolk squadron to CINCLANT;
3. from CINCLANT to chief, bureau of naval personnel;
4. from chief, bureau naval personnel to Navy liaison to Congress;
5. from Navy liaison to congressman; and, finally;
6. from congressman to ABC Cleaners.

By the time ABC Cleaners received its response—that its remedy, if any, was to sue seaman apprentice Flanigan—ABC's initial letter had expanded into a thirteen-page conglomeration of Navy protocol. The *Forrestal*'s captain, however, was pleased because, miraculously, his legal eagle had indeed made that jumble of worrisome correspondence from higher Naval authorities and Congress go away.

So long as he kept his captain out of trouble, the legal officer of a large aircraft carrier enjoyed life more than any other LTJG aboard ship. Some in the ship's enlisted complement (in anticipation for any possible future misadventure on their part) tried to build up good will with the legal officer by reporting to him anything that might be of special interest. For example, in keeping with the captain's promise that (so long as I did not screw up) I would enjoy the best duty in the Navy, I was the only line officer aboard the *Forrestal* who did not stand deck watch—I was not on the *Forrestal*'s watch bill. This enormously irritated LT. Bigelow, senior watch officer, a Naval Academy graduate. From the executive officer's chief yeoman, Carter, my leading petty officer, learned that Bigelow was trying to get the executive officer to make me stand deck watches in addition to my duties as legal officer. I quickly drafted an order (by direction, commanding officer, *Forrestal*), appointing Bigelow a summary court-martial officer. Thenceforth, Bigelow could not even go on leave without my approval, since I might be assigning him summary court-martials to hear during his hoped-for leave. An unspoken pact was forged—so long as he stopped pushing for me to stand deck watches, I never assigned him any summary court-martials.

The legal officer also enjoyed special shipboard privileges. Enlisted personnel, seeking to curry future favor, would, for example, endow the legal officer with benefits—the *Forrestal*'s bake shop periodically delighted the legal office by delivering freshly-baked chocolate donuts. The officers' barber offered me a standing appointment for a trim every other Friday at 12:00 noon. One Friday noon, I went for my standing appointment, but the regular officers' barber was not in the shop; instead, a young sailor stood in his place. While shaving the back of my neck, he cut me. I felt the cut, and soon I sensed a little trickle of blood. The barber quickly dabbed it with alcohol and held a hot towel to it. Soon it stopped bleeding. About five minutes later, he nicked my neck on the other side. Half jokingly, I asked, "Did you graduate from Navy barber school?"

"The Navy doesn't have a barber school, sir."

"What barbering training have you had?"

"None, sir."

"Oh come now, the Navy must have sent you to some sort of school."

"Oh, the Navy did. They sent me to pipefitter's school, but I flunked out. That's why they made me a barber."

Surprise

Mothers of young women in Norfolk, San Diego and other Naval base cities have been giving their daughters the same advice since the beginning of World War I.

"Beware of Navy officers, particularly those who have been to sea. You've got to catch them either early in their Navy service or before they have gone to sea. Once they've gone to sea, they become obsessed with this idea that young women should be available to them in every port. Officers who have always been stationed ashore are much better husband-material."

The question that invariably followed was, "But Mom, how can I tell whether a particular officer has been to sea?"

"That's easy. Navy regulations forbid a uniformed officer from going around bare-headed. He must always wear a cap. Just look at the gold insignia attached to the cap he's wearing. If he's been to sea, instead of the insignia on his cap being gleaming gold, it will have become tarnished. The salt air at sea turns the gold insignia greenish. The brighter his cap insignia is, the safer bet he is."

Generations of young women hearing this same advice have decided one course of action—go after the officer with the greenest cap insignia!

~ ~ ~ ~ ~

Peter was emphatic: "It's difficult to like the guy. I've stood one four-hour watch with him, and I know more about him than I do about my own brother."

Jason chimed in, "He's *my* roommate, and he's always babbling about his grandfather and father having been admirals. He is actually delighted to be the most junior ensign aboard the *Forrestal*."

"Listen, you guys," Bob offered. "I think we ought to give Cad time to acclimate."

"That's another thing," Peter complained. "Imagine having a nickname of 'Cad,' short for 'Academy.'"

"That's just because he wanted, as a toddler, to go to the 'Cademy,'" defended Bob.

Peter interrupted: "How about all of Cad's drivel about cutting a wide social swath while at Annapolis:" Peter continued that Cad had confessed—quite seriously—that there were no fewer than three voluptuous beauties, awaiting his first shore leave, eager to hear every detail about his first sea duty. They delighted, he said, in his salty language—'deck' for 'floor' and 'ladder' for 'steps.' Peter said that the most outrageous thing about Cad was that, to impress those naïve fertility statues, he'd brought aboard that extra gold insignia to wear on his cap when he went ashore. He planned to fasten the extra insignia somewhere on the open bridge, where it would be exposed to salt spray twenty-four hours a day. Cad had explained to his harem that they could tell how much sea duty an officer had had by how green the salt spray had turned the gold in his cap insignia.

"You guys sound jealous," Bob said.

"Of course, we're jealous!" admitted Peter, "but I would like to take Cad down a peg or two. In fact, I have a fabulous idea. Suppose, while Cad is not on bridge watch, one of us takes down the cap insignia he's posted on the open bridge, polishes it and then replaces it exactly where Cad had originally posted it."

"Peter, that is really mean-spirited," Bob said. With a smile, "I'm in."

Jason made it unanimous.

The *Forrestal* began a four-week cruise, and Cad carefully affixed his extra cap insignia on the open bridge. Each day, as Cad assumed the watch, he would go to the open bridge and look at his cap insignia. He tried not to act surprised, but his keen disappointment at the still-gleaming gold was apparent to all. Of course, when Cad was not on bridge duty, Peter, Bob and Jason were punctiliously polishing Cad's insignia back to its original golden sheen.

Finally, at the end of the first week at sea, Cad complained openly to his watch-mates that his regular cap insignia (the one he wore *inside* the ship) was greener than the insignia he had exposed to salt air twenty-four hours a day. Cad was perplexed.

Soon, long discussions ensued. Cad ultimately rejected his initial suspicion that the gold in the exposed insignia was fake. His having moved the insignia to different parts of the open bridge had brought no positive results. Cad was stumped as the *Forrestal* headed into its second week at sea. It was then that Cad's friends stopped polishing the gold insignia Cad had affixed to the open bridge.

Cad began to notice that, at last, his bridge insignia was indeed beginning to turn slightly green. Each watch, his enthusiasm increased as he witnessed the ever-increasing greening of his gold cap insignia. By the middle of the fourth (and final) week of the cruise, the insignia was decidedly green, and Cad was ecstatic, whistling "Anchors Away" and anticipating his coming amorous conquests—facilitated by his seadog cap insignia.

Cad informed his friends that he planned to place the green insignia to his cap during his watch duty on the day the *Forrestal* docked at Norfolk. The next day Peter and Jason were on watch with Cad when he almost ceremoniously announced that he was going out on to the open bridge to retrieve his salty cap insignia. An uncustomary expletive emanated from Cad, who, moments later, entered the closed bridge, clutching his exposed cap insignia, glistening bright gold in his shuddering hand.

For the first time, Cad glowered suspiciously at his watch mates, realizing that his friends had just re-polished to gleaming gold what had been his greenish cap insignia.

The Navy's Best Baker

Napoleon Denby was the best baker in the U.S. Navy. That's why, everywhere that Admiral Taft went, Denby was sure to go. Admiral Taft was a gourmand of quite excessive proportion. When Admiral Taft established his flag aboard the *Forrestal*, Captain Engle made my future quite clear. "George, my legal eagle, Napoleon Denby has been Admiral Taft's personal baker for over seven years. If you like your job as legal officer aboard the *Forrestal*, I'd protect Napoleon Denby with your life."

Only seven days later, I was informed by the officer of the deck that the sheriff from Norfolk had requested permission to come aboard to arrest and take into his custody one Napoleon Denby. Since the *Forrestal* was to embark the very next day on its shake-down cruise to the Caribbean, I said simply, "Permission to come aboard, denied."

Three weeks later, as the *Forrestal* steamed toward Port-au-Prince, Haiti, in my capacity as legal officer, I received a letter concerning Napoleon Denby. The letter, from the States Attorney of Norfolk, informed me that a criminal non-support action had been filed against one Napoleon Denby in Des Moines, Iowa. Within an hour, Napoleon Denby was sitting in front of my desk. I had previously checked his service record and had learned that Denby's net pay amounted to no more than twenty-two dollars each payday, with the balance divided between the two illegitimate children he had fathered.

"Denby, have you ever been in Des Moines, Iowa?"

"No sir, I have never ever been in Des Moines, Iowa."

"Denby, I've checked your service record, and I find that you were stationed at the Naval air station, Des Moines, Iowa, two years ago. Isn't that true?"

"Yes sir, now that you reminded me, I was stationed in Des Moines."

"Denby, while in Des Moines, did you make the acquaintance of a lady named Jessica Baines?"

"No sir, I've never known any lady named Jessica Baines."

"Denby, Ms. Baines has enclosed this picture of herself with someone who looks very much like you. Take a look at this picture."

"Yes sir, now that I see her picture, I do recognize I did know Jessica Baines."

"Denby, did you 'know' her in the Biblical sense?"

"Sir, I don't understand what you mean."

"Denby, in her letter, Jessica Baines says that you are the father of her eighteen-month old child. Did you have sex with Jessica Baines?"

"No sir, I never touched the lady."

"Denby, Ms. Baines has sent this picture of her baby, and I can't help but notice that the baby has a mole on his right cheek exactly where you have a mole."

"May I see the picture, sir? Well, he sure is a handsome fellow, isn't he, sir?"

"Denby, he is indeed a handsome fellow. Are you his father?"

"Yes, sir, I'm the father."

"Denby, commencing next payday, you will receive fifteen dollars and seventeen cents. The balance of your pay will be apportioned among the mothers of your children."

Seaman Simon

Seaman Simon had joined the Navy at seventeen to see the world. He craved a life of travel and adventure—anything to get away from Haw River, North Carolina. He had been fortunate in being assigned to the U.S.S. *Forrestal* just as the largest warship in the world was departing Mayport, Florida for its shakedown cruise in the Caribbean Sea.

The only unfortunate thing about Seaman Simon's being aboard the *Forrestal* was his job. He had to endure seemingly interminable four-hour watches alone in an isolated small space on the hangar deck level. There was nothing in the small space except a red button which he was to push in the unlikely event of a fire on the hangar deck. Once the button was pushed, enormous amounts of chemical foam would come cascading down from large sprinkler heads located on the hangar deck overhead, dousing any fire among the planes parked on the hangar deck. Simon had been aboard the *Forrestal* for seven months, but he had yet to push the red button.

One day while Simon was on watch, he was visited by his good friend, Seaman Apprentice Darrell, who had only recently come aboard the *Forrestal*. Darrell asked, "Just exactly what are you supposed to do while you stand watch here for four hours?"

"In case of a fire on the hangar deck, I'm supposed to push this red button,"

Simon said, as he pointed his finger close to the button. In fact, it was too close—Simon, horrified, suddenly realized that he had unintentionally pushed the red button. Everyone on the crowded hangar deck also realized that the button had been pushed. Deafening alarm bells began clanging, and the entire hangar deck was suddenly awash in torrents of thick, sticky chemical foam.

No one escaped—every single officer and enlisted man on the hangar deck was drenched in foam, which also covered the thirty-five planes which were parked on the deck.

As legal officer, I was summoned to the bridge. Captain Engle was erupting in a paroxysm of anger. "That stupid SOB! I want to slap that dumb bastard into the brig for two weeks on bread and water—and, then, I'll court-martial him."

"Captain, you know that if you handle the case at captain's mast, you can't also court-martial him."

"You're right, George. Get him before me at captain's mast. I'll throw the book at him. In fact, I'm going to make an example of him."

The captain paused for a moment, "George, I want you to have the supply officer conduct an investigation to ascertain precisely how much money that idiot cost the Navy by his incompetence. I want to have that sum available to me at captain's mast."

The supply officer groaned when I told him of the captain's order. "We'll spend more time figuring out the cost than we did in cleaning up the mess." Nevertheless, the supply officer knew that he had better start working on the figures pronto. Soon, the *Forrestal* was buzzing with talk of the Grand Inquisition being conducted by the supply officer. The number of man hours involved in the wash down of planes on deck, plus the cost of cleansing materials utilized, the cost of laundering the uniforms of the personnel drenched with foam—all were being carefully tabulated by the supply officer. The final figure was being kept confidential by the supply officer—at the captain's order. All over the ship, a huge betting pool sprang up, the closest guesstimate to the final figure taking the pot.

I met with Captain Engle just before captain's mast.

"George, do you have know the figure?"

"No, sir."

"That vacuous nitwit's stupidity cost the taxpayers about eleven thousand dollars. I've thought about it a lot, and I've decided that I'm sentencing him to seven days in the brig, and, if I could, I would have topped it off with three days bread and water. But, by heaven, he'll spend seven miserable days and nights in the brig."

All were assembled for captain's mast. The captain stood behind a podium, and the sailors on report took their turn in standing before him. At last, it was Seaman Simon's turn. I noticed that, as he took his place in front of the podium, his knees were visibly shaking in his bell bottoms. No doubt he had heard about the Grand Inquisition and dreaded the captain's certain wrath.

I read the charge and specification against Seaman Simon. Thus far during the mast, the captain had been very calm and deliberate in dispensing his justice. However, now, with Simon literally trembling in front of him, the captain's face began to redden. When the captain spoke, his tone was angry and hostile, and his voice grew louder until he thundered,

"Do you know how much money your stupidity and incompetence cost the Navy?"

Terrified, Simon blurted out: "Five million dollars, sir?"

Visibly taken aback, the captain, after a moment, said, "Well, not *that* much." Several moments passed.

"Case dismissed!"

The Portuguese Interpreter

Chris Sakellis was a Naval Academy graduate of Greek descent, recently assigned to the U.S.S. *Forrestal*. He and I became good friends. Now, the *Forrestal* was two days sailing from Lisbon, Portugal, and, as the legal officer of the largest ship in the flotilla, I had received orders appointing me foreign claims officer in Lisbon.

The foreign claims officer, once the ship had anchored in a foreign port, would establish the foreign claims commission, the mission of which was to hear complaints by foreign civilians, seeking payment for damages caused the civilians (or their businesses, taxi cabs, etc.) by American sailors on liberty in the foreign port. For example, if a sailor broke a store window, the owner of the store would appear before the foreign claims commission, tell his story and ask for payment to replace or repair the window. If the claim was granted by the commission, money was paid (hopefully reduced from the amount asked), after the complainant had first signed a release to the United States government.

The foreign claims officer enjoyed the greatest duty in the sea-going Navy. First, although all other junior officers aboard ship were subject to "port and starboard shore leave" (while the ship was in a foreign port, officers could go ashore only every other day, having to stand duty aboard ship on alternate days), the foreign claims officer spent every single day and night ashore. Second, the foreign claims officer established the commission in the very best hotel in the port. Additionally, a group of the wives of some of the younger officers aboard had come to Europe to follow the *Forrestal* from port to port in order to be with their husbands on shore leave. Unfortunately, of course, their husbands could get shore leave only every other day and night, and one of the more pleasant duties of the foreign claims officer was, as best he could, to care for the needs of those wives whose husbands had duty and had had to remain on board ship.

In any event, as the *Forrestal* approached Lisbon, my first task was to locate a Portuguese interpreter. Unfortunately, I found that no one aboard the *Forrestal* spoke Portuguese. Knowing that the commission's interpreter shared the good fortune and aforementioned advantages of the foreign claims officer, my friend, Chris, made his pitch. "Bud, I don't speak Portuguese, but I am totally fluent in Spanish. I can act as your Portuguese interpreter because the languages are incredibly similar. Please, please, please, as a friend, make me your Portuguese interpreter."

Convinced that Chris could do the job, I arranged for him to accompany me ashore as foreign claims Portuguese interpreter. Although we partied the first night ashore with those officers on starboard shore leave, Chris and I both knew that the next morning, at 1000 sharp, I would convene the foreign claims commission, and Chris would be my official Portuguese interpreter.

The purpose of the foreign claims commission was to create good will and respect for the United States government among foreign civilians. Accordingly, the next morning, in an impressive meeting room furnished by the hotel, at 0945, an American flag was unfurled, and two marines in dress uniform arrived to stand at attention on each side of the commission's table. In dress blues, I sat behind the table, and Chris sat to my right. Although the *Forrestal* had been in Lisbon less than one full day, I was informed that twelve Portuguese civilians were waiting in the next room to present their claims.

At precisely 1000 one of the marines escorted a middle-aged man, the first complainant, into the commission's room, pointed to where the complainant was to stand and took his position beside the table, at attention. The man began to speak in Portuguese, a language I had never before heard. I kept my eyes on the man until, after about four minutes, he stopped talking.

Matter-of-factly, I turned to Chris and asked him what the man had said. "I haven't the remotest idea" was the chilling response I got from Chris. In a subdued tone, I whispered, "Chris, this is terribly embarrassing! We are sitting here with the American flag behind us, two marines at attention on either side of us, and you are *now* telling me that, although you speak fluent Spanish, you did not understand anything the man just said in Portuguese?"

"Bud, I'm sorry, I did not understand *one word*. I'm afraid that Portuguese is nothing like Spanish."

I called a recess—which was difficult to communicate to the complainant. I stood up, gave a little wave good-bye to the man and walked toward the door. I went to the hotel lobby and spoke to the concierge. In several minutes, the hotel supplied me with an interpreter—who happened to be an attractive young lady.

The Commission re-convened, the middle-aged man again spoke in Portuguese, and I learned from my interpreter that he was a pianist who played in a restaurant which had been frequented by American sailors the night before. Unfortunately, a sailor had, as a lark, put on the pianist's coat, which had been hanging on a hook. The sailor and his shipmates, who had had much to drink, left the restaurant with the man's coat.

The man volunteered that the coat was old and not worth very much, but, it being the only one he had, he would like to get it back. Impressed with the complainant's honesty, I asked my interpreter how much a new coat would cost in Lisbon, and she told me that the man would be very happy with fifteen American dollars. A deal was struck, a release was signed and the *Forrestal*'s first foreign claims commission case in Lisbon had been settled!

The rest of the morning went smoothly, and, having learned that the interpreter was unmarried, I asked her if she and a girlfriend would join Chris and me for dinner that evening. She said that she would make a call and let me know. Just before the commission re-convened at 1350, she informed me that she and a friend would be delighted to join us that evening.

Her friend turned out to be charming and personable. The four of us were dining at the Rio Lisboa, and the conversation was spirited and congenial. All of our conversation was in English until—suddenly, the friend said something in Portuguese to the interpreter, who laughed and spoke a few Portuguese words in response. For the next three or four minutes, Portuguese was the only language spoken at the table, with both girls giggling sporadically.

Finally, I looked at Chris and said *"Toe tra-pai-zee ee-nai ko-kee-noe"* ("the table is red"). Chris burst into uproarious laughter. In fact, he almost fell out of his chair before answering *"Toe a-go-ree ee-nai psee-los"* ("the boy is tall"). I guffawed loudly and responded, *"Toe af-toe-kee-nee-toe ee-nai mai-ga-low"* ("the car is big"). The girls, stunned, stared, first at us, and then at each other. One asked (in English), "Hey, guys, are you talking about *us*? What's so funny?"

"Of course, we're not talking about you. But, if you two are going to talk in Portuguese, Chris and I will speak in Greek."

A truce was quickly effected, and the evening progressed pleasurably—and only in English.

Rel

Needing the captain's signature on some papers, I went to the bridge. Commander DiNardo, the gun boss was standing next to Captain Engle, who saw me and said, "Wait one, George. The Air Force is towing a target, and we are about to commence a firing drill."

The command duty officer's voice sounded on the bridge: "Ten seconds to firing! 9, 8, 7, 6, 5, 4, 3, 2, 1"

Captain Engle gave the order, "Commence firing!"

Instantaneously, the *Forrestal*'s anti-aircraft batteries began firing at a tan oblong target at the end of a long towline attached to an Air Force plane. All binoculars and eyes (including mine) were fixed on the target. Strange, I thought, I heard the guns go off, but I see no explosions. Suddenly, a voice screamed from the bridge's radio: "YAAA!! You dumb Navy bastards! You've locked on to my tow plane instead of the target!"

All binoculars and eyes quickly shifted to the front end of the towline. There, the small plane was engulfed in puffs of black. Shells were exploding all around it.

"Cease firing! Cease firing!" shrieked Captain Engle, leaping from his chair.

"Cease firing" was the word passed on all circuits.

"Identify the control battery," yelled Captain Engle, his face red with rage.

"Starboard #4," someone answered.

"George, come with me," said the captain, as he scurried off the bridge, down the ladder and sprinted across the flight deck. Other officers and I were following close behind. When we reached the starboard edge of the flight deck, we peered down at 5" battery #4.

The tarpaulin cover had been pulled partly off of the battery, exposing the 5" gun. We saw two enlisted personnel manning the gun. The microphone and earphones, which should have been on the gunnery officer-in-charge, were instead on an enlisted man. The gunnery officer-in-charge had crawled under the tarpaulin, and only the backs of his khakied legs were visible.

"Who is the officer-in-charge of starboard battery #4?" demanded Captain Engle.

The gun boss answered, "Ensign Calhoun, sir."

"Have him report to the bridge immediately," said the captain as he stalked off across the flight deck.

Rel Calhoun was a notorious and legendary character among *Forrestal* officers. His mother had been the longest-tenured President in the history of the Temperance Union of South Carolina, and Rel (acronym for Robert E. Lee) had grown up in Walterboro, South Carolina, in a home in which the high alcoholic content of vanilla extract had prohibited its use in baking. Rel and I had identified each other as fellow "Dookies." In fact, Rel had boastfully informed me that, while attending Duke University, Rel had quickly immersed himself in alcohol's excesses, joined the KA fraternity ("knights of alcohol"), and had spent some of his days and many of his nights in a quasi-inebriated state.

Rel had even been disciplined at Duke for instigating what became a three-fraternity fracas-turned-riot. It seemed that Rel, along with three of his KA brothers, returning from a Saturday night binge about 0300, had painted red a small white stone lion outside the SAE house, following which they had dripped red paint to the front door of the adjoining Sigma Nu house. SAEs awakening Sunday morning had followed the drip-trail to the SN house, where yelling turned physical, and a fight ensued. Rel and a few of his KA brothers had gathered to watch the brawl until one of the SAEs noticed that Rel's hand was splattered the same shade of red as the lion, whereupon the SAEs and SNs joined forces to attack Rel and his KA brothers.

Upon his graduation from Duke, Rel had became a naval officer. But binges remained his big problem. In the *Forrestal*'s visit to Gibraltar, trying to impress two female tavern acquaintances with his bravado, Rel had tried to sneak up behind a kilted Royal Highland Fusilier, standing, statue-like, as sentry in front of the Military Prison. Rel, intent on lifting the Fusilier's kilt, had failed to note that the Fusilier had surreptitiously unbuckled his belt. As Rel's hand reached for the kilt, the Fusilier suddenly wheeled about and flung his belt which unfurled and rapidly wrapped around Rel's head, the weighty buckle impacting bloodily against Rel's cheek. The Fusilier quickly re-cinched the belt and resumed his erect sentry-posture. Although Rel was in civilian clothes, his escapade had been witnessed by Commander Wilcox, the *Forrestal*'s navigator, who reported the incident to Captain Engle. Rel was deprived of going ashore on the *Forrestal*'s next two ports of call, Cannes and Naples.

My other experience with Rel occurred at escalator #1, a very long escalator which traversed three decks. Escalator #1 had buttons at each end which directed it to go up or down. A month or so before, I entered the escalator #1 space and saw Commander Bitner, the *Forrestal*'s executive officer, descending on the escalator, about half-way down. Rel had entered the space before me. Without looking at the escalator, he first pushed the STOP button and then the UP button. Commander Bitner jolted to a stop and then found himself going back up escalator #1.

"Hey there, Ensign! What the hell are you doing?"

Rel looked up at the escalator and was shocked to see the angry face of his executive officer, traveling backwards. Again, Rel depressed the STOP button. The escalator stopped. Although intending to push the DOWN button, Rel, in nervous confusion, unintentionally again pushed the UP button. Once more, Commander Bitner found himself traveling backwards up the escalator. "JEE-ZUSS Christ," Commander Bitner's voice boomed.

Finally, Rel composed himself and pushed the STOP button yet again. Commander Bitner had braced himself for this stop. Carefully, Rel pushed the DOWN button and stood at attention as escalator #1 delivered the executive officer to the lower deck.

Mindful of Rel's Gibraltar escapade, remembering his own escalator reversal, and having just witnessed Rel's wrong target fiasco, Commander Bitner promptly issued a request to the chief of naval personnel to transfer Ensign Robert E. Lee Calhoun from the *Forrestal*.

Liaison to Athens

It is 1956, and, as the *Forrestal* left Naples, with Athens its next port of call, I was worried. With Chris Sakellis on leave, I was the only officer of Greek descent aboard, and I had been informally appointed by the captain as what he had called the "*Forrestal*'s liaison to Athens." The *Forrestal* was the world's first supercarrier. Everywhere it went, it drew intense interest. What would I find in Athens? I had never been to Greece. How would I be received? I could speak a little Greek, and I could understand more Greek than I could speak. But would either be enough? What did the captain expect from me as the *Forrestal*'s liaison to Athens?

On the morning we anchored in Piraeus' harbor, I was on the flight deck looking shoreward, and I saw a large group of small boats heading toward the *Forrestal*.

"Why are all those boats coming to the *Forrestal*?" I asked.

"They are the Athens news media, radio, TV and newspapers."

Forty-five minutes later, I entered the *Forrestal*'s largest ready room. The din was deafening—it sounded like seventy or so people all jabbering at once—everyone was talking, and no one was listening. How Greek, I thought. No one took notice of me when I entered, dressed in my khaki uniform. I ascended the podium and stood there for several moments, trying to determine how to get everyone's attention. I was ignored.

"*Pa-tree-oh-tee*" ("countrymen"), I shouted in Greek over the loudspeaker.

Immediately, all noise ceased! Every person in that ready room stopped talking at once and was now gawking at me. I was shocked at the sudden silence. Then, as if by pre-arrangement, they all began clapping and whistling loudly. As one body, they surged forward, rushed up the steps of the podium and surrounded me. Some grabbed my right hand and began shaking it. Others were hugging me and slapping me affectionately on the back. A man spoke: "My name is Spiro Hondris. We are so proud to find a Greek-American officer to greet us on the largest warship in the world. You must tell us about yourself and about this supercarrier."

"My name is Harris George. I am the *Forrestal*'s legal officer and its liaison to Athens. But, unfortunately, I cannot speak Greek well."

Softly, Spiro said, "Don't worry. Elia Kazan was here last month, and he could say only a few words. I will be your translator. You answer my questions in English, and I will translate them into Greek. Everyone will want to know about *you*. In our group are Radio Athens, all of the Athens newspapers, and all TV stations of Greece."

Spiro then spoke over the loudspeaker—in Greek. Happily, I understood what he said, "This Greek-American officer—Harris George—has consented to my interviewing him. Please show him respect by being quiet. I will translate into Greek his English answers to my questions."

The room quieted. Spiro slowly asked his first question in English: "Where were your parents born?"

"My parents were born on the island of Kythera."

Very deliberately, Spiro turned to the audience and, in Greek, said: "Mr. George's parents were born on the island of Kythera."

Polite clapping emanated from the crowd.

"Quiet. Quiet, we must continue" Spiro said. "And where were you born?" Spiro asked me almost in a whisper.

I whispered back, "I was born in America."

Spiro turned, and, in Greek, announced loudly, "Mr. George was also born on the island of Kythera."

Thunderous clapping and whistling erupted! But, I, having understood what Spiro had said, leaned over to him and, in a low voice, said, "No, no, you misunderstood, I was born in *America*."

Spiro's response was not reassuring. "Sh, sh, please. It makes a better story if you were born on Kythera."

That set the tone for the remainder of my interview. Spiro "translated" into Greek whatever answer made the better story. All during the interview, flashbulbs were blinding me as my picture was being taken. When Spiro's interview finally concluded, I was separately interviewed by Radio Athens.

The next morning when I went ashore in Athens, I found huge pictures of myself on the front page of every newspaper in Athens. There were also pictures of the *Forrestal*, but my pictures were much bigger than the *Forrestal*'s. The media hype which had preceded the *Forrestal*'s arrival as the World's First Supercarrier and the Largest Ship in the World was culminated—in all Athenian newspapers, on Athenian TV and on Radio Athens—by the startling revelation that a Greek-American officer— *born on the island of Kythera*—was part of the complement of the U.S.S. *Forrestal*.

Everywhere in Athens that I went in my Navy uniform, I was instantly recognized. I walked into a restaurant, and the band began playing "The Star

Spangled Banner." Bottles of champagne were sent to my table. On the streets, people grabbed my right hand to shake it, asking, "Do you know my cousin, Gus Pappas, in Cincinnati?"

As I walked into stores, I was greeted with smiles and affectionate hugs. Free merchandise was continually being pressed into my hands—"a gift for our Greek-American."

In Piraeus that evening, on my way back to the ship, I came upon a sailor arguing loudly with a young woman.

"What's the trouble, sailor?" I asked "Perhaps I can help."

"This bar girl has taken my watch, denies that she has it, and won't give it back."

I turned to the young woman, and, in my broken Greek, exclaimed, "As a Greek-American, I am ashamed to learn that a Greek girl has taken this American sailor's watch."

The girl immediately reached into her purse and handed the sailor his watch. "I am not Greek. I am really Italian. I am just a visitor here in Athens," she lied.

The next day, I received a note from Spiro, thanking me for the interview, scribbled in English, attached to a large newspaper clipping containing my picture and Spiro's article—in Greek, of course. Being unable to read Greek, I immediately airmailed the article to my father.

Weeks later, I received a letter from my father. You are the biggest liar the family has ever had! You told the reporter that you were born on Kythera, and, although only twenty-five years old, you are already the executive officer of the U.S.S. *Forrestal*, second in command of the largest ship in the world!

Secret Things

For almost all of my Navy commitment, I had been stationed aboard ships, first aboard the *Midway* and then aboard the *Forrestal*. While awaiting my discharge, I had been assigned for the last month as an assistant legal officer, in the office of commandant, fifth naval district, in Norfolk, Virginia. I had finally achieved much-coveted but seldom-attained shore duty.

There were four civilian secretaries, all female and two over sixty, in the commandant's office. This was a change for me, because, aboard ship, I had always had male yeomen as legal secretaries. After only one week on the job, I yearned for a return to the shipboard legal office. I had spent almost three full years aboard ships with complements of five thousand men. The ships had been at sea, sometimes continuously for long periods of time, under stressful conditions—general quarters exercises, round-the-clock flight operations, battle readiness exercises with flotillas of ships—and, in all that time and under those stringent conditions, I had *never* heard a cross word pass between two men in a Navy legal office.

But, ashore, the two older civilian secretaries were constantly at war. It was clear that each disliked the other intensely, and each was trying to make *me* her ultimate weapon to destroy the other. Upon my return from lunch one day, Mrs. Rogers was waiting for me in my office doorway. "May I please see you, sir?"

"Of course."

Mrs. Rogers entered my office, closed the door and proclaimed loudly, "Well, I want you to know that I was working in the file cabinet area when I saw Mrs. Talbott go to my desk, rummage through all my drawers and look at all of my secret things. Sir, she has no right to look at my secret things, and I request that you reprimand Mrs. Talbott and order her never to do it again."

"Mrs. Rogers, the Navy doesn't pay me to mediate civilian disputes such as the one between Mrs. Talbott and you. I suggest that you keep no secret things in your desk."

I opened my office door to let Mrs. Rogers out, and, standing there, was Mrs. Talbott.

"May I please see you, sir?"

"Yes, Mrs. Talbott, come in."

Mrs. Rogers departed, and I once again closed my office door.

"Well, sir, I want you to know that I have never in my life been so mortified as I was today."

"What happened, Mrs. Talbott?"

"Well, I had a terrible headache around noon today, and I said to one of the younger secretaries, 'Where are those aspirin that we girls chip in for, for headaches in the office?' and I was told that Mrs. Rogers keeps them in her desk. So, naturally, I went to Mrs. Rogers' desk and opened the top drawer. Well, Mrs. Rogers, who had been hiding behind some file cabinets, leaped out and screamed at the top of her voice, 'I knew that you've been going through my desk, looking at all of my secret things.' Everybody in the office looked at me as if I were a thief. Well, sir, I request that you reprimand Mrs. Rogers and order her never to do it again."

"Mrs. Talbott, the Navy doesn't pay me to mediate civilian disputes. I suggest that you and the other secretaries find another place to keep the aspirin."

I left the Navy three weeks later, but I'm certain that a state of war still exists between Mrs. Rogers and Mrs. Talbott.

Curtis McCarthy

Curtis McCarthy was bigger than any of the other boys in Towson Elementary School, and he was rough and physical. He *always* won the king of the mountain games at recess, and no classmate wanted to be hit by a dodge ball thrown by Curtis. As we progressed through elementary school, he remained bruising in competition, and, whatever game he played, sometimes one of his classmates ended up crying. He was often chastised by the teachers, "You'd better change your ways, Curtis, or you'll end up in jail."

I lost track of Curtis McCarthy when I went away to college. After that, I went to law school and into the Navy. I never thought about Curtis again. As a young attorney, I was walking down a corridor in the Towson courthouse when I looked into a courtroom and noticed Curtis McCarthy, handcuffed to another man standing in open court before a judge. I walked into the courtroom.

Poor Curtis, I thought. Way back in Towson Elementary School, the teachers had always said that he would end up this way. When the judge had finished imposing sentence, Curtis, still handcuffed to the other man, turned and started to leave the courtroom. As he saw me, Curtis flashed a happy grin. Same Curtis, I thought. He's not even ashamed that I have seen him ending up this way.

A few moments later, I learned that Curtis McCarthy was a Baltimore county deputy sheriff, and the criminal was the other guy.

Mr. Lawrence Goes to Spring Grove

In the early 1960s in Towson, attorneys who wanted to get routine orders signed by a judge would go to a courtroom, take a seat in the back, and, at a recess, ask the judge to sign the order. As a young attorney, I had an order requiring a judge's signature, and I took my seat in the rear of Judge G.'s courtroom. Judge G. was a kindly, white-haired gentleman, with courtly manners and a gracious style. He did, however, have the reputation that—every now and then—he would get a strange look in his eyes.

Judge G. disposed of the matter before him, and gestured for me to approach the bench. Before I could present him with the order I wished signed, Judge G. said, "Bud, I would like to appoint you to a case." In those early days, young attorneys appreciated getting cases through court appointment because, although the fee was invariably small, such appointments represented a welcome source of income. I said, "Thank you, Your Honor. When is this case scheduled to be heard?"

Judge G. answered, "In about twenty minutes. It's that fellow sitting in the front bench. He has been acting quite peculiarly, and two doctors' certificates have already been tendered, calling for guardianship. I just need an attorney to represent him at the guardianship hearing."

Shocked, I said, "Judge, I can't represent someone in twenty minutes. I have to study the file, interview the client, and talk to his family."

Judge G. got that strange look in his eyes and said, "Mr. George, you'll represent that gentleman in twenty minutes."

Flustered, I blurted out, "Then Judge G., I pray a jury trial," which was a desperate ploy on my part since I had not yet participated in a jury trial. Judge G. looked at me, perturbed. "Bud, if you pray a jury trial, I will not be able to hear this case in twenty minutes."

"I'm sorry, your Honor, but I insist on a jury."

The judge's face softened. "Perhaps if I ask him if he will go voluntarily, he will consent." Judge G. then said in a loud voice, "Bring Mr. Lawrence before the bench."

The man in the front row got up, and, escorted by a deputy sheriff, stood in front of Judge G., who said, "Would you like to go to Spring Grove Hospital? It's a very nice place, and it will be helpful to you."

Mr. Lawrence answered, "I don't mind."

The judge said, "Then it is done. You are hereby remanded to the Spring Grove Hospital. Next case."

I had been standing by the bench during this exchange. I leaned over to the court reporter and whispered, "You didn't enter my appearance as having represented Mr. Lawrence in this matter, did you?"

Cow Poke

"Mr. Campbell, I've just been retained by a farmer who is foreclosing a chattel mortgage on a herd of cattle. I've never handled such a case, and I'm wondering if you can think of a similar case that's been filed here in the circuit court for Baltimore County. I'd certainly like to look at some experienced Towson lawyer's petition to foreclose a chattel mortgage."

"Bud, I remember Lawrence Ensor filing such a suit about ten, twelve years ago. I'll see if I can't find that case file for you."

Mr. Campbell was in charge of all civil cases in the clerk's office of the circuit court for Baltimore County, and he had been in the clerk's office for the past twenty years. He was an extremely polite gentleman, eager to be helpful to young lawyers who were just starting practice. He returned about ten minutes later and handed me a dog-eared case file. With sincere thanks, I headed for a counter on which I could study the file.

David S. owned a large farm which bordered on York Road in Lutherville, just a couple miles north of Towson. He had made a lot of money selling off small pieces of his farm to business entrepreneurs who wanted commercial locations along the York Road corridor between Towson and Timonium. In fact, S. had made so much money selling parts of his land that he had begun to lend money to other farmers. One of the farmers he'd loaned money to was Derwood Carson, and, as security for the loan, S. had taken back a chattel mortgage on Carson's herd of cattle. Carson couldn't keep up the loan payments, and S. had retained me to foreclose his mortgage on Carson's herd.

"You don't know anything about cattle, so you ought to meet me out at Carson's farm. Pending the sale, those cows are in legal custody of the sheriff, and I'm responsible for taking care of them until they're ready to be sold, pending the trial."

In my three-piece suit and shoes polished to a high sheen, I met Dave S. at the Carson farm, and we began walking toward the barn. I was totally unprepared for the pervasive manure smell of one hundred and twelve cows. I had to walk very carefully to avoid stepping into one of the seemingly hundreds of manure deposits between the barn and us. When I walked into the barn, the stench was so overpowering I almost passed out. I tried to pretend that I did not notice the smell, but I was relieved when I finally got back into my car to head for my Towson office.

I had filed a request for admissions, compelling Carson's attorney to admit that S. had loaned Carson the money, that the herd had been security for the loan, and that the loan was currently in default. The case came before Judge John E. Raine, Jr., who was known as a smart and practical judge. On the day of the trial, Jack Hessian, Carson's attorney, surprised me by putting Carson's young daughter on the stand. Her testimony revealed that she was fourteen years old, a long-standing member of the 4-H club, and that she had helped her father around the farm since she was a tot.

"I raised nine of those cows from the day they were born. I took care of them every day of my life. My father always said those cows belonged to me."

I turned to Dave S. sitting next to me at the trial table. "You've just lost nine cows."

S. gave me a bewildered look and murmured, "What are you talking about? Those nine cows are on the mortgage."

"Yes, but Judge Raine has a very soft spot in his heart for children. He's not going to take those cows away from a fourteen year-old, 4-H girl who's raised them since they were born, and he knows that it will cost you a heck of a lot more than the value of nine cows to take an appeal from his decision."

"Mr. George, if I lose those nine cows, you're fired."

I was unemployed the instant after Judge Raine had ruled that S.'s mortgage covered only one hundred and three cows. Fortunately, the next morning, I was re-hired by Mrs. S., who had been sitting in the courtroom and had convinced her husband that it had not been my fault that he had lost nine cows.

The mortgage sale of one hundred and three cows was conducted by an auctioneer on a Saturday morning. Dave S. was in charge of bringing each cow into a fenced-in area, with about eight bidders standing outside the fence. S. was holding a rolled-up black whip with a small yellow handle, and he prodded each cow into the ring, whereupon the auctioneer, after consulting with Carson and S., would start the bidding. During the course of the auction, many of the eight present entered a bid at some time or other. S. had earlier announced that he personally would not be buying any of the cattle being auctioned.

I reported the results of the action sale to the court, and, thirty days later, the report was ratified without exception. Several months later, as I was taking a walk after lunch in Towson, I was stopped by an elderly stranger. "Hey, aren't you the lawyer who conducted the auction sale on the Carson herd?"

"Yes, I am. Were you there?"

"Yes. You know that S. ended up buying the best in the herd."

"No, he didn't," I said. "He announced that he wasn't bidding on any of the cattle offered for sale that day."

"Son, do you remember the whip he used the day of the sale to poke the cows into the circle? Well, he had his man planted among the bidders. He knew those cows well since he had taken care of them pending the auction sale. When S. brought a cow in that he wanted to bid on, he had moved his hand from the yellow handle to the black part of the whip. As long as he held the black part of the whip, his man continued to bid. As soon as S. believed that the price had gone too high for that particular cow, he moved his hand back to the yellow handle, and his man stopped bidding. Son, you, S.'s attorney, were probably the only one at the sale who didn't know what the hell was really going on."

The Towson Hapsburg

When I was a young lawyer, I shared office space with an attorney named Will Jacobson, who had one annoying habit—on Saturdays, he would unlock the door to our office suite, invariably placing his keys into his jacket pocket. He would then hang his jacket on a hanger. Later, when he would go to the lavatory (which was located outside the suite), the door would lock behind him and, when he tried to reenter, he would suddenly remember that he had left his keys in his jacket inside the suite. He would then go to a phone to try to locate me. After some anguish, he would finally find me, and I, like a good and faithful suite-mate, would drive to the suite and unlock the front door, according him his newly-recovered ability to drive home. This happened on three different Saturdays.

The last time it happened, I told Will, "I'm not coming again. Never again put your office keys into your jacket pocket; *always, always* put your keys into your trouser pocket. That way, unless you leave the suite without your trousers, you will always have your keys with you."

Will never again called me on a weekend.

Will had pallid skin, his sparse hair was lighter than blond, and he was short and chubby. One Friday after work, we stopped at the Penn Hotel for a martini. I noticed that Will had long facial hair (obviously he hadn't shaved for a while), but, since his hair color matched his skin, one would not notice that he needed a shave unless one got close to him.

"Will, how long has it been since you've shaved?"

"At least a week or two."

"Wow, if I don't shave twice a day, my Greek heritage reveals my heavy beard a block away."

"That's because you were not born to the purple."

"Born to the purple? You mean that you are of royal blood?"

"Precisely.... I was baptized Wilhelm Von Jacob Von Hapsburg."

"You are a descendant of the Hapsburgs?"

"Yes I am. I am the sterile fruition of centuries of fastidiously-orchestrated inbreeding, first cousins marrying first cousins! I think of myself as the sorry caboose on what was once the most powerful imperial engine of Europe. But I never married, and I don't have any siblings, so my imperial branch will die with me."

"America," I said, "What a country! Bud George, son of an impoverished and orphaned Greek immigrant, sharing office space with Will Jacobson, the last of the Hapsburgs."

"You've got it right—only in America."

"But, Will, why have you kept it such a secret? If I were a Hapsburg, all of Towson...indeed all of Maryland would know."

"I'm not eager to spread the word. A Hapsburg should have done better at law than I have done."

"Nonsense. You are the best title attorney in Towson."

"Bud, it's my martini talking. You are the first person I've told this to in years."

"Have you told anyone else about your Hapsburg heritage?"

"Actually," Will said, "I remember one occasion when I disgorged my Hapsburg heritage in one big stream-of-consciousness."

"When was that?"

"My best friend, all through high school, was named Bushrod Allen. His friends called him Rod. He was a nice guy, he and I were great buddies, but his mother was a colossal pain. Every time Rod had friends to his house, his mother would, at some point, announce to everyone that Rod had the name of Bushrod because he was a descendant of Bushrod Washington, a cousin to George. Every one of Rod's friends had heard the story from Mrs. Allen many times over our high school years, but that never deterred her from continually repeating the story.

"One day I had had enough. As my friends and I were about to hear for the umpteenth time about Rod's being related to George Washington, I interrupted Rod's mother and launched into my family history of the Hapsburg dynasty. I explained how the Hapsburgs had championed Christianity against the Ottoman Turks, how we had supplied four centuries of Holy Roman Emperors and were recognized as the social pinnacle of European royalty. Poor Mrs. Allen. She may never even have heard of the Hapsburgs, but, until I finished, she stood, mouth hanging open, dumbstruck. From that day forward, Mrs. Allen never again mentioned Bushrod Washington to any of Rod's friends, I guess because Bushrod Washington seemed so french fries compared to the Hapsburg big mac."

Try, Try Again

I received an order of court, appointing me to represent a lady named Harriet D., who was at the time occupying a cell in the Baltimore County jail. Ms. D. was charged with making alcoholic beverages in her private still and illegally selling them from her house in Turner Station, an economically challenged neighborhood in Baltimore County. When I reviewed the file of *State of Maryland v. Harriet D.* in the state's attorney's office, I ascertained that an informant had alerted police to the fact that Ms. D. was making and selling "hooch" from the back door of her cottage, known locally as Harriet's Hooch House.

The police had then obtained a search warrant which recited the following facts:

1. A police agent went to the back door of Ms. D.'s cottage, knocked, and, when a lady appeared, said that he wanted to buy liquor.
2. The lady closed the door for a moment and then re-opened it, handing the agent an Old Stag bottle containing clear contents. The agent paid Ms. D. one dollar.
3. The Old Stag bottle did not bear a Maryland alcoholic tax stamp.
4. The Baltimore county police quickly obtained a search warrant, returned to Ms. D.'s house, arrested her and carted away twenty-seven assorted Coca Cola bottles, pickle jars, wine and whiskey bottles, all filled with liquids.

I then interviewed Ms. D. at the Towson jail. She was an uneducated woman, but, though she was without sufficient funds to retain an attorney (hence my court appointment), she informed me that her neighbors had missed her so much that they would soon be bailing her out of jail. In researching Ms. D.'s case, I decided to argue that the search warrant was legally invalid because it did not state that the police had either tasted, smelled or chemically analyzed the "clear contents" of the Old Stag bottle, which had been the sole basis for obtainment of the search warrant. Ms. D. did indeed make bail, and she was released from jail to return to Harriet's Hooch House.

On the morning of her trial, my client needed to be driven to my office by a neighbor, Mrs. Watts, because Ms. D. was totally inebriated. Her breath reeked of alcohol, her speech was slurred, her eyes were glassy, and she walked unsteadily—not the best presentation for a defendant charged with illegally selling homemade hooch. *State v. D.* being the first case scheduled at 9:00 a.m., I decided that I should get my client to the courtroom early so that I could situate her in a sturdy arm chair, the arms of which would, hopefully, prevent her from collapsing to the courtroom floor in front of the judge.

Ms. D. and I arrived in the empty courtroom at 8:30 a.m. I found a narrow arm chair which I placed behind my trial table. I told Ms. D. to sit in the chair and clutch its arms to steady herself. I instructed her to say absolutely nothing and explained that if she fell out of the chair, it would convince the judge that she was indeed guilty of illegally selling hooch.

The presiding judge was to be the Honorable John Grason Turnbull, Sr., and Paul Feeley, Sr., was the prosecutor. I knew that Judge Turnbull was not a teetotaler. Judge Turnbull called the first case, *State of Maryland v. Harriet D.* For the next fifteen minutes, states attorney personnel carried into the courtroom and placed on a large table cartons and cases containing the twenty-seven bottles and jars confiscated at Harriet's Hooch House - an impressive inaugural parade to commence the prosecutor's case,

I stood. "Your Honor, I wish to present to the court a motion to quash the search warrant and to exclude the evidence seized thereunder."

Judge Turnbull looked at my motion and asked me to proceed.

"Your Honor, the search warrant is invalid on its face. The warrant states simply that a police agent asked Ms. D. for liquor, and she handed him an Old Stag bottle 'containing clear contents.' Those 'clear contents' could have been water. The warrant does not state that the police smelled the liquid, and it smelled like alcohol. They didn't taste it and have the warrant state that the liquid tasted like alcohol. They didn't chemically analyze the liquid, determine that the liquid was indeed alcohol, and have the warrant make that assertion. Your Honor, *you* know that you can't tell alcohol by looking at it. You've got to smell it, taste it, analyze it."

I presented the judge with a legal memorandum, citing a number of cases from the prohibition era. The prosecutor, Mr. Feeley, made his argument to counter mine.

Judge Turnbull did not take long to rule that the warrant was quashed and that the evidence seized thereunder would be excluded from any consideration. State's attorney office personnel were summoned, and, for the next fifteen minutes, the twenty-seven bottles and jars were removed from the courtroom.

The prosecutor informed the court that, without the excluded evidence, he would have to dismiss the charge against Ms. D., who had sat rigidly in her chair, her hands clutching its arms. I walked over to her, "We won."

Dazed, she asked, "What do you mean?"

"You are free to leave with Mrs. Watts."

"You mean I'm not guilty?"

"Yes, that's what I mean."

"You mean that I can get back all of my goods."

"Well, I guess so."

"Mr. George, you got to help me get my goods back to my neighbor's car."

At that moment a uniformed police corporal approached me. "Mr. George, I'm Corporal Armand Elliott. I prepared the search warrant in this case, which you have just quashed. I want to congratulate you. I've been preparing search warrants for a long time, and this is only the second one that has been found defective. The other one was successfully attacked by Judge Menchine about seven years ago, before he went on the bench."

Sincerely flattered, I thanked Corporal Elliott for his kind words. I then arranged with the prosecutor to deliver the twenty-seven bottles and jars to Mrs. Watt's car.

About a month later, I heard that my client, Harriet D., had again been arrested on the same charge. Because of the generosity of her clientele, she had made bail and, this time, had hired a private attorney to defend her, no longer requiring court-appointed defense counsel. Nonetheless, I went promptly to the state's attorney's office and reviewed the case file of *State of Maryland v. Harriet D.* I examined the search warrant, which, I noted, stated, in detail, that the bottle of "clear contents" purchased from Ms. D. had been taken immediately to a chemical laboratory where, upon verified analysis, it had been determined to be alcohol. Thereafter, the "clear contents" had been smelled, and the smell was clearly alcoholic. Finally, the contents had been tasted, and the taste was distinctly alcoholic.

I thought, bravo, Corporal Elliott, that's the way the justice system is supposed to work—the invalid first warrant made valid the second time. You've begun another seven-year run.

Lawyers' Liquid Lunches

I was getting a haircut in Ken Smith's Barber Shop around 11:45 a.m. Ten minutes into the haircut, Ken said, "If you keep looking out the front window, you'll see one of Towson's most prominent lawyers coming out of the Loyola Federal Building going to lunch."

Sure enough, at precisely 12 o'clock noon, I saw Tom S., Esquire, walking toward York Road. Ken said, "Every day at lunchtime, Tom S. goes to lunch at Souris' Saloon. However, when he returns *from* lunch, he never walks as steadily as when he walked *to* lunch.

~ ~ ~ ~ ~

The drinking headquarters for Towson's judges, lawyers and politicians was the Quill Club, a stag bar the walls of which were covered with pictures, plats and maps of old Towson. The Quill Club was located on the basement floor of the Penn Hotel, Towson's most popular restaurant, directly adjacent to Ken's Barber Shop. Patrons of the Quill often stopped by Ken's in various stages of inebriation, and, from them, Ken heard many Towson rumors. The Quill could be entered directly from the sidewalk via thirteen concrete steps that went down between the restaurant and Ken's.

Several Towson lawyers spent a good portion of their working day at the Quill. One of them was John M., Esquire. John, who was divorced, was a prodigious drinker who regularly imbibed breakfast, lunch and dinner at the Quill. He also spent much of his time between meals there. The Towson legal community knew that the only exercise John ever got was going up and down the thirteen steps leading to the Quill. Since John had practiced law in Towson for many years, it had been estimated that he had utilized the thirteen steps at least thirty thousand times.

One day, Towson was shocked to learn that the Quill had suddenly closed its doors. The Penn Hotel building was to be torn down to make way for a new restaurant. John was distraught. His refuge was being taken away. His bereavement was profound. He felt compelled to see the Quill just one more time. He had to walk down those thirteen steps. Perhaps the door would be open, and he could take one last, lingering look at his beloved home hangout.

As John approached the stairwell leading to the Quill, he was saddened to see a locked gate at the top of the thirteen steps bearing a sign
     The Quill Club is closed.

Almost in tears, John quickened his pace and walked past the gate. And then a strange thing happened—just as John took his fourteenth step beyond the stairwell, he realized that he had begun to salivate.

~ ~ ~ ~ ~

Gordon G. was the shortest and most corpulent lawyer in Towson, and his drinking feats were legendary. He and I were on the opposite sides of a contested divorce case, and, one day, I received a phone call from Gordon. "Bud, I want to take you to lunch and settle this Harbaugh case."

"Okay by me, Gordon. Where shall I meet you for lunch?"

"I'll pick you up at 12:00 tomorrow."

Promptly at noon the next day, I found myself a passenger in Gordon's car, heading north towards the Tail of the Fox, a private club frequented by many of Towson's politicians, judges and attorneys. As we headed into the dining room, Gordon suddenly turned left and said, "Let's have a drink before we have lunch."

A waitress asked, "The usual, Mr. G.?"

"Yep, a double martini. What are you going to have, Bud?"

I ordered an iced tea, but Gordon would not allow it.

"We'll never settle this case unless you order something alcoholic."

"I'll take a scotch and soda."

We began discussing the case, and soon our drinks were placed on our table. In two quick gulps, Gordon had drained his martini glass, and he held up two fingers to the waitress, signifying two more drinks. In what seemed like only a minute, another double martini and scotch and soda were placed on our table. I had barely sipped my first.

We haggled over the amount of the alimony and child support. We argued about property division. Gordon downed a third double martini. I was sipping my second scotch and soda, while ignoring the third one waiting on our table. As we continued negotiating, I became conscious of the fact that my speech was becoming slurred, whereas Gordon, *au contraire*, with six martinis in him (and nothing to eat), was enunciating perfectly, not affected one whit by the enormous amount of gin he had consumed.

While we were haggling, the bar had become crowded. Joe Webster, a Towson lawyer, approached our table. "Hi Gordon, Hi Bud, you two are drinking your lunch?"

"Gordon is drinking, and I'm trying to keep up," I answered.

"Joe, believe it or not, Bud and I are trying to settle a case," Gordon interjected.

"Are you that busy that you have to work even at lunch?" Joe asked.

Gordon responded, "Joe, I'm up to my ass in work."

"Then you're not very busy" was Joe's parting shot as he headed back to the bar.

Finally, we settled our remaining issues in the case. Gordon asked if I wanted another round to celebrate settling the case, but I declined. As we got into Gordon's car, I was conscious of the fact that my speech was practically unintelligible. Gordon continued to pronounce each word clearly. He drove slowly and carefully back to Towson, dropping me at my office.

That evening, I felt embarrassed by my inability to hold my scotch. The next day, a lawyer in Gordon's firm called me, "What did you do to Gordon at lunch yesterday?"

"What did *I* do? Why do you ask?"

"Well, Gordon had a 4:00 appointment. He had laid down on the sofa in his office, and we couldn't awaken him to meet his client. From time to time, he would murmur, 'lunch with Bud George,' and then he would lapse back into a stupor."

Maryland's First Savings and Loan Scandal

It was 1964, and I was thrilled as I hung up the telephone following my call from Carl F., Towson's attorney/banker, who was retaining *me* as his attorney for the appeal. F., who had flown his defense counsel, Gregory Welsh, in from Chicago for F.'s trial in Baltimore federal court on mail fraud charges, had been convicted after a five-week long trial. The federal prosecutor had been Stephen Sachs, hyper-aggressive, brilliant and articulate, the darling of the local media. The case had gotten front-page press coverage every day of the trial, along with daily news blurbs on television and radio. Carl had told me that he was not going to retain Greg Welsh for the appeal; instead, he was hiring *me* to try to reverse his conviction.

Since that evening I was to have dinner with Mom and Dad, I walked to their Towson apartment from my office. I found Mom and Dad sitting in their living room watching a commentator on TV, "The jury convicted Carl F. on two counts of mail fraud. This conviction brings to an end the career of Carl F., the Towson attorney who masterminded the establishment of numerous savings and loan associations, all of which have gone bankrupt. People had been enticed to deposit money into F.'s savings and loans by high interest rates and appliances as gifts for opening accounts. But Security Financial Corporation, the company supposedly insuring deposits in F.'s Maryland banks, was based in Tangier, North Africa. When the first claims were filed against that company, it was discovered that Security Financial had no assets."

Mom spoke. "I hope he goes to jail for a long time. Elderly people, churches, everybody has been victimized by that crook."

"Mom, I have just been hired by Carl F. to represent him on appeal of his conviction. Please don't go around Towson saying he's a crook."

"Why not? He has just been convicted."

"Mom, if people around Towson hear *you* saying that 'Carl F. is a crook', they will think that you learned that from me, as his attorney. Whether you believe it's the truth or not, please don't talk about Carl F. to anybody, whether in Towson or at the Greek church on Sunday."

"Well, okay, I understand your predicament."

I met with Carl the next morning. Bartley Connor had been presiding judge at his trial, and Carl said that, from the very beginning, Connor had been nasty, hostile and prejudiced against Carl in all rulings on the evidence. In fact, one of the grounds for appeal was going to be Judge Connor's bias and hostility against Carl F., preventing his fair trial. "We'll never reverse the conviction on that ground, but it will lend perspective to our more substantive grounds for appeal," Carl explained to me.

Carl said that, as additional grounds for appealing had become evident, Welsh had filed three motions for new trial before Judge Connor. The last thing F. wanted, of course, was a new trial with Connor presiding, but filing such motions allowed those additional grounds to be raised on appeal. "In fact, Bud, you'll soon be filing still another motion for new trial, because I've uncovered another point not raised in our previous motions."

I filed the new motion, along with the striking of Carl's representation by Welsh and entry of my name as F.'s new attorney. News of my becoming F.'s attorney spread around Towson, and my motion for new trial was reported in the *Baltimore Sun*. Judge Connor's chambers set a prompt date for hearing on my motion. At lunch one day at the Towson House, Speed Hanley asked me, "Have you ever appeared before Judge Connor?"

"No, I haven't."

"Well, he has a nervous condition, some sort of facial tick, that makes his face turn red and contort. Don't be surprised if that happens when you appear before him."

"Well, thanks for the warning. I'll be on the lookout for it."

Soon thereafter, Carl F. and I were sitting in federal court in Baltimore City, awaiting Judge Connor's arrival on the bench. Stephen Sachs having retired from the prosecutor's office, the federal prosecutor was now Ben Civiletti, Sachs' chief assistant throughout F.'s trial. The clerk entered the courtroom and intoned, "All rise. This court is now in session, Judge Bartley Connor presiding."

F. and I stood up behind our trial table, as did Civiletti behind his. Judge Connor entered the courtroom and took his chair behind the bench. He immediately looked at the prosecutor, smiled, and directed a few preliminary remarks to him. Civiletti responded, also smiling. Their conversation lasted several minutes.

That Speed Hanley, I thought. Where did he get the idea that Judge Connor had some sort of nervous facial tick. The smiling Judge Connor concluded his remarks with the prosecutor and turned toward F. and me. "And *you*, Mr. George, you are now representing Mr. F., and you appear before me today having filed a *third* motion for new trial in this case."

The smile had disappeared from Judge Connor's face, which was now rapidly reddening as he spoke. Muscles in his face began twitching. Thinking that I might bait Judge Connor into some conduct which could add more substance to our bias argument on appeal, I asserted, "With *all* due respect, your Honor, you are mistaken. This is actually the *fourth* motion for new trial filed in this case on behalf of Mr. F."

Judge Connor exploded. "You're *right*. This *is* the fourth motion filed."

Angrily, Judge Connor flung a pencil he had been holding toward the bench in front of him. The pencil rocketed off of the bench and landed on the floor near Civiletti's trial table. He rose from his chair, picked up the pencil, and placed it on the bench in front of Judge Connor.

The words instantaneously formed in my mind:

LET THE RECORD REFLECT THAT JUDGE CONNOR, IN A PAROXYSM OF UNBRIDLED AND BIASED RAGE AGAINST THE DEFENDANT, HAS JUST FLUNG HIS PENCIL AGAINST THE BENCH SO VIOLENTLY THAT THE PENCIL FLEW FULLY TEN FEET UNTIL IT LANDED NEAR THE DESK OF THE PROSECUTOR, WHO HAS SPRUNG TO HIS FEET AND HAS REPLACED THE PENCIL ON THE BENCH IN FRONT OF A SCARLET-FACED AND INFURIATED JUDGE CONNOR.

I opened my mouth to speak, but no words emerged. After a moment, the hearing commenced, and, not surprisingly, I lost the motion for new trial.

F.'s Conviction Appealed

I had learned early on that Judge Simon Sobeloff would be one of the three judges hearing the F. appeal before the fourth circuit. In doing my research for the brief, I had happened upon a case in which Judge Sobeloff had been the attorney representing a client who had been convicted of mail fraud. Sobeloff had won his case on appeal. I obtained a copy of Sobeloff's brief in that case. His arguments were articulate and convincing. I copied verbatim many of Sobeloff's words from his own brief.

The day of the hearing arrived in Richmond, Virginia. I had learned from the clerk which one of the three judges was Judge Sobeloff, and, during most of my argument, I fixed my eyes directly into Sobeloff's. Some of my argument was framed in Sobeloff's exact wordage. Unfortunately, not the slightest hint of recognition ever manifested itself in Sobeloff's eyes. F. had been sitting in the courtroom, and, on our drive back to Baltimore, we discussed whether Sobeloff had recognized his own verbiage.

A month or so after the hearing, the ruling from the fourth circuit was handed down. F.'s conviction on mail fraud had been reversed by a divided court, two judges going for the reversal, and one judge dissenting. Judge Sobeloff had been one of the judges for reversal. The dissenting Judge Haynesworth was, years later, nominated to the Supreme Court of the United States by President Nixon, but his nomination was rejected by the Senate.

Sly

Several years after I had started my law practice in Towson, I drove by a charming house within ten minutes walking distance from my office, on the front lawn of which was a sign:

For Sale
Slago Realty, Chartered
823-1000

I had heard of a Towson attorney named Sylvester Slago. He had a bad reputation. In fact, Slago's nickname was "Sly."

I called Slago Realty and asked for information about the house for sale on Georgia Court in Towson. The secretary said that she would have Mr. Slago call me back. An hour later, I received a call: "Hello. This is Slago of Slago Realty, Chartered. How can I be of service to you?" I told Mr. Slago that I would like to see the house on Georgia Court, and we agreed to meet there the following day.

Mr. Slago was an unusual looking man. His body frame seemed slender, but his belly protruded above his tightly cinched belt. The top of his head was bald, and he had allowed the hair on the side of his head to grow long. These long hairs he combed tortuously across the top of his bald scalp. He had a bushy mustache and a short multi-colored beard.

"Are you related to the Towson lawyer Sylvester Slago?", I asked.

"I am the Towson lawyer Sylvester Slago."

We went through the house, and, deciding that I wanted to buy it, I said, "Mr. Slago, I too am an attorney, and, as you know, under Maryland law, attorneys are permitted to share real estate commissions with real estate brokers. If I buy the house, I want half the real estate commission as your cooperating broker/attorney."

"No problem. If we agree on price, I will send you a contract for purchase of the house, and, in that contract, I will expressly provide that you and I will split the commissions."

"That's fine with me," I said.

In the next several days, we agreed on price, and I received the contract. The real estate commission amounted to one thousand three hundred eighty dollars. The contract provided for a deposit of five thousand dollars, payable at the signing of the contract. The contract also said that Slago Realty, Chartered, and the attorney/ cooperating broker, Harris George, would split the commission.

I signed both copies of the contract and my check in the amount of five thousand dollars, all of which I mailed back to Sylvester Slago. My half of the commission would amount to six hundred ninety dollars. About a week later, I received my duplicate original of the contract back, signed by the seller, along with a check drawn on Slago Realty, in the amount of four hundred dollars payable to me. Since the commission check was two hundred ninety dollars short the six hundred ninety dollars he owed me, I called Slago on the telephone.

"Mr. Slago, the commissions are one thousand three hundred eighty dollars, which we agreed to split, and yet I received a check in the amount of only four hundred dollars."

"What's wrong with that?" asked Mr. Slago.

"I was supposed to get six hundred ninety dollars. That's the split of one thousand three hundred eighty dollars."

"Mr. George, I never said we'd split fifty-fifty on the commission ."

I was dumbfounded. Calling to mind Slago's reputation, I said, "Mr. Slago, the contract expressly provides that the real estate commissions shall be split between Slago Realty, and Harris George. 'Split' means fifty-fifty, and, even if there were any ambiguity, it would be construed against Slago Realty, since you drew the contract. I am returning your check for four hundred dollars, and I demand, promptly, your check for six hundred ninety dollars."

"Well, I'm shocked. You're being unreasonable, and your offensive tone is making me angry. You shall hear from me shortly," Sly said, as he slammed down his receiver.

I quickly wrote Slago a letter, enclosing his four hundred dollar check and setting forth my entitlement to six hundred ninety dollars. Five days later, I received a letter from Slago Realty, Chartered. Opening it, I found a Slago Realty check in the amount of six hundred ninety dollars , payable to me. I quickly deposited the check. About five days later, Slago Realty's check was returned to me, marked "insufficient funds."

I called Slago.

"Mr. Slago, this is Harris George. My five thousand dollar check to you was good, wasn't it?"

"Yes."

"How come your check to me for six hundred ninety dollars out of my five thousand dollars bounced?"

"Mr. George, you're becoming offensive again. If there has been an error, it's obviously on the part of the bank."

Ultimately, I got a check for six hundred ninety dollars which did not bounce. I told my experiences with Sly to Jim McCarthy, another lawyer friend of mine who had grown up in Towson. "Sylvester Slago," he said, "would rather climb a tree to tell a lie than stand on the ground and tell the truth."

Sly Slago had worked to elect Bunky Fuller to be state's attorney of Baltimore County. Bunky had won, and Sly had been rewarded by being appointed an assistant state's attorney. He appeared every day in the office in a three-piece suit, with a vest, either matching or starkly contrasting the suit he was wearing. The job of an assistant state's attorney was full-time. Upon arriving at the office each morning, Sylvester would first hang his jacket on the hook behind his door, and he would then drape his vest on the back of the swivel chair behind his desk. For the first month, he worked assiduously. During his second month, anyone looking for Sylvester, and, not finding him in his office, would ask, "Where is Sylvester?" The office staff would answer, "Well, Mr. Slago must be here. There's his vest on the back of his chair." Soon people began to say, "Sylvester's vest is always on the back of his chair, but where is Sylvester?"

The deputy state's attorney, Bill Mackey, became suspicious and mounted a secret surveillance of Sylvester's activities. Mackey learned that Sylvester was the first assistant to arrive each morning at the state's attorney's office. He quickly took off his vest, hung it on the back of his chair, and, after varied forays into different parts of the office (obviously to be seen), Sly would slip out of the office. Mackey learned that Slago had use of an office in a building across the street from the courthouse, where the state's attorney's office was located. Apparently, Sylvester would go to this private office where he was conducting a private practice, although showing up from time to time during the working day in the state's attorney's office. Sylvester's vest was his omnipresent stand-in in the state's attorney's office. Deputy Mackey confronted Sylvester with the facts and offered to let Sylvester resign rather than be fired. Sly did not hesitate. He resigned.

Sylvester disliked Bill Mackey for having uncovered Sly's gambit. One day, Sylvester was representing a defendant in an armed robbery case in which Bill Mackey was the prosecutor. During a motions hearing, Mackey had showed up early and placed on his trial table three *Maryland Reports* case books with yellow strips protruding, marking in each volume the Maryland case upon which Mackey would rely during the hearing. Sly, representing the defendant, had entered the courtroom after Mackey had left. The courtroom being empty, Sylvester pulled the yellow slips from each of the law books on Mackey's trial table.

The hearing commenced, and the prosecution began its argument. Soon, Sylvester challenged a certain point, to which Mackey responded, "I've got a case right on that point, Your Honor." The deputy went to his *Maryland Reports*, and for the first time—to his horror—realized that the yellow strips marking the relevant cases were no longer in the books on his desk. The prosecutor looked angrily at Sylvester who stared straight ahead at the court.

At the annual Baltimore county bar association golf outing, Sylvester Slago and Bill Mackey happened to be the last two attorneys to sign up for the tournament. The attorney in charge of the tournament asked Slago whether he was going to walk or ride in a golf cart. Without hesitation, Sylvester said, "I always walk." Bill Mackey always rode, and he paid the cost of a golf cart, since his partner, Slago, would be walking. After the first hole, Slago jauntily tied his golf bag onto the cart and jumped into the passenger seat, saying, "No sense you riding alone."

The Minority Stockholder

A handsome client of mine of Italian extraction, Francis A., had gone into the radio dispatching business with his highly volatile but wealthy lady friend, Janet. Janet had contributed the money, and Francis the looks. Janet made Francis a twenty-five percent stockholder, and she had held the other seventy-five percent.

One day, Francis rushed into my office, "Bud, you've got to help me. Janet just threw me out of the office, and she's threatened to destroy all of my personal property, radio equipment, everything I've got in my private office."

"Francis, what do you want me to do?"

"Just telephone her—right now and tell her not to destroy my stuff."

"Francis, attorneys do not *telephone* opposing parties. We write to them or send telegrams. I communicate with their attorneys, and we settle things, all in due time."

"Bud, if you don't call her *right now*, it will be too late. She was frothing at the mouth when she threw me out."

"Francis, she'll never pay attention to a telephone call."

"Bud, please, for me, do it! Telephone her now, or it'll be too late."

I picked up the phone and dialed the company number. I then asked for Janet C. "This is Janet C."

"Miss C., this is Harris George. I am Francis A.'s attorney, and Francis, who is in my office, tells me that you have evicted him from his office and threatened to destroy his personal property."

"It's *my* company, I paid for all of his stuff, and I can do with it what I please."

"Well, I respectfully disagree with you. It is not *your* company. Francis A. is a minority stockholder, and your conduct is oppressing his rights as a minority stockholder."

"Francis is *not* a minority stockholder", was Janet's reply.

Flustered, I asked, "What are you saying? Francis has showed me the corporate papers. He owns twenty-five percent of the company."

Janet repeated, "Francis is *not* a minority stockholder. He was born in *this* country."

Taken aback, I could say only, "Miss C., oppressing the rights of stockholders like Francis can make you responsible for punitive as well as compensatory damages. Please don't do anything rash until you have talked to your attorney."

The Flea

A man, small in stature, paused in front of the show window on which a huge sign proclaimed

E. J. KORVETTE
GOING OUT OF BUSINESS
Everything must go for pennies on the dollar!

He scanned all the merchandise in the window (mostly luggage and patio furniture), but he stared at one particular background fixture. It was a realistic-looking small tree. He went into the store, chatted briefly with a salesperson and walked out with a hollow tree.

The man was Frank Alessi, my private detective. He was conducting a surveillance on Phyllis N., wife of Dr. Anthony N., my client. Phyllis had been described to me by her husband as "flirtatious, attractive, with a great body." Frank described her as a woman who wore clothes that clutched her body in a death grip. Phyllis seemed to be giving off some sort of signal, that caused men to come on to her constantly. She also disproved the adage that drugs and alcohol don't mix. In fact, they *did* mix, in Phyllis, copiously and often. She seemed to thrive on the combination.

One late afternoon in western Maryland near the Newton vacation lodge, one tree among many seemed to be inching closer to the window of a first floor bedroom. From within the hollow tree, Frank spotted a man through the window. The tree stopped. Moments later, Phyllis, within the house, appeared in the window. There she paused, nude, and the man, also nude, embraced her. The tree had done its job, and Korvette had paid its latest posthumous dividend.

~ ~ ~ ~ ~

Alessi has been my private detective for over twenty-five years. In my early law practice, private detectives had a bad reputation. They were often ex-policemen kicked off the force or drunks unable to hold a steady job. In fact, in those days, Maryland cases involving private detectives could be found in the *Maryland Law Digest* under the generic title, "Private Detectives, Prostitutes and Other Persons of Dubious Character."

Frank was always different. Judges in Baltimore county learned that he would not exaggerate on the witness stand. It became known around Towson (through Ken Smith's lawyer-friendly barber shop) that Frank had actually threatened violence to a politician who had offered Frank a bribe to forget something that he had seen. Alessi had an ingenious mind, boundless optimism, and, as his most salient characteristic, dogged persistence. I called Alessi "the Flea" because, once he got on you, you couldn't get him off.

～ ～ ～ ～ ～

In another divorce case, I represented a wife whose businessman husband had a paramour in Montreal, Canada. Mr. Business did not know that we knew about his French connection. When he booked a flight to Montreal, I called the Flea to tell him to get a ticket on the same flight.

"Bud, you realize that I will have to travel first class."

"First class?"

"Of course. I'll have to go first class if I'm going to get off the plane before our quarry. Then I can meet our Montreal detective. Together, we'll await the merchant prince's departure from the plane and then follow him to his love nest."

The Flea's plan worked perfectly, and, soon thereafter, Technicolor film displayed Mr. Business and his lady friend on her terrace, in bathrobes, toasting each other with champagne glasses before they embraced.

～ ～ ～ ～ ～

Mrs. B. was a pleasant seventy-five year old lady who had been married to Mr. B. for fifty-three years. He too was seventy-five. Mrs. B. suspected that her husband was "keeping time with another woman." For one thing, he always left the senior center early, and, when Mrs. B. arrived home, he was never there. He would always come in later, looking exhausted.

"Mrs. B., do you really think that your husband, at his age, is seeing another woman?"

"Yes, in fact, I had been warned that I should never have let him go alone on a certain bus trip that the senior center sponsored. You may not know it, but there are five times more women than men at the senior center. My friends warned me, if I didn't go along on that bus trip, the barracudas on the bus would get him."

I said that I would call the Flea.

The following day, Mrs. B. called me, very excited. She had accidentally hit speed dial on her phone, and a woman's voice had answered on the other end. She looked at caller ID and discovered the name and phone number of Wanda F. The Flea began his surveillance of Mr. B. as he left the senior center. Each day, Mr. B.

would park his car outside Towson's high-rise Penthouse condominium, and he would disappear inside. The Flea had tried to follow Mr. B. inside the Penthouse, but there was security above the seventh floor, and public access was denied. Alessi could never get above the seventh floor, although Mr. B. did so repeatedly. After an hour or two, the Flea would see Mr. B. emerge from the Penthouse.

I told Alessi, "You know, it does no good to track Mr. B. into and out of the Penthouse high-rise. We must show some connection, some show of affection between Mr. B. and Wanda F."

"Bud, I know that."

An exhilarated Flea called me a week later. "Bud, about an hour ago, Mr. B. came out of the Penthouse, and, as he was about to enter his car parked across the street, he looked up to a balcony where a lady was standing. He blew her a kiss, and she blew one back. I've got them connected, affectionately."

"Fabulous," I said. "But, Frank, how are you going to serve her with a subpoena for my deposition? You can't get above the seventh floor."

"Leave it to me."

A couple of days later, upon returning to my office, I received a fax from the Flea—SIGHTED SUB, SANK SAME!

"Frank, how did you serve her?"

"Well, through the department of motor vehicles, I got the license plate of her automobile, which I located in the Penthouse garage. I then called her on the phone and told her that I had collided with her automobile in the garage. When she came down to meet me, I said, 'I have good news and bad news. The good news is that I did not hit your car; the bad news is that you are hereby served with a subpoena for a deposition.'"

~ ~ ~ ~ ~

Sidney G., a pious man staunch in his Orthodox Jewish faith, suspected his wife Ruth of being unfaithful to him with Marvin S., a man who lived in Kansas City. One day, an excited Sidney called me. While his wife was showering, he had rummaged through her purse and had found a matchbook from the Airport Motel. As Ruth emerged from her shower, she informed Sidney that she was going to accompany her sister to New York Friday and stay overnight to catch a Broadway show. They would return on Saturday. This was the first time in their seventeen years of marriage that Ruth was planning to overnight with her sister.

Sidney suspected that perhaps Marvin S. was intending to spend Friday night at the Airport Motel with Ruth. I called the Flea to see if he was available for surveillance on Friday night. Frank said that he was, and I arranged that Sidney, Alessi and I meet in my office Friday afternoon. The meeting commenced, and Frank announced that he had had his assistant call the Airport Motel, pretending to be Marvin S.'s secretary. The Airport Motel had confirmed a reservation for Marvin S. As the conference was about to conclude, Sidney suddenly said, "Mr. Alessi, I don't want you to go. Ruth will not be there."

I was shocked. "Sidney, what are you talking about? Of course Ruth will be there. Frank has confirmed that Marvin S. is going to be at the Airport Motel tonight. Why else would Ruth give you an excuse about going to New York with her sister to catch a Broadway show *this same Friday night*?"

"It would be a waste of my money to send Mr. Alessi to the Airport Motel. Ruth will not be there. Ruth would *never* commit adultery on the Sabbath."

The Flea interjected, "Mr. G., you are forgetting that there are ten commandments. We strongly suspect Ruth of adultery. If she would break the commandment against committing adultery, don't you think that she would also break the commandment concerning the Sabbath?"

After a prolonged exchange, Sidney relented, and the Flea went about his business—as a result of which we all learned that Ruth was not as religiously observant as Sidney had hoped she would be.

The Snatch

I got a call from a corporate lawyer acquaintance of mine telling me that he was sending his sister-in-law, Suzanne T., to see me. Suzanne's husband had left their home in Milwaukee, Wisconsin, taking with him the couple's only child, a seven-year old girl, Amanda. Suzanne did not know where her husband was, but his mother (Amanda's grandmother) lived in Baltimore County.

Suzanne T. looked anorexic and distraught, explaining that she was unable to sleep because she didn't know where her daughter was or who was taking care of her. Suzanne informed me that the grandmother, Gretchen T., had three children (other than Suzanne's husband) living in three different states, and Suzanne didn't know which one had Amanda.

Suzanne had come to Baltimore to plead with the grandmother to tell Suzanne where Amanda was, but Gretchen T. had refused to speak with Suzanne.

I had Suzanne retain my private detective, Frank Alessi, to conduct surveillance on the grandmother in Baltimore County. If Amanda was not with the grandmother, it could take a lot of time and money to conduct surveillance in Alabama, Pennsylvania, and Colorado, where Gretchen's children lived.

My first priority was to obtain an order of the circuit court for Baltimore County, awarding temporary custody of Amanda to her mother, Suzanne T.. Unfortunately, since I did not know where Thomas T. (Suzanne's husband) was or even whether he was in the State of Maryland, I could not serve him with papers to give the Baltimore County courts jurisdiction over the custody matter.

I finally decided to file a complaint, asking for temporary custody, serving two defendants. I sued the grandmother, alleging that she had engaged in a conspiracy with her son, co-defendant Thomas T., to deprive Suzanne T. of the custody and companionship of her daughter Amanda T. In desperation, not knowing of Thomas' whereabouts, I decided to try to serve him, as defendant, by serving his mother, Gretchen T., as his agent, alleging her to be his co-conspirator.

I told my law partner of my plan to serve the grandmother as the father's agent and co-conspirator. My partner smiled and suggested that I was trying to hook a big fish with a paperclip. Since I was unable to come up with any other alternative, I drafted and filed the complaint. In less than a month, I received two responses to my complaint. The grandmother denied any such conspiracy with her son. However, I was pleasantly surprised when a Baltimore County attorney filed a "special appearance" on behalf of Thomas T., the defendant father, denying, first, that Gretchen T. was his agent for service of process, and, second, that he had been properly served. Since Maryland had, some years before, abolished special appearances, Thomas T. had, in effect, entered his appearance for suit purposes, thereby subjecting himself to the jurisdiction of the Baltimore County court. Shortly thereafter, I obtained an ex parte temporary custody order, and my partner was delighted that my paperclip had indeed hooked the big fish.

Locating Amanda was the next problem. I noted the grandmother's deposition along with a lengthy document subpoena, which required her to bring to the deposition a plethora of documents—all of her financial, household, and personal records, including her checkbook, her bank account statements, her gas and electric bills, her telephone bills, her credit card records, and every other document I could think of. I had asked for a hundred pages of documents to disguise the fact that I was genuinely interested in only two documents:

1. Gretchen's checkbook (particularly entries shortly before and after Thomas had taken Amanda from the home) to see whether the grandmother had made any loans to any of her children; and
2. her telephone records to see to whom she had made phone calls shortly before and after her granddaughter's having been taken from her mother in Milwaukee.

My examination of the relevant documents revealed no payments from Gretchen to any of her children, but, in the several days after the father had taken Amanda from their Milwaukee home, I did note five calls from the grandmother to her son, Stanley, who lived in Alabama with his wife and two small children. The grandmother had made only two calls to her daughter, Phyllis, in Colorado and one call to Grace in Pennsylvania. Amanda was probably with Stanley, I thought.

The next morning Suzanne and Alessi flew to Mobile, Alabama, where Suzanne rented an automobile and Frank put Stanley T.'s home under surveillance. Three days later I received a phone call from Frank, informing me that Suzanne and he had located the school which Amanda was attending. Frank and Suzanne waited for a recess period, Suzanne got out of the automobile and called Amanda, who ran to hug her mother. Suzanne got Amanda into the automobile, Alessi raced the car toward Mississippi, and the snatch was successfully concluded when Frank's automobile crossed Mississippi's border.

The Horse Auctioneer

Earl S. had established Earl's Sales Agency, a horse auctioneering business in Towson, Maryland. This was not an easy field to break into because the auction sale of horses was dominated by a national organization with offices scattered throughout the country. Still, Earl was a third generation Maryland horseman, and he was determined to succeed in the horse auction business.

In order to establish his business, Earl had loosened the credit requirements for buyers at his auction sales, and, not surprisingly, he was owed money by buyers who had bought a horse on credit at Earl's auction in Towson and transported the horse to the buyer's home state. However, the time for payment passed, and no payment had been forthcoming from numerous buyers. Earl found the consignors of horses to his sales clamoring for their money.

I could readily understand Earl's problem. I imagined that if a non-paying San Antonio buyer of a horse at Earl's auction were to receive a certified letter from a Maryland lawyer, for which the buyer was asked to sign a return receipt, he would certainly refuse to do so since, knowing that he owed money to a Maryland horse auctioneer, he could easily guess that the letter was probably a summons to a Maryland court. He would be correct in his thinking, because his signature for the certified letter would indeed accord jurisdiction to the Maryland court over a buyer in Texas under the Maryland long-arm statute.

I told Earl that I would represent him in trying to collect monies from out-of-state buyers of his horses. I looked at a calendar and saw that Valentine's Day was approaching. I obtained three shoeboxes and three blocks of wood. I waited until a week before Valentine's Day and then filed three suits against three defendants who lived in three different states: Virginia, South Carolina and Tennessee.

The Baltimore County district court papers I filed under affidavit consisted of a declaration, which stated the facts of the case and a request for admission of facts, which required the defendant to admit or deny under oath the facts set forth in the request. For each defendant, I wrapped his summons, a copy of his declaration, and his request for admissions around a block of wood (binding them with a rubber band) and placed the block inside a shoebox. I then stuffed crumpled newspapers inside the box to hold the block steady.

My secretary then wrapped the box, and, on the outside, she *wrote* the defendant's name and address. I also had her write "love and kisses," "Happy

Valentine's Day," and "with all my love" on the package. She omitted any return address. I sent the box certified, return receipt requested.

Obviously overcome by curiosity, all three of the defendants readily signed for their respective packages, and I visualized them eagerly tearing apart the wrapping paper only to find a summons to the Maryland district court, along with a declaration and request for admissions banded to a block of wood. Once the defendants had been served, each paid for his horse because his only alternative would have been to retain a lawyer in Maryland to appear for him and try to defend the case. But the defendants had no defense on the merits of the case, since each had the horse, had failed and/or refused to pay for it, and could not deny under oath any of the facts set forth in the declaration. I collected the full amount from all three defendants.

Just prior to succeeding holidays, squadrons of blocks of wood were sent in the same manner (no return address, my secretary writing—rather than typing—the defendant's name and address, and the envelope containing handwritten slogans or greetings for the appropriate holiday) to nonresident buyers of horses from Earl's Sales Agency. Around each block was wrapped a summons to the appropriate Maryland court and a copy of the relevant pleadings.

The summons packages were particularly irresistible during the Christmas season, and many nonresident defendants unknowingly subjected themselves to Maryland jurisdiction in order to satisfy the "visions of sugarplums" that "danced in their heads."*

* *A Visit from St. Nicholas*, Clement C. Moore.

The Tower

I had been hired by Baltelco to obtain the proper zoning to erect a tower which was to be the last link needed to connect the transmission line through Baltimore county. I was told that the tower needed to be one hundred forty feet tall. I informed Baltelco that it needed to be absolutely certain about the maximum height required for the tower because, if I obtained zoning for a one hundred forty foot tower, the tower could not go one foot higher than one hundred forty feet without another zoning hearing. Baltelco wrote me that it had confirmed that the tower needed to be only hundred forty feet high, max.

In my zoning application, I requested permission for a tower one hundred fifty feet high. With Mr. and Mrs. Rosenberg, owners of the property, I visited the tower site, which was a large clearing in a heavily wooded area in northern Baltimore county. I advised Baltelco that opponents of the tower could appear at the hearing to object to the zoning, although there was no residential development in the vicinity of the tower site.

The property was posted with notice of the hearing on February 11, 1983, and notice of the hearing was also advertised in a local newspaper. I arranged for the Rosenbergs to appear as witnesses, and Baltelco provided the engineers who would testify on its behalf. It started snowing heavily in Baltimore county early on February 8. The snow continued unabated for the next several days. Many county roads became impassable. County schools closed. Power outages were rampant.

The zoning commissioner convened the hearing promptly at 10:00 a.m. on February 11. I had prepared Baltelco's two engineers to testify. Mr. and Mrs. Rosenberg, the owners of the property, were snowed in and unable to appear at the hearing. Fortunately, no protesters were present, and that enabled the hearing to proceed expeditiously. The commissioner allowed me to proffer the testimony of the owners, and I put on my engineering witnesses. In short order, the commissioner granted my zoning application, giving Baltelco permission to proceed with erection of its one hundred fifty foot tower. I closed my file and thought no more of Baltelco— until, about a month later, I received a call from one of Baltelco's engineers. "Mr. George, we have now learned that the tower needs to be one hundred sixty-eight feet high in order to work."

I scheduled another zoning hearing. Once again, the property was posted with notice of the new hearing, and the hearing was advertised in the newspaper. On the morning of the new hearing, the property owners, Baltelco's engineers, and I walked into a hearing room filled to capacity with noisy, hostile opponents. Their leader was a feisty and disagreeable lady, Mrs. W., a lawyer, who lived in a development called Tall Oaks.

As the protesters registered with the zoning commissioner, I learned from the Rosenbergs that all of the protesters also lived in the Tall Oaks development, and, further, that Mrs. W. was a consummate rabble-rouser. I asked the commissioner to have the opponents mark on the map where they lived in relation to the tower site. It seemed that the nearest protester lived perhaps two miles from the tower site.

I asked, "What is your complaint? The tower itself will be totally surrounded by huge trees and could not even be seen by anyone in the Tall Oaks development."

Mrs. W. erupted: "Mr. George, the residents of Tall Oaks will see the blinking red lights on top of the tower. Those lights will destroy our rural vista, depress our property values, and ruin the aesthetics of the Tall Oaks community."

"But you won't ever see the red lights at the top of the tower because of the surrounding trees and the topography of the land," I insisted.

"Prove that," snarled Mrs. W.

Baltelco was under enormous time pressure, to get this last tower built, without which the line could not be connected. Baltelco was already behind schedule and would soon be in contractual breach with several parties. I also knew that, even if I won the hearing before the zoning commissioner, the protesters could take an appeal and delay the project for many months.

"If I prove that Tall Oaks cannot see the tower, Mrs. W., will you withdraw the protesters' opposition to the one hundred sixty-eight foot tower?"

Sneering with confidence, Mrs. W. said, "Yes."

I came up with a possible solution to the problem. I decided to hire Harry Carter, an engineer, who, at the tower site, would release a helium-filled balloon at the end of a one hundred sixty-eight foot line. Mrs. W. and I would then leave the tower site and drive to Mrs. W.'s home. Once there, we would look in the direction of the tower, and, if we could see the balloon, Mrs. W. would be able to see the red lights.

Mrs. W. insisted that the test be conducted on a Saturday. That was agreeable to me, and Baltelco's president, Larry Hite, decided that he would like to attend. Two Saturdays later, Larry Hite met me at my office at 10:00 a.m. He was accompanied by his six year old daughter, Tracey. Larry said, "This being Saturday, Tracey's not in school, and I thought she might enjoy seeing the test."

The three of us got into my car, and I drove to the tower site. Harry Carter was there, as were four protesters, including Mrs. W. The protesters had already verified that the balloon was attached to a line that measured one hundred sixty-eight feet. It was a very windy day.

The plan was that three protesters would stay at the tower site with the engineer, while Mrs. W. led Mr. Hite, his daughter and me back to her house for the viewing. Harry Carter inflated the balloon with helium. When he released it, instead of going straight up, strong gusts of wind caused the balloon to veer to one side of the clearing and then careen to the other side.

Nevertheless, Larry Hite, Tracey and I got into my automobile and began following Mrs. W. We reached her home in about fifteen minutes, where we were greeted by Mrs. W.'s husband, her six year old daughter, Chloe, and the W. family dog, Poochie. Larry, Mrs. W. and I sat on porch chairs and looked in the direction of the tower site. After a while, Tracey, Chloe and Poochie went downstairs to play.

We made small talk for about fifteen minutes. Finally, I said, "Well, I don't see any balloon."

"Of course you don't, Mr. George," Mrs. W. retorted. "The heavy winds have prevented that balloon from going up."

Suddenly, we heard a young girl's scream. Mrs. W. leaped from her chair and headed downstairs, Larry and I following close behind her. We found Tracey crying and holding her left arm. Chloe explained, "Tracey tried to grab Poochie's ball, and Poochie bit her."

Tracey's skin had been punctured, and there was a small amount of blood where Tracey was holding her arm. Solemnly, I said, "Larry, let's quickly get Tracey to the emergency room of Greater Baltimore Medical Center."

The three of us departed with a hasty goodbye to Mrs. W.

The following Monday, at 9:01 a.m., I received a call from Mrs. W. She seemed troubled, first asking how Tracey was feeling and what had happened at the hospital. She then apologized profusely for Poochie, although quickly pointing out that Poochie had never bitten anyone before. I sensed that Mrs. W. might fear possible repercussions from Poochie's having bitten Tracey. Finally, Mrs. W. said that she had talked to her neighbors, and they had all agreed—since she never did see that balloon—to withdraw any protest to Baltelco's tower.

Dragon Lady

This was my first day in Baltimore county's office of law, and I was leaning back in the swivel chair in my new office, my feet propped upon my desk, reviewing the first of five files which have just been assigned to me. Into my office swept Mrs. D., for twenty-two years secretary to the county attorney and the deputy county attorney. Her desk was between both of their offices, and she had been lead secretary to five previous county attorneys, as well as to the deputy county attorney. I had been forewarned about Mrs. D. She ran the office of law, and she delighted in terrorizing young assistant county attorneys. "The county attorney, Mr. Moore, does not permit assistants to put their feet on the desks, and, besides, we girls chip in out of our own money to buy the polish to keep all the desks polished and shiny."

Girls, I thought, she's sixty-three if she's a day. "Mrs. D., I'm going to save you girls a lot of money because I don't want my desk polished—*ever!* It makes my sleeves shiny."

"Well, I never...," and she stormed out of my office.

I continued reviewing the file, until I heard, about ten minutes later, someone slamming doors elsewhere in the suite. Suddenly, Mrs. D., clutching some papers in one hand, surged into my office, dropped a paper on to my desk and departed without saying a word. I picked up the paper.

> From: E. Scott Moore, County Attorney
> To: All Assistant County Attorneys
>
> Assistant County Attorneys shall not put their feet
> on their desks.

There was a rubber stamp where the signature should have been:

> The County Attorney
> by Ruth D.
> Administrative Assistant

Mrs. D. was heading down the corridor, obviously to place her directive on other desks, but, as I heard her coming back my way to leave the suite, I quickly make a paper airplane out of her directive and sailed it out of my door, across her bow. Mrs. D. paused outside my office and glared at me. Both of us, I am certain, had identical thoughts: This is war!

Mrs. D. and I crossed swords many times over the course of the next year. She won almost all of the battles, but I won a few. We were most assuredly not each other's favorite person in the office of law. But then, something occurred which was to affect profoundly the relationship between Mrs. D. and me. Walter R. Haile, who had been deputy county attorney for fifteen years (and whom Mrs. D. idolized) was appointed a judge of the circuit court for Baltimore county. To everyone's surprise (including mine), I was appointed his successor as deputy county attorney.

Casually, on the Tuesday after Easter, I sauntered toward Judge Haile's former office. Mrs. D. was seated at her desk, just outside Judge Haile's office. I paused in the office doorway—which was now to be *my* office—and said softly, "Mrs. D., would you kindly arrange to have *my* desk brought over to the deputy's office and Judge Haile's desk moved into my old office?"

Mrs. D.'s eyes opened wider than I would have thought possible, and, with incredulous annoyance, she asked, "You are getting rid of Judge Haile's desk?"

"Mrs. D., he is not here. He is risen!"

Gossip Central

The gossip center of Towson remained Ken Smith's barbershop. Since Ken cut the hair of all the politicians, judges and lawyers in Towson, you had to get your hair cut by Ken just to make sure you kept up with the latest rumors around Towson— particularly since some of them might involve you.

One day, Ken told me about how the marriage of one of Towson's most prominent lawyers, Bill Armstrong, had just been saved. Bill was married to Frances, but everyone in Towson (including Frances) knew that Bill was carrying on with Polly, who was a flashy blonde who drove around Towson in an old convertible with the top down, even in winter (when she kept the heater on, full blast). From time to time, Polly would stop by Bill's office, which was in the Masonic Building at the corner of Washington and Chesapeake Avenues. Bill's office, which was on the first floor of the Masonic building, had big windows, facing the courthouse square. But Bill had assured Frances on several occasions that he was no longer seeing Polly.

Bill was looking out his office window one morning, and he saw Polly stop her convertible (top down, of course), across the street from his office in front of the courthouse. Bill immediately left his office, walked across Washington Avenue to Polly's convertible, and began chatting with Polly. Several moments later, Polly said, "Hey Bill, Frances has just pulled up in front of your office across the street, but she hasn't looked our way."

Bill froze in place, his back to Frances, trying to decide what to do.

Just at that moment, the streetcar started up from in front of the courthouse and, several seconds later, passed between Frances' car and Polly's convertible.

Bill suddenly broke into a trot behind the streetcar as it traveled away from the Masonic building.

Ken told me that Bill didn't stop running for two blocks.

~ ~ ~ ~ ~

In 1966, Dale Anderson had just been elected county executive of Baltimore county, and the Towson legal community couldn't decide whom he would pick as his county attorney. There were many things about Steve Kirk which commended him for the job. He was mature, experienced, and had been helpful in Dale's campaign for county executive. On the other hand, Bruce Alderman was young, energetic and likeable. All of Towson was debating whether Dale Anderson's county attorney would be Steve Kirk or Bruce Alderman.

One afternoon, as Ken was cutting my hair, he asked, "Bud, who is it going to be, Kirk or Alderman? You are in the county attorney's office. Who is Dale going to pick?"

Having just the day before completed a deposition with an attorney named David R. Finkleberg, I said, "Ken, if I tell you, I've got to swear you to secrecy. I'm one of the few who know."

Ken's eyes widened. "You can trust me, Bud. You know that I won't tell a soul. Which one is it, Kirk or Alderman?"

Holding my hand in front of my mouth so that no one could read my lips, I whispered, "The new county attorney is going to be David R. Finkleberg."

"David R. Finkleberg! I've never even heard of him."

"Ken, remember, you must keep it secret."

"You know you can trust me, Bud."

Ken finished cutting my hair, and I left the shop, thinking no more about our conversation. Two weeks later, as I was about to enter the Towson House for lunch, an attorney friend, Harrison Stone, burst out the door, and announced, "I know who the county attorney is going to be."

Excitedly, I asked, "Is it Kirk or Alderman?"

"It's going to be someone named David R. Finkleberg."

The Deputy

Dale Anderson had just won the election to be county executive of Baltimore county by defeating Scott Moore, the Republican candidate who had been county attorney under the previous administration and who had previously appointed me to be an assistant county attorney. Word had reached me that I was going to be the first assistant fired when Dale Anderson took office, since I was a Democrat who had accepted an appointment to the office of law from a Republican. This word circulated around Towson, and I received an offer to become an assistant state's attorney under Sam Green, who had just won a tight three-man race for state's attorney.

One week after the election, Walter R. Haile, who had been Baltimore county's deputy county attorney for fifteen years, was, quite unexpectedly, appointed a judge of the circuit court. I was on a stool in the stag bar of the Penn Hotel one late Friday afternoon after work when into the bar stepped Dale Anderson. He walked over to me and asked if I would join him at a small table away from the bar. Once seated, Dale said, "Bud, I hear you're going to be an assistant state's attorney under Sam Green."

"That is true."

"Well, wouldn't you prefer to be deputy county attorney in charge of a thirteen-man office of law rather than one of fifteen assistant state's attorneys who do nothing but criminal work? Walter Haile has been appointed judge, and that means that I will be needing a new deputy county attorney. I've asked around, and people I respect say you should be the next deputy. I'm offering you that job. Are you interested?"

"Well, thank you very much. Yes, I am interested in becoming the new deputy county attorney."

"Well, there's only one catch. In order to take care of political commitments, I've got to appoint *three* deputy attorneys. You will be the *real* deputy, but I have to appoint two other attorneys who will be also designated deputy county attorneys. That's okay with you, isn't it?"

"No, frankly, that's not okay with me. Walter Haile has been deputy for fifteen years, and he's been the *only* deputy. I would really not be interested in becoming one of three deputies taking the place of one deputy. I would rather be an assistant state's attorney."

"Why is that? You'd be the *real* deputy."

"Well, I don't want to be standing in a circle with two other deputies, each pointing to another, saying, 'that was his responsibility'. My feeling is that you should have one deputy. If that deputy does his job, fine; if he doesn't, fire him, and get one who does."

Dale thought for a moment and said, "You know, dammit, you are right. All right. I'm going to appoint you the only deputy attorney. However, don't tell anyone yet. I'll have to find other jobs for the two attorneys who have been promised a deputy's job." Shortly thereafter, Dale announced that Bruce Alderman was going to be his county attorney. Bruce then appointed me his deputy.

Dale Anderson had won election as county executive of Baltimore county primarily because of the very heavy vote he had received from the eastern side of the county, particularly Dundalk, Essex, and Middle River. An unpopular man in Dundalk was Spence B., who owned acreage of land east of Dundalk which, for many years, he had been utilizing as a sanitary landfill for the disposal of garbage and refuse. Mr. B. also owned Baltimore county's largest garbage and trash collector. For twenty years, trash and garbage from all over the county was hauled to the landfill.

According to the residents, disgusting odors constantly emanated from Mr. B.'s landfill at all hours of the day and night. Most homes in the neighborhoods nearest the landfill had no air-conditioning. These residents had to open their windows, and smells soon permeated the insides of their houses. Their choice was between the rock and the whirlpool—either keep the windows closed and suffer from oppressive humidity, or open the windows and breathe in the stench-filled air.

Dale Anderson had campaigned extensively in Dundalk, and to receptive ears he had promised to close down the landfill. Not surprisingly therefore, several months after the election, B.'s company's routine permit for annual renewal of landfill operations was denied by Baltimore county's department of permits and licenses, based on several technicalities. Mr. B. promptly filed a petition for mandamus (a pleading aimed at requiring a government to perform a specified act) to compel the county to issue the renewal permit.

I was defending the county against the mandamus. I interviewed a number of residents who lived near the landfill, listening to their tales of living in malodorous discomfort for many years. I picked three residents who would testify about their experiences in having lived in the area of the landfill. I had sent each of them a list of questions that I proposed to ask, and I had reviewed their answers with them. I had also prepared two county officials as witnesses. The trial date arrived, and my three Dundalk witnesses and I proceeded to the courtroom. They were eager to testify, jocular in mood, feeling that at last they would get a chance to tell the world the misery caused them by Mr. B. and the landfill. On the sidewalk in front of the courthouse, a group of Dundalk residents was demonstrating, carrying signs proclaiming, "Dundalk, not Dumpdalk".

The trial began with the courtroom almost filled with Dundalk residents. Mr. B., petitioner's first witness, answered a number of questions from his counsel regarding his history of having filled out the applications for annual permits and submitting them to Baltimore county. His testimony was clear—for years, he had filled out precisely the same permit application, supplied precisely the same answers, and all of the previous applications, without exception, had been granted. This time, as B. emphasized, under the "new" county executive, the renewal permit had been denied.

When B.'s testimony ended, his attorney surprised me by resting his case. I moved to dismiss the case, pointing out that B. had not proved that the county's denial of the renewal application had been arbitrary and/or unjustified. Argument between counsel started in a civil manner, but, after a few exchanges, became quite vociferous, at which point Judge W. Mitchell Jenifer interjected, "You gentlemen are generating a lot of heat but not much light." Finally, Judge Jenifer stated that, in ruling on a motion to dismiss in a non-jury case, the evidence must be construed most favorably to the petitioner/B. Therefore, he denied my motion to dismiss and called a fifteen minute recess.

I left the courtroom and joined my three Dundalk witnesses-to-be, who had been sequestered from the courtroom pursuant to a motion by B.'s attorney. They were impatient to get on the stand and tell their story. I returned to the courtroom, sat in my chair behind the trial table, and realized that something was troubling me. Pondering for a moment, I decided that, to my way of thinking, B.'s attorney had not produced enough evidence to sustain his petition for mandamus. Judge Jenifer was extremely bright, scholarly and even-handed. I had a strong visceral feeling that, if I rested my case, the county would win because there had been no direct proof that the county's denial of the application for renewal of permit had been unjustified or arbitrary.

On the other hand, three long-suffering and enthusiastic witnesses from Dundalk were sitting outside the courtroom, eager to disgorge the tales of the misery caused their lives by the landfill. Additionally, the courtroom was crowded with those demonstrators from Dundalk. My thoughts were interrupted when the court clerk announced, "All rise. This Honorable Court is now in session, Judge Jenifer presiding."

Judge Jenifer took his seat behind the bench and asked, "Mr. George, is the county ready to proceed?"

"Yes, your Honor. The county rests."

The words left my mouth instinctively. Once out, I was suddenly aware that I had never consciously made the decision *not* to put witnesses on the stand. The words just came out, and I stood there. There was a considerable stir in the courtroom behind me, where the Dundalk residents were buzzing among themselves. Judge Jenifer's expression never changed. He announced that he would take a half hour recess before rendering an opinion, and he left the courtroom. The buzzing behind me ceased. I was still standing.

During the next half hour, sitting in my chair behind my trial table, I rebuked myself repeatedly for having rested my case. What a dumb move! I had three witnesses from Dundalk who had spent their lives preparing to give testimony, for which I had prepared them, and I had denied them their opportunity to get on the stand to vent their anger and outrage. I had two county witnesses prepared to testify that there were indeed some technical reasons which could have been advanced for not approving the renewal permit. I could have easily given the citizens their opportunity to air their passions; instead, I had acted on a gut belief that I could win the case based solely on the insufficiency of the other lawyer's proof. Gosh, this was no time for me to try to be a *smart* lawyer; this was the time to be a *political* lawyer, which was exactly what I was—the deputy county attorney for Baltimore county.

Judge Jenifer returned to the bench. The courtroom was now empty except for the attorneys, court personnel and the judge. The citizens from Dundalk had all departed. Judge Jenifer announced that, based upon the totality of evidence presented, he agreed with the county's position that petitioner had failed to meet its required burden of proof to overcome the county's denial of the renewal permit. Therefore, Mr. B.'s petition for mandamus was denied.

Elated, I returned to my office and found a large scribbled message in the middle of my desk: Dale Anderson wants to see you *NOW.* After being announced, I walked into Anderson's office. Angrily, he asked, "What happened in court?"

"The county won."

"The county *won?*"

"Yes, the county won."

"Well, I've just had about thirty constituents of Dundalk in my office for the last half hour, screaming that you had tricked them into believing that they were going to be witnesses, and then you never put them on. Bud, you realize that, if you had lost the case, I would have to fire you."

"Well, Dale, honestly, I hadn't even thought of that."

"Bud, *you* are the one who advised me to get *one* deputy, and, if he doesn't do the job, fire him and get someone who would."

Note: Richard A. Reid, Esq., attorney for the petitioner, filed an appeal from Judge Jenifer's ruling and was successful in having the case remanded for further proceedings, which I ultimately lost.

The Secret Investigation

Bill Farley, administrative officer for Baltimore county, was known as the guy who gets things done. On his desk were two signs, one saying "Do It Now" and the other, against a sailboat background, "If there is no wind, ROW!" Once, when neighborhood opposition was building against the paving of a long dirt road, Farley organized the county workforces so that they could begin a surprise paving operation at 4:00 a.m., the job to continue that day and into the night until completed, so that, by the time the citizens had organized, hired an attorney, and filed an injunction to stop the paving, the road would be a *fait accompli*.

As deputy county attorney, I received a call around 11:00 a.m. "Mr. Farley would like to see you in his office right away." I entered Farley's office, and he asked me to follow him. He opened the door to his private conference room. When I entered, he closed the door. There, seated at the table, was a young woman. Farley said, "Bud, this is Paula Raymond, a reporter for the *Baltimore News American*. She has brought me a county story that is so hypersensitive that you and I are the only two Baltimore county personnel who are going to know about it. I'm not telling Dale, the county executive, and you are not to tell anyone in your office. Ms. Raymond has agreed to divulge the story to us solely on condition that we keep it absolutely secret while you investigate it. When you have completed your investigation, she is to get an exclusive release, which I've agreed to give her. Ms. Raymond, please tell us the story."

"If either of you leak the story, my source will be blown. I will trust both of you to keep your word."

Farley reassured her, "You can rely upon us, Ms. Raymond."

Ms. Raymond began. "A man named Joseph Ferino was sentenced to three months at the Towson jail for gambling and distribution violations. He started his sentence on March first and has been in the jail for about three weeks. My source reliably informs me that, several nights each week, an automobile pulls into the darkest part of the jail parking lot and that Ferino is allowed to leave the jail and enter the automobile, where a lady is waiting to grant him sexual favors. She also brings him drugs which he not only uses himself but distributes to other prisoners in the jail."

"Wow," was my reaction.

Farley spoke. "Bud, I want you, personally, to conduct the entire investigation of this matter. I don't want anyone in Baltimore county government to get wind of this. Ferino has gotten to someone at the jail who could be doing the same sort of thing for other prisoners, besides engaging in who knows what other illegal activities. Incidentally, don't even tell me how you are going to investigate this matter. Use non-county resources, and do it entirely on your own. I've given Ms. Raymond my assurance that her information will be treated with the highest degree of secrecy and that she will be the first to break the story."

As I emerged from Farley's office at almost noon, I decided to go to lunch at the Towson House, where lawyers and judges ate regularly. During lunch, I gave no thought to my newest assignment, but, as I was returning to the county law office, I decided that I had better call Frank Alessi, the private detective I used in my divorce cases. I was reaching for my phone when it rang. A lawyer friend of mine asked, "Bud, how's the investigation coming?"

I was dumbfounded!

"What investigation?"

"The one in which you're checking about the prisoner who's getting sex and drugs while locked up in the Towson jail."

"Where on earth did you ever hear such a wild story?"

"Bud, I'm looking at the story in this afternoon's *Baltimore News American*. It says that Farley has appointed you to investigate the shenanigans, and you are to report only to him."

"Is there a by-line on the story?"

"Let me look. Yes, the by-line is Paula Raymond, exclusive to the *News American*."

Non-Legal Advice

Gisele G., looking bereft, sat across from my desk. She was a tall lady, slightly overweight, her hair hanging in short unkempt clumps. She certainly doesn't look like a woman named Gisele, I thought.

"Donald left me exactly twenty-two days ago. We have no children. It wasn't that we had had a loving, exciting marriage. We were just sort of comfortable. I am principal of a high school, Donald is a graphic designer and very artsy, but he handled all the business affairs for both of us. In fact, I don't even know how to take care of a checkbook. I would give my paycheck to Donald. He would deposit it, pay all of the bills, and take care of our financial affairs."

"Why did Donald leave?"

"We lived at an apartment complex in Towson. I didn't want to move there, but Donald insisted. He loved to mingle with the younger crowd that lived there. He spent every available moment at the pool, even when I was at school. His hours were much more flexible than mine."

"Tell me your respective salaries."

"I make about fifty thousand dollars per year, and Donald made, I believe, about twenty to twenty-five thousand dollars."

"You haven't told me why Donald left."

"Last year, a couple of attractive females moved into our complex. One had just gotten a divorce, and she moved in with a single friend of hers. I could tell that Donald was particularly intrigued with the recent divorcee. After he met her, he became even more obsessed with going to the pool. I'm sure that they met to swim together while I was at work. I had to go away for a three-day teachers' convention, and, when I returned, Donald's belongings were gone, and he had left this note for me."

I read the note:

Gisele,

Carol has been transferred to New York by her company, and I'm going with her. I've always felt that I needed to get myself into the New York market, and Carol and I are in love. I don't want to hurt you, but, as I look down the road

*of our marriage, I know what's in store. You are satisfied
with being comfortable, but I want a more exciting and
fulfilling life, which I anticipate having with Carol in New
York.*

*I won't contest your getting a divorce. You make more money
than I, you have your career in education, and I must now
follow my love and begin pursuing my career in earnest. As
soon as Carol and I settle, I'll let you know how you can get
in touch with me.*

Have a good life.

Donald

I looked up at Gisele. Slouched in her chair, she had a forlorn look about her.
"I was so shocked when I got that letter. My first feeling was overpowering fear and
insecurity. I am afraid to sleep in the apartment alone, just because Donald isn't there.
I know that I have a master's degree in education, I'm working on my doctorate, and
I'm principal of a school. But Donald handled all the taxes, paid the bills, and made
all the important decisions in my life. I have been seriously thinking about suicide. I
go to the library to read books about suicide, although I am careful not to check them
out."

She slumped into her chair, exhausted by her stream-of-consciousness
revelation.

"Well, I believe that you are wrong to blame yourself for Donald's leaving. I see
Donald leaving for entirely different reasons."

Gisele came slightly out of her slouch and asked, "For example?"

"I believe that Donald felt himself a kept man. You were earning substantially
more money than he, you had a job in which you were in charge of an entire school,
whereas he worked, catch-as-catch-can, sporadically. Basically, Donald was simply
trading one meal ticket for another, and...."

Gisele interrupted me. "Okay. What should I do now?"

"You should leave my office, resolved to begin a new life of pretense. If you are
afraid, pretend to be fearless. If you feel weak, pretend to be strong. Eventually, your
pretenses will become realities - if you consistently pretend."

"How can I develop the strength to pretend? I really am afraid of the future."

"Well, you're about to get non-legal advice from a lawyer. First, I suggest that you should sign up for a course offered by Goucher College called, "What Women Should Know About Their Finances." This course is designed to help women who are recently widowed or divorced acclimate themselves to the realities of the financial world. You will learn how to budget expenses, do your banking, and how to handle your investments. I've sent previous clients to the course, and they have told me that it is worthwhile. Additionally, I just saw in the *Baltimore Sun* that Montgomery Ward is offering a modeling course, which teaches ladies how to walk, how to do makeup, and good posture. As to clothes, ask any friend whose wardrobe you admire where she shops. Think about all of your friends and decide which of them you think has hair which is most attractive. Go to her hairdresser. A new hairstyle may make you feel better about yourself. Join a fitness center and hire a personal trainer who can teach you exercises that will make you feel better about yourself."

"Well, you've given me a lot to think about. Thank you."

A year later, the requisite separation period had elapsed, and the parties were ready to sign a marital settlement agreement. My secretary informed me that Donald G. and his attorney had arrived. I asked her to send them both into my office. Seconds later, I was buzzed again. "Mrs. G. is here."

"Send her in also."

The door opened, and Donald G.'s attorney entered, followed by a balding and stoopshouldered man, who closed the door behind him. A moment later, the door opened again, and into the office strode an erect Gisele G., her hair stylishly coifed, a sleek suit setting off her statuesque and slender body. She smiled condescendingly at her husband, whose eyes opened wide.

Divorce Sampler

In 1960, I had just opened my office in Towson, and Mr. B. came in to see me about his divorce problem. Mr. B. and his wife had no children, and they lived in a rural section of upper Baltimore county, where Mr. B. owned and operated a general store, which was open seven days a week and sold fresh produce, groceries, clothing and hardware. Mr. B. worked about ten hours a day, seven days a week, and Mrs. B. was not employed. Mr. B. said "In a small town, everyone gets to know everything. I'd heard that my wife was fooling around with John Bishop, the town barber. I confronted her, and she admitted it. I can't stay married to her, so I came to see you about getting a divorce."

I explained that, ethically, my first duty as an attorney was to try to reconcile the parties and save the marriage. Mr. B. admitted that this had been Mrs. B.'s first indiscretion, and that the barber was a notorious ladies' man. Still, Mr. B. did not feel that he could forgive his wife. I advised that he should make one attempt to try to reconcile the marriage. In about a week, Mr. B. called to let me know that he had indeed forgiven his wife and that they were now fully reconciled. Mr. B. thanked me for saving his marriage. Gosh, I thought, in my first divorce case, I saved the marriage, but I didn't make any money.

A couple of weeks later, I received another call from Mr. B., informing me that, even though Mrs. B. had given up the barber, she had now taken up with the owner of the only filling station in town. "This time I'm going to go ahead and file the suit. Don't talk to me anymore about reconciliation. All my wife did was move from the barber shop to the gas station."

In short order, I filed a complaint for divorce against Mrs. B., charging her with adultery with a man who would be identified at the hearing of this case. About two weeks later, I received another call from Mr. B.: "Word has gotten around town that I have filed suit charging my wife with adultery."

"Well, that was to be expected. You certainly understood that when you left my office the last time."

Mr. B. replied, "Well, of course, I expected you to file suit. What I didn't expect was that, in four days, three different married men in town would come to my store, each of them pleading with me not to name him as the one carrying on with my wife, and the gas station jockey and the barber were not among the three."

~ ~ ~ ~ ~

Just after my marriage in 1969, I was an associate with a firm which concentrated its practice in divorce and custody cases. My bride met me for lunch one day, following which we returned to my office at 1:00 p.m., where I was told, "Bud, you've got to hop into your car and get to Annapolis by 2:15. Our client is being deposed by Joel Hartz. Wally was supposed to defend the deposition, but he's tied up."

"What's the case about?," I asked.

"Divorce, of course. We represent the wife, and, as you may know, Hartz is a very tough and experienced hombre."

As Joan and I entered my office, I asked her: "Hey, why not drive to Annapolis with me? You can go shopping, while I attend the deposition. When the deposition is over, we can stroll around the harbor and have a romantic dinner overlooking the water."

"Great," Joan responded.

I grabbed the file, and, with Joan, raced to Annapolis, arriving at Hartz's office three minutes before the deposition was scheduled to begin. I introduced myself to my client, Mrs. M., a rotund, unpleasant-looking woman. The deposition began, and, after the usual preliminaries, a line of questions from Hartz caught my attention.

"On September twenty-fourth of this year, did you happen to be driving your car on Doyle Road just outside of Glen Burnie?"

"Yes," answered Mrs. M.

"What happened?"

"I lost control of my car."

"And?"

"My car went off of Doyle Road."

"When your car left Doyle Road, where did it go?"

"Onto someone's property."

"Please describe what happened."

"Well, my car was out of control and on this lawn."

"Where was your out-of-control car headed?"

"My car was heading towards a white-haired lady."

"What was this lady doing at the time?"

"This lady was tending to a rather pathetic garden."

"Can you identify this lady for the record?"

"Yes, the lady is my mother-in-law."

Although the office was air-conditioned, I sensed perspiration on my brow.

"What did your mother-in-law do?"

"When my mother-in-law saw my car approaching, she began hobbling as rapidly as she could toward the steps of her house."

"Do you know your mother-in-law's age?"

"I believe that she is eighty-four."

"What happened then?"

"My car was getting close to her, but my mother-in-law reached her steps and started up to her porch. I was suddenly able to re-gain control of my car and guided it back on to Doyle Road. Then, I drove home."

That colloquy set the tone for the rest of Mrs. M.'s deposition, which, unfortunately for me (and Mrs. M.), lasted four more hours. Before dinner that evening, overlooking the beautiful Severn River, instead of my usual scotch and soda, I opted for a martini.

~ ~ ~ ~ ~

In 1979, Mr. W. came to see me about his divorce case. He and his wife had had no children, and, after seven years of marriage, his wife had suddenly left him and gone to live with a high school sweetheart who had recently been divorced in South Carolina. As Mr. W. told the story, he began crying.

"I can see that you cared for your wife very much."

Mr. W.'s eyes opened wide. He stopped crying. "Well, Mr. George, actually, no. My wife and I were miserably unhappy living together. In fact, we didn't even like each other."

"Well, if you were miserable living together as husband and wife, why are you crying now that she's left?"

Mr. W. hesitated before answering. "Well, I was miserable being married, but at least it was something."

"Mr. W., tell me about the high school boyfriend with whom she's now living in South Carolina."

"I know his name, and I know that he has a lot of money which he inherited from his father."

"Well, I'll tell you what I think we should do. I think I should contact him in South Carolina and inform him that Maryland allows a lawsuit called criminal conversation, which makes a man who is having a sexual relationship with a married woman responsible in money damages to her husband. Actually, looking at your case information sheet, your wife and you own your house as tenants by the entireties, and you and she have bought some stock together. How about if I offer to forego the criminal conversation action on your part against him, in return for your wife's conveying to you her interest in the house and the stock you own jointly."

Mr. W. suddenly became enthusiastic about his case. "Hey, that would be great!"

Within three weeks, I had contacted the South Carolina boyfriend and Mrs. W., and an agreement was quickly signed. Mr. W. would file suit for divorce on adultery, and the property settlement agreement provided that Mrs. W. would give Mr. W. her interest in the W. house and the jointly held stock, in return for which Mr. W. released all of his rights and remedies under Maryland's criminal conversation law.

Three weeks after Mrs. W.'s deed to Mr. W. of her interest in the house property had been recorded, the jointly-held stock had been re-issued to Mr. W.'s sole name, and the divorce had been granted, my morning mail brought me the *Daily Record* (Maryland's legal newspaper), and I saw, emblazoned as a headline, Criminal Conversation Abolished in Maryland. Since only a man could sue or be sued for criminal conversation, the Maryland Court of Appeals had just declared criminal conversation unconstitutional because women could not participate in its benefits.

~ ~ ~ ~ ~

Jim P., a manufacturers' rep., told me why he needed a lawyer. "I have just established my first business on my own, and I want you to draw me up a contract which will prevent my salesmen from doing to me what I just did to my boss."

Jim was an athletic and handsome man who, although married, bragged openly about how women could not stay away from him. His wife Doris was well aware of the fact that Jim was unfaithful. Jim would run two miles every morning. Dressed in sweats, he would jog into nearby neighborhoods, hoping to chance upon an attractive female jogger.

One day, as Jim was running through a neighborhood at around 6:00 a.m., he was stopped by the police.

"There have been some break-ins in this neighborhood. Would you please show us some identification?"

"I have sweats on. I don't have any place to carry identification."

"Where do you live?"

"About a mile from here."

"Please get into the car. We will take you to your home."

Jim got into the police car, which he directed to the front of his home. He strode confidently to the front door of his house and rang the doorbell. After a few moments, Doris opened the door. One of the policemen asked, "Ma'am, can you identify this gentleman?"

"I've never seen this man before in my life."

"Doris, this is *no* time to try to be funny."

Doris stood there for a moment, staring blankly at Jim, but she finally relented and admitted, reluctantly, that Jim was her husband. It wasn't long thereafter that Doris and Jim parted marital ways.

~ ~ ~ ~ ~

The early days of my practice included many nights working in my office on Washington Avenue, across the street from the Towson courthouse. Asbill's Pharmacy remained open until 10:00 p.m., and my habit was to go into Asbill's about 9:30 p.m. to get an iced tea that would help me work until perhaps midnight. One night, I noticed a new customer at Asbill's. The next night, the man was not there. One night the following week, the same man was sitting at Asbill's soda fountain. He was not there the next night, but I asked the fountain attendant whether he knew who the man was who had been there the night before. He did not.

My client, Fern F., was a lady who exuded sex appeal. She wore short skirts, black stockings and tight sweaters. She was married to an ex-policeman who had been discharged from the force for psychiatric reasons. Fern's husband suspected that she was cheating on him. Although they still lived together, I was trying to negotiate a separation agreement with her husband's attorney.

One morning I received a call from an excited Fern, "My husband has threatened to kill you."

"Why would your husband want to kill me?"

"He thinks you and I are having an affair."

"Why does he think that?"

"Because, when I go out at night, he asks me where I'm going, and I tell him I'm going to see my lawyer."

I asked Fern to bring me a picture of her husband, and it had been he who had been frequenting Asbill's Pharmacy late at night.

I stopped night work until I had settled Fern's case.

~ ~ ~ ~ ~

I represented Elizabeth M., who was divorced from Reverend John M., Pastor of St. Edward's Episcopal Church, a small parish in a poor section of Baltimore city.

Reverend M. was consistently delinquent in his child support payments for Matthew, the couple's only child. Elizabeth M. had retained me to collect the arrearage and to seek an increase in child support. At trial, Reverend M. testified that his only source of income was his salary of five thousand five hundred dollars per year and that he had not had an increase in the two years he had been at St. Edward's. On cross-examination, I asked, "How many weddings have you performed during the last year at St. Edward's?"

"About seven."

"How many baptisms have you performed during the last year?"

"About the same number."

"And how many funerals?"

"About ten."

"Reverend M., in the joy of the seven weddings you performed last year, didn't anyone ever offer you a gratuity in any amount?"

"No."

"Reverend M., in the glee of the seven new baptisms, didn't anyone ever press some paper money into your hand?"

"No."

"Reverend M., in appreciation of a comforting eulogy, didn't anyone ever hand you an envelope with some money in it?"

"You know, Mr. George, I would prefer that you call me *Father* M."

"I'll call you *Father* M. when you pay up your child support."

~ ~ ~ ~ ~

Franklin W. was a successful stockbroker who had moved out of his home, leaving there his wife Laura, and their two girls, aged five and seven. Franklin, represented by Jim Turner, an aggressive divorce specialist, was seeking divorce and custody of his two children. He had gotten into a fee dispute with Turner, had terminated his services and had brought his file to me. I was amazed at the plethora of pleadings. I noted that Laura was also being represented by a contentious divorce specialist. During my first interview with Franklin following my review of his file, I gave him my opinion.

"Mr. W., I've got to tell you that, in my view, unless I am missing something about your wife, I don't believe that you are going to get custody. Frankly, I was surprised to see that without explanation, you had missed your five-year old's birthday party. You failed to show up for your seven-year old's first day at her new school.

You've almost completely ignored your children until you separated from your wife. You don't seem to have a great interest in doing what's important for the children."

"I've tried to settled this case. Jim Turner, my previous attorney, has had a number of cases against my wife's lawyer and is certain that he's not even passing on to my wife the numerous letters we've sent, trying to settle this case. What do you suggest we do?"

"Well, if your wife's attorney is not communicating with her, I suggest we ask promptly for a four-way conference, with both attorneys and both clients in the same room. That's the only way I can talk directly to your wife. Perhaps we can settle your case, but you will not get custody. You should make the best deal you can."

Ten days later, following a tortuous five-hour conference, the W. case was settled, wife getting sole custody, generous child support and abundant alimony. The essentials of the agreement were immediately typed up and signed by both parties. As she was leaving the conference room, Laura W. paused, looked at me and said, "If you had been his attorney at the beginning of this case, we wouldn't be getting a divorce."

~ ~ ~ ~ ~

Jenifer B. was a tall bulky woman who looked as if she could take care of herself in a fight. She and her husband Larry had been married for many years, and they lived in Hampton, an affluent section of Towson. Larry had always been physically abusive to Jenifer, and, on several occasions, Jenifer had gone to a hospital to be treated for injuries inflicted by Larry. On the day that Jenifer came to see me about her divorce case, she had already moved out of the house and was living in an apartment.

"Larry has always had a mean streak and a terrible temper," Jenifer said. "He's alienated himself from the children, and, as far as I know, he lives alone in the big house. He spends a lot of time hunting and skeet shooting. He is a genuine gun nut. I told him that I was coming to see you today so that you can file for divorce. I have been separated over a year, and I want to get on with my life."

Around 3:00 a.m. on the night following my meeting with Jenifer B., I was awakened from a deep sleep by my phone ringing. I picked up the phone, and, before I could say hello, the caller had hung up. The same thing happened the following two nights, with the calls coming in between 2:00 a.m. and 4:00 a.m. After the third call, they stopped. There was no caller ID in those days. I had contacted the telephone company after the second call and had tracers attached to my line, but they revealed only that the phone calls were coming from different public phone booths in the Towson area.

I had no more late-night phone calls until Jenifer came to see me for another appointment. Following that appointment, I received another three consecutive early morning phone calls. One didn't have to be high on the intellectual food chain to know that Larry B. was making the calls.

"Mr. George, that's typical of Larry and the way that his mind works. He wants to harass and annoy anyone he thinks is helping me."

Although I had never seen Larry B., I could visualize his evil face, grinning maniacally, as he got out of bed at 2:00 a.m., dressed, got into his car and drove to some remote public phone booth just so that he could awaken me in the middle of the night. Three days after the last series of phone calls to me had stopped, I arose from bed at 2:30 a.m., dressed, got into my automobile and drove to a public phone booth in a remote section of Towson. I inserted the coins, dialed Larry B.'s telephone number, and, when a sleepy voice mumbled hello, I hung up. I made other early morning calls to Larry B., but sporadically.

As often happens with men who beat up their wives, Larry B. was represented by a female attorney, Carol Bigel. The B. case basically boiled down to simply dividing the assets. Still, the process took months, during which, from time to time, I would get that 3:00 a.m. phone call. Once I got the first phone call, I would turn off my phone for the next several nights, chuckling to myself that I had thwarted Larry B., whom I could visualize leaving home in the middle of the night in order to call me, only to be disappointed by not hearing me being awakened by his mischief. On the other hand, I would make an infrequent early morning phone call to Larry, just to let him know that I was alive and well. After a call or two, Larry unlisted his number.

Carol Bigel and I had agreed on the basic essentials of a property settlement agreement. The only thing that remained was division of the household goods. Bigel and I agreed that the two attorneys and their clients should meet at Larry B.'s house on Wednesday afternoon at 3:00 p.m. Jenifer B. came to my office at 2:30 p.m. "It's going to be strange for me to be in the house again. I haven't been there for almost two years."

"Well, I think your husband is off mentally, and you are lucky to get out of this marriage alive."

With Jenifer sitting beside me, my car turned into the driveway of B.'s property. You could not see the house from the road, but, as we proceeded along the driveway, Jenifer and I saw, mounted above the garage, a huge, professionally-painted sign,

ANYONE ON THIS PROPERTY WITHOUT PERMISSION OF
LARRY B. IS A TRESPASSER.
TRESPASSERS WILL BE SHOT.

"Mr. George, that sign wasn't there when I was living in the house. I think he's really gone off the deep end."

"Well, Jenifer, I certainly hope that he didn't fake this meeting as a ruse to kill us. I still have two children in school."

Warily, I parked my car, and Jenifer and I approached the front door. I pushed the doorbell. The door opened quickly, and there stood a skinny man, barely five and a half feet tall. He turned away quickly, and Carol Bigel appeared in the doorway.

"Come in. Mr. B. has told me that he will not talk to either of you. He will speak to you only through me."

Jenifer and I entered the house. Bigel and I had an inventory list, and, as we entered the living room, Jenifer whispered to me, "Look, by every window, there is a rifle or shotgun, and on each windowsill there are shells."

When I asked, "Who gets the fireplace implements in the living room?", Larry said, "Ms. Bigel, tell them that she can have these, and I will take the ones in the study."

We went through the house, room by room. In a bedroom, we opened a closet, in which I saw a boy scout sash, bearing innumerable merit badges. Jenifer announced, almost proudly, "Larry was an eagle scout."

Looking at Larry, I asked, incredulously, "You... *you* were an eagle scout?"

As we entered the study, I saw a wall covered with pictures of U.S. Navy ships. I paused to look at them and saw a picture of Larry B. in Navy dress whites.

"You... *you* were a United States Naval officer and gentleman?"

Finally, Jenifer and I were in my car, heading toward my office.

"Jenifer, now that I have seen your husband, I cannot understand how you would have permitted that runt of a man to beat you repeatedly over the years. He sent you to the hospital, but you could have mauled him if you had wished. How come you never once beat *him* up or called the police and had him arrested?"

I will never forget Jenifer's answer:

"I love the man."

I have not restricted my life to dissolving marriages; indeed, I have often served as a

Matchmaker

At eighteen, I was required to register for the draft. I entered the draft office and was assigned a number. When my number was called, I was directed to a desk, behind which sat an attractive young lady whose nametag identified her as "Ginny." Ginny had a pleasant personality, and, during the interview, I invited Ginny to lunch. Ginny accepted, and we became friends.

I was attending Duke at the time, but, when I returned to Baltimore for holidays and summer vacation, I went out with Ginny from time to time. I dated Ginny sporadically during law school. Ginny was a smart gal. On our last date before I left Baltimore to go into the Navy, Ginny gave me a large bottle of Bay Rum aftershave lotion, saying, "Every day, when you slap this lotion on your face, think of me." Ginny's ploy worked.

Ultimately, I established my law office in Towson, and, more than occasionally, Ginny would stop by around 4:30 p.m. I would sometimes invite Ginny out for a drink. On one occasion, Ginny told me that she was tired of being single and wanted to get married. I immediately thought about Jim, a bachelor friend of mine, who had recently confessed to me that, since he was getting bald, he needed to get married soon. No girl would want to marry a bald-headed man.

I arranged a blind date, and the happy couple recently celebrated their forty-first anniversary.

~ ~ ~ ~ ~

Charlie, another friend of mine who wanted to get married, would tell me about young women who had almost met his exacting standards. One Monday, Charlie telephoned me. "Bud, I've met the perfect one. I went to New York to be an usher in the wedding of my college roommate, and one of the bridesmaids was really lovely, really personable. I could tell that she really liked me."

"Charlie, what's the problem? She's everything you want, and she likes you."

"Unfortunately, Bud, Kate is engaged to another usher. I got to know her at the rehearsal party where everyone was dancing with everyone else."

"Charlie, if she's engaged, how could you tell that she really liked *you*?"

"That's the fabulous thing, Bud. At the wedding reception, the bridal party were all seated at one table. When Kate's fiancé asked her if she would like to dance, she shouted, 'Yes, I would like to dance, but with Charlie.'"

"Charlie, if you are convinced that Kate prefers you to her fiancé, get on the phone to your roommate. Tell him that you are interested in Kate, and ask him to find out whether Kate is more interested in you than in her fiancé."

Charlie and Kate have now been married for over thirty-five years.

~ ~ ~ ~ ~

Jamie, my brother-in-law, wanted very much to find the right girl and start raising a family. One Saturday, at dinner at my house, he said, quite casually: "Oh, incidentally, I met a really great girl named Mamie from Scranton, Pennsylvania. She's a good-looking nurse with a great personality."

"Jamie, when's your next date?"

"Oh, I don't have any definite plans. Scranton is not nearby, you know."

"Jamie, why are you having dinner, *here* in Baltimore, on a weekend? You should be having dinner with that young lady in Scranton, Pennsylvania. As you and I are speaking, she could be meeting the guy of her dreams. Call her and book Mamie for the next three weekends. If she is the right one, you'll know soon enough."

Jamie, married for twenty-five years, has three statuesque, beautiful daughters who look very much like Mamie.

~ ~ ~ ~ ~

Arnold, my friend and trusted accountant of many years, died suddenly, leaving Miriam, his attractive wife, a widow after forty-two years of marriage. For soft-spoken, feminine Miriam, Arnold's loss was a terrible blow. Two years later, my client, Howard, lost his wife in an automobile accident. Howard's marriage had lasted forty-five years. Several months after his wife's death, I said to Howard, "When you are ready to start socializing again, there's a lovely lady I would like you to meet. I believe that you and she would find each other quite attractive."

Howard replied, "I'm not ready to start dating yet, but, when I am, I'll give you a call."

I ultimately arranged a blind date between Howard, seventy and Miriam, aged sixty-four. Four months later, I heard from Howard. "Harris, Miriam and I are getting married, and, in honor of your having introduced us, we plan to name our firstborn after you."

The Greeks of Gdansk

In the early 1960s, I got a call from a doctor friend of mine. "Bud, for the last couple of weeks, I've been working at Hopkins with a Polish surgeon who's going to be in Baltimore only for a few more days. She's been working day and night, trying to learn as much as she can to take back to Poland."

"She?" I asked.

"Yes, she's an attractive woman, and, you being one of my few bachelor friends, I wonder if you would take her out to dinner, sort of show her the Baltimore flag."

That evening, I greeted Dr. Hedwig Romanski in the lobby of the Hopkins medical quarters. She was indeed attractive, with dark hair and eyes, and distinctively high cheek bones. With a charming accent, she said, "Mr. George, I thank you for your kindness in showing me some of Baltimore."

"I assure you that the pleasure is mine."

I had decided on Baltimore's unique Haussner's Restaurant, renowned for its statuary, artwork, and bronzes, and she was impressed. "This restaurant is also an art gallery," she said, as we walked about, pausing from time to time at a particular painting or bronze.

When we were seated, for the first time there was a lull in our conversation.

"So," I ventured, not knowing what I was going to say next, "are you a Communist?"

"Yes."

"Do you like Communism?"

"Yes."

"You like Communism? May I ask why?"

"Well, before Communism, my parents and grandparents had been peasants. If it were not for Communism, I would be a peasant's wife, and my brother would be a peasant; instead, I am a surgeon, and my brother is an engineer, in charge of a factory outside Gdansk."

"Gdansk," I said, "isn't that the seaport that used to be called Danzig?"

"Yes, it is."

"Is there any down-side to being Communist?"

She did not hesitate. "Yes, Communism works socially, transforming peasants into doctors and engineers, but it doesn't work economically."

"What do you mean?"

She paused for a moment, "Well, for example, my brother's factory manufactures farm tractors. If everyone worked a normal work day at the factory, it would manufacture, let's say, one hundred tractors a month."

"Okay?"

"The Communist government would say that one hundred tractors a month is fine for this year, but, next year, we must raise the quota by ten percent—so next year the factory would have to produce one hundred ten tractors each month."

"That seems quite reasonable to me."

"Oh, but that's because you don't understand workers in a Communist factory. They would anticipate that the government would raise the quota each year by ten percent. Therefore, instead of working efficiently to produce one hundred tractors a month this year, the workers would work only hard enough to produce forty tractors monthly. This would mean that, next year, the factory would have to produce only forty-four tractors a month, instead of the one hundred ten which it could produce. "

"My brother, who is really a brilliant engineer, knows that his factory is producing far fewer tractors than it could—in fact, everyone in the factory—everyone in Gdansk—everyone in the government—*everybody knows that the factory is producing less than half of what it could produce*. But everyone accepts that fact, and lives with it, year after year. My brother is not challenged by being head of the factory. Instead, he is terribly bored, and he drinks to excess."

She seemed suddenly depressed and distracted. Thinking that a change of subject would help, I asked, "This, I understand, has been your first visit to America. Did you have any pre-conceived notions before your visit that you found to be false?"

"Yes, I expected almost everyone in America to be poor."

"Did you find any of your pre-conceived notions to be true?"

"Yes, there is much racial prejudice here."

Her tone seemed to become more upbeat. She continued, "It seems strange to find racial prejudice in America because, except for the aboriginal Indians, all Americans are foreigners."

She paused for a moment. "Where did your ancestors come from?"

I said, "My parents came from Greece."

Her face registered instant distress.

I said, "Does that startle you?"

She hesitated, but I urged her on.

"Well, in Gdansk, everyone hates Greeks."

"What? Why on earth would the Polish people in Gdansk hate Greeks?"

She answered coolly, "Gdansk is a seaport. When the Greek Communists lost the civil war, they fled by the hundreds from Greece. All the Communist countries were asked to find a place for them to settle. Some of the Greek Communists, who were seamen, were accepted by Poland, and they were settled in Gdansk."

"So?"

"After they came, we found out that they were not really good Communists."

"What do you mean?"

"Well, while all the Polish men would go off on ships from Gdansk, these Greek seamen refused to do the same. Once they learned that the government would feed and house them, they refused to go to sea. Instead, they opened coffee houses and sat around all day and all night, listening to loud Greek music, playing cards and drinking. Not only that, since many of the Polish men were away at sea, these Greek men began having liaisons with the Polish women whose men were not there."

She paused. "The Greeks of Gdansk are not liked at all."

I must have seemed amused, for she asked, "Why are you smiling?"

"I just realized that Greeks seem to be defined by the economic system in which they live. I know only Greeks who have come to the United States. They understood that if they wanted to succeed and to give their children a good education, they would have to work seven days a week, ten hours a day. They did it —and became ideal capitalists! On the other hand, I have just learned that if Greeks live in Communist Gdansk where the government will supply their food and shelter while they listen to Greek music and play cards—well, they won't work at all, these Greeks of Gdansk."

Gold Is Where You Find It!

It was hot and humid, as only an August noon in Washington, D.C. could be. I had just come down from my friend's apartment and was eager to get to the pool. I noticed that a guy lying on a towel near me seemed extremely fidgety. "Have you seen that beauty in the gold bikini on the other side of the pool?" he suddenly asked me.

"No, I can't say that I have."

"Well, she has a spectacular body. I've been here about an hour, and, from time to time, I swim across the pool just so I can get a really close gander."

I glanced across the pool at the beauty in the gold bikini and said, "I'll take a closer look," I jumped into the pool. Pulling myself up on the other side, I studied the bikini-figure—a cute face, but, to me, she was too well-endowed for the tight bikini into which she had squeezed her body.

I returned to my towel.

"What did you think? I saw you gaping at her. She's stunning, isn't she?" he asked excitedly.

"Well, for my taste, she is too Rubenesque for that bikini."

"Too Rubenesque?" he repeated incredulously.

"Well, that's why we'll never get in each other's way. We have different tastes."

"Yeah, but man, you are crazy. That gal is terrific."

We chatted amiably for the next hour. From time to time, my companion leaped into the pool, and I watched him pause at the opposite side, drinking in the beauty in the gold bikini.

When he returned to his towel, he said, "Man, that gal is super."

The door from the apartment building opened and through it came the lithe figure of a truly attractive young woman. Although she was wearing a modest one-piece bathing suit, I sensed something truly sensual about her. My friend was still staring across the pool, and I interrupted his reverie. "You can have the gold bikini. Here comes the one I want."

He glanced in my direction and looked at the approaching young woman. He was dumbstruck. "Not that woman—that's my wife!" He introduced us, as she spread her towel in front of both of us. Funny, but for the remainder of the afternoon, my friend never ventured into the pool; instead, he devoted all of his attention to the two of us.

Their Uncle, the Stock Starter

As a bachelor, I had always hated shopping in general and Christmas shopping in particular. After all, at Christmas time, I had thirteen Christmas presents to buy—for my parents, my three siblings, their spouses, and my five nieces and nephews. In 1966, I decided to Christmas shop for my nieces and nephews (aged six through twelve) from my desk, rather than by plunging into crowded stores. I called my stockbroker and bought shares of stock for each niece and nephew in some company I thought could be especially meaningful to them. I obtained all five stock certificates in early December, and, to each niece and nephew, I wrote a letter enclosing the certificate. Each letter contained the admonition that companies are like people—some turn out to be good and others bad.

I had selected only companies which paid dividends, and I explained that, even though their dividend checks would be small, good companies would increase their dividends over time, whereas bad companies might reduce or even stop their dividends altogether. Since Valerie's father was sales manger for Bethlehem Steel, I gave Valerie shares of Detroit Steel. In my letter to Valerie, I told her that she was now an owner of a company in competition with her father's company. When she received Detroit Steel's annual report, she should let her father read it and give her his insight as to how Detroit Steel was really doing.

My letter suggested: you should start to keep a chart, comparing the stock prices of Bethlehem Steel and Detroit Steel to see which stock outperforms the other over several years. Perhaps your mom and dad might match whatever dividend you receive, and you could buy more shares of Detroit Steel.

To nephew "Little Jim," I gave shares of Hess Oil because there was a Hess Oil station near his home. My letter to Jim advised him that, as a shareholder of Hess Oil, he should ask his father and mother to make a special effort to buy gas at the Hess station, and, while there, Jim should inspect the men's room to make sure that it was clean. If it wasn't, Jim, in the company of his parent, should ask to speak to the manager, and tell him that, as a Hess shareholder, Jim was dissatisfied with the condition of the men's room. Further, the manager should be put on notice that Jim (and his parents) would be back to take a second look.

My letter said: Jim, the future of the world depends upon oil, and the certificate enclosed with this letter makes you part owner of that future. Cars run on oil, homes are heated by oil, and wars are fought over oil. If you keep your eye on the oil ball—

and perhaps use your summer job earnings to buy more shares of Hess Oil, you could accumulate substantial wealth.

Nicky was an avid bowler, and he got shares of Brunswick Corporation. My letter to Nicky informed him that Brunswick owned a large chain of bowling alleys and pointed out which alleys near his home were owned by Brunswick. I advised him that, since he was now an owner of Brunswick Corporation, he should make a special effort to patronize Brunswick's alleys, and he should also encourage his friends to bowl there. I encouraged him to try the food. If the burgers were not as good as McDonald's, he should ask to speak to the manager, identify himself as a shareholder of Brunswick and ask him why.

I continued: periodically, visit other bowling alleys and see whether they have more customers than Brunswick's. If they do, try to discover why, and be sure to tell the manager at Brunswick Lanes why bowlers are going to Brunswick's competitors. Perhaps your mom and dad can help you write a letter to the President of Brunswick, telling him how he can attract more bowlers to Brunswick's alleys.

To my nephew "Big Jim," since he was an inveterate TV watcher, I gave shares of Warner Pictures, maker of TV programming. My letter to Big Jim said that television was in its infancy, and that, as owner of shares of Warner Pictures, he was in on the ground floor of an industry certain to flourish. Get your mom and dad to help you identify which TV shows are produced by Warner Pictures. Compare those shows with similar shows produced by Warner's competitors. Your mom, dad and friends can help you with their thoughts on comparing the shows. Maybe, in a year or so, your mom and dad could help you write a letter to the president of Warner, giving him the benefit of your comparisons. Getting the attention of Warner's president, could propel you to a career in the TV industry.

The Baltimore Hilton Hotel was being built in 1966, and I gave shares of Hilton to my niece, Tessa, with the advice that, once the hotel opened, she should make it a point to inspect the hotel, ask her parents to take her to lunch there, following which she should give the manager her input. Tessa, Hilton is one of the largest hotel chains in the world. People are vacationing and traveling much more now than they have in the past. As you get older, you too will stay at hotels. Every major city and resort in the world has a Hilton Hotel. Whenever possible, stay at Hilton Hotels and urge your parents, teachers and friends to do the same. Since you are an owner, this will put increasing amounts of money into your pocket.

Stock performances do indeed vary: Hilton, Hess, and Brunswick did well, but Detroit Steel and Warner Pictures went bankrupt.

Passengers

As a bachelor in 1969, I had decided to go to Greece about ten days before the family arrived for the trip to take Dad back to Kythera. I wanted to revisit Athens on my own—my first visit since my Navy days—and then I intended to fly to Rhodes for three or four days because Rhodes (I understood) was the summer destination of hordes of beautiful Danish girls. In the Greek Archdiocese newspaper, I found a charter flight departing from New York on an appropriate day, flying directly to Athens. I bought my ticket, and, when the date arrived, I flew first to New York. As I awaited boarding the plane, I discovered that all of the passengers on the charter flight were Greek, although the pilot and crew were American.

The flight was noisy but otherwise uneventful until we were approaching Athens. The pilot announced that, in ten minutes, our plane would be flying over the Acropolis. Although the fasten seatbelt sign was on, almost every aisle seat passenger unhooked his seatbelt and got out of his seat to begin peering through some window on the plane. The inboard passengers were, of course, already looking out of their windows.

It was night as the plane flew over the Acropolis, with spotlights highlighting the Parthenon and other temples. Pandemonium suddenly erupted. The passengers began whistling loudly, cheering and clapping. Someone started to sing the Greek national anthem. All seatbelts (but mine) were quickly unfastened. The aisles were filled with Greeks, singing. I was stunned.

For a moment, so too were the stewardesses. Then, they began pleading with the passengers to sit down and re-fasten their seatbelts. No one listened. The passengers continued singing loudly, and now they joined hands and began single-line Greek dancing in the narrow aisle. A stewardess must have alerted the pilot to what was occurring. I could just hear his voice above the din, "Please, be seated. Fasten your seatbelts. We cannot land until everyone is seated."

Still, the raucous celebration continued. No one made a move to sit down. Stewardesses were now struggling, physically, to push passengers into seats. The stewardesses succeeded with a few passengers, but, after being seated for only a short time, the recently-seated passengers would again jump up and join those surging up and down the aisle.

The pilot's voice screamed above the noise, "Dammit! Sit down! I'm not going to land this plane until every passenger is seated and belted. We will stay in the air for another hour, if necessary, but we will not land in Athens until everyone is seated."

Now, some of the seated passengers began shouting in Greek to those still dancing. Very slowly, with stewardesses pushing and pulling those still in the aisle—eventually—all passengers were seated, and the plane landed in Athens. I checked into the Athens Hilton Hotel and spent the next several days revisiting the archeological museum and the Acropolis. Finally, I was ready to go to Rhodes. I packed my bag, paid my bill at the cashier's desk, and, bag in hand, walked to the Olympic Airlines desk in the Athens Hilton lobby.

"One ticket to Rhodes, please."

"I'm sorry, sir, but all tickets to Rhodes have been sold. There are no tickets available today, or, in fact, for the next two weeks."

"What? I thought planes would be flying from Athens to Rhodes every several hours."

"Sir, to fly to Rhodes in August, one must buy his ticket weeks in advance."

"Does any airline other than Olympic fly to Rhodes?"

"No, sir."

I thought for a moment about those Danish girls cavorting in Rhodes.

"Can I get a ticket to Copenhagen?"

"Yes, sir."

"I'll take one."

Soon, I was on a Lufthansa flight heading to Frankfurt, where I would change planes to Copenhagen. As I looked around at the other passengers, I realized that no Greeks were flying to Germany. These were all Germans, returning from their vacations in Greece.

An air of relaxation pervaded the plane. Small groups of passengers were standing around the stewardess stations, chatting in German. The pilot said something in German. The small groups dispersed immediately, each passenger racing to his seat, and immediately buckling his seatbelt. Gosh, I wondered, is the plane in trouble? The pilot then said something in French, but, by this time, everyone was now seated and buckled in.

Getting alarmed, I was about to ask someone what the problem was, when the pilot, in English, said,

"Ladies and gentlemen, please be seated."

I had to smile, as I realized how differently Greek and German passengers reacted to requests from their pilot.

The Picnic

Mom had died suddenly in 1968, and the family decided that it would perk up Dad's spirits for the family to take Dad back to the island of Kythera, the island of his birth. The family was excited because, except for Ted, none of us had ever been to Kythera. In 1969, thirteen of us landed at Kapsali, Kythera's only port—Dad, my siblings, their spouses, children and I. Although we stayed at Kapsali's only motel, we were all eager to go to Karava, the village in which both Mom and Dad had been born. We chartered a bus for the next day.

Vasili, who owned the bus, was also its driver. We crowded around the bus and saw that it was old and its tires bald. Vasili, sensing some apprehension, quickly assured us that he was an excellent driver, as well as a master carpenter, expert fisherman, learned scholar of Greek antiquity, and a superb musician. "Besides," Vasili said, "this is the only bus on this side of the island." Thus reassured, we boarded the bus.

The trip was exhilarating. The road was unpaved, consisting only of two deep ruts winding through the mountains. We could see the valley far below, and the view was spectacular. Suddenly, my sister, Mary, who was sitting in the front seat of the bus, squealed. An old truck was coming down the mountain at high speed toward us, its wheels in the same two ruts as our bus's wheels. How could we pass each other? The road was only one lane wide. Neither vehicle slowed. All eyes were peering out the front window of the bus. Collision seemed inevitable. When the vehicles were about ten feet apart, our bus veered to its right, as did the truck. Our bus's wheels were now on the road edge of the mountain and on the ridge in the road between the two ruts.

There was no guardrail. Everyone on the right side of the bus, looking at the valley perhaps three hundred feet below, screeched simultaneously. It was a long way down. The bus then lurched left, its wheels again finding the two ruts. Miraculously, the vehicles had somehow passed each other. Vasili's voice boomed, "I told you I'm a good driver. I haven't had an accident....for at least two weeks."

The road became even narrower. Vasili announced that he would be stopping for a few minutes to pick up something from a relative who lived on the way to Karava. Five minutes later, Vasili pulled to a stop in front of three small houses and said that anyone wanting to stretch should do so. My nephews and I emerged from the bus. I saw three old men drinking coffee around a small table on a stone ledge outside one of the houses. Recognizing me as an American, they smiled. I sauntered up to them, and, endeavoring to make polite conversation, in my broken Greek, I asked them whether this was the road to Karava. The oldest of the three smiled even more broadly and said, "Monsieur, this is not Paris. There is only one road to Karava."

Vasili emerged from a house and headed for the bus, as did my nephews and I. The journey resumed, and the bus entered Karava and came to a stop at the village square, where villagers were waiting to greet us. We got off the bus, and the villagers, most of whom were aged, began hugging and kissing Dad and Ted. Soon, the George family was introduced to the villagers, some of whom were our relatives who had not seen Dad or Ted since 1933, when Dad, Mom and Ted (then sixteen) had visited Kythera.

I began chatting with *Thee-ah Ma-ria* ("Aunt Mary") who, when a little girl, had been a playmate of my mother's. Aunt Mary told me that, when she was a child, her parents had left Karava to emigrate to Australia, where she had spent most of her life. When she was sixty, she had been diagnosed with a terminal illness and given only six months to live. She decided to spend those last six months on Kythera—and she was now seventy-five! Although frail-looking, she spoke with conviction and passion, constantly gesticulating.

The villagers had gathered because they were preparing to take the George family on a picnic. Unfortunately, Dad felt tired, and he decided to remain in the village. The picnic had been Aunt Mary's idea. She would lead us to the miraculous spring, the waters of which had cured her of her fatal illness fifteen years ago and had kept her healthy and vigorous ever since. Baskets of food and drink, watermelons, various breads and Greek pastries had been assembled, and, at last, Aunt Mary gave the word—*Ba-mai*" ("We go"). I asked Aunt Mary, "How far are the picnic grounds?" She answered, *"Ai-na vee-ma"* ("one step").

Since I, at six feet two inches, towered over everyone else going on the picnic, I decided to take two large watermelons, one in each arm. As I picked them up, I saw that Aunt Mary, carrying a basket, was heading toward the edge of the square, away from the village. Carrying a watermelon in each arm, I hurried to take my place right behind her. She left the square and started down the mountain. I was amazed at Aunt Mary's sprightly pace. After some ten minutes of descent, the ground leveled, and we came upon a rather wide stream. There being no bridge, I assumed that this was the picnic site. I was shocked to see Aunt Mary jump onto a rock in the stream and then another until she landed, completely dry, on the other side of the stream. Undaunted, and carefully balancing the two watermelons, I too jumped from rock to rock and crossed the stream.

Aunt Mary, who had waited for me, now started up a small hill. The watermelons were beginning to feel heavy, and I called out to her, "How far are we from the picnic?"

"Ai-*na vee-ma*," came her prompt response.

Cresting that hill, we came upon a stony down slope. It was difficult to get secure footing, and, cradling a watermelon in each of my arms, I carefully made my way behind Aunt Mary, whose pace seemed to have quickened. I looked behind me and saw that the procession was moving steadily, lugging baskets of food and drink. At the bottom of that hill, my arms really began to ache. I couldn't stop now to put the watermelons down and give my arms a rest, I thought. I was the biggest guy in this whole group, and I've got to keep up with Aunt Mary. As we began ascending the second hill, I called out, "*Thee-ah*, how far?"

"*Ai-na vee-ma.*"

Both of my arms were now absolutely numb. Desperately, I clutched the two watermelons as I struggled up the hill, which was somewhat steeper than the previous one. I was silently exhorting myself to keep up with Aunt Mary. Finally, I saw Aunt Mary, ahead of me, put her basket on the ground. NIRVANA! I thought. I made it! I have kept up with (seventy-five year old) Aunt Mary. I put the watermelons down and flexed my arms several times to restore feeling. The miraculous spring was in a rock outcropping amid a grove of trees beside a swiftly running stream. Some of the villagers had brought musical instruments—a bouzouki, a flute and a mandolin.

Aunt Mary insisted that the first thing to occur was that each member of the George family should drink from the spring. Once that had been accomplished, the George family and the villagers feasted, drank and enjoyed the music and the comradery. After a half hour or so, my arms began to feel normal again. I chuckled to myself as I thought of the ordeal my arms had endured because of those watermelons. *Ai-na vee-ma*, indeed!

Soon, it was time to go. Everyone began collecting baskets, food and trash. I saw a small, old villager struggling to bring a metal canister to the spring. "What are you going to do with that canister?" I asked.

"I'm going to fill it with spring water to take to your father in the village" was his answer.

Inwardly shuddering, I said, "I will carry it to my father."

We retraced our route, up and down the steep second hill, up and down the stony first hill, jumping on the rocks to cross the stream and—at last—up the final slope to the village square. This time, I was hauling a metal canister heavy with miraculous spring water. This time, my ego did not get in my way. I stopped from time to time to put the canister down and to rest my arms. The villagers offered to help me carry the water, but I refused. Some of the villagers kept my pace and, when I stopped, they stopped too. By the time I reached the village square and put down the canister of water, I was exhausted, and my arms were aching painfully.

Many other villagers had now gathered at the square, eager to glimpse the newly-arrived Americans. There also stood Dad and black-robed, bearded Father Gregory, St. Charalampos' priest, clutching stalks of basil leaves in one hand and a small silver bowl in the other. Father Gregory made the sign of the cross three times over the canister and began chanting in Greek. The villagers bowed their heads, and the George family followed suit. After five minutes, Father Gregory spoke softly to a villager, who picked up the canister and poured water into the silver bowl.

Aunt Mary quietly instructed the George family to line up next to Dad. The priest, with Aunt Mary holding the silver bowl filled with water, approached Dad. Father Gregory dipped his index finger into the bowl and made a tiny sign of the cross on Dad's forehead, chin and two cheeks, murmuring the names of the Holy Trinity. Ted's forehead, chin and cheeks were next, and Father Gregory continued down the line until all of the George family had been blessed. He then dipped the stalks of basil into the bowl and began sprinkling the villagers, again intoning the Holy Trinity.

Father Gregory smiled, proclaiming, "Today the blessed waters have united the George family from America with those who welcome them to their ancestral home of Karava." A smiling Aunt Mary, putting her arm around Dad's shoulder, shouted to me, "Bud, your father has been blessed and is now fully rested. Grab some watermelons, and let's have another picnic."

Joan

In my mid-thirties, I had been a bachelor a long time and had dated many young ladies. I had decided that I wanted to marry a DAFI female—someone who was Decent, Attractive, Feminine and Intelligent. I pursued girls who were attractive and hoped that they would prove to have the other three qualities. I also hoped that if I ever found a DAFI female I wanted to marry, I would be lucky enough to have her want to marry me.

One evening, I took a date to Beaver Dam Dinner Theater. In those days, one brought his own alcoholic beverages, a buffet dinner would be offered, and then the theater show would follow. I noticed, as soon as we were shown to our table, that, on the other side of the theater was another larger table, around which sat seven older men and women and an attractive young lady. Since the young lady was attractive, I had a feeling that she was also decent, feminine, and intelligent. The problem was, of course, how to meet her. My date and I finished dinner, and the show began.

An acquaintance of mine, Richard Byrd, was the producer of the show that we were watching. He was also an attorney, whose day job was working as an attorney for Baltimore County. I was an attorney in the same office. During the show's first intermission, Richard walked over to the other table and began speaking animatedly to one of the older gentlemen. I thought that perhaps Richard could be my introduction to the young lady.

The next day in the county law office, I went to see Richard, asked him about the table he had visited, and learned that it was a group he had invited to the theater as his guests. He said that the wife of one of his guests happened to be sick, and the young lady was the daughter of the lawyer. She had attended in place of her mother. The next day, I called the lawyer, identified myself, and told him that I had seen his group and daughter at the dinner theater. I wondered if he would ask his daughter if she would agree to go to lunch with me on a blind date. The lawyer said that he would check with his daughter and that I should call him the following day at 2:00 p.m. I did, his daughter said she would go to lunch with me, and thus I met Joan.

Joan was as DAFI as I had hoped. In fact, Joan was so DAFI that, on our third date, I asked her to marry me. I assumed that she would turn me down, but, at the very least, she would know that I was thinking seriously about a relationship. Joan was taken aback. "How can you ask me to marry you on our third date? Let me consider carefully, and, when I'm ready to give an answer, I'll tell you. We need to get to know each other better."

Joan and I had been dating for about eight months, when, one evening over dinner, while I was expressing my intense displeasure about the Baltimore Orioles' latest trade, Joan interjected, "Incidentally, the answer to your question is yes."

"What question?"

"You asked me to marry you, and my answer is yes."

I was thrilled. We decided to get married sometime in June. Joan was Roman Catholic, I was Greek Orthodox, but neither of us went to church every Sunday. I said to Joan, "You know, if you, as a Roman Catholic, were to get married in the Greek Orthodox church, your marriage would be recognized by the Roman church. However, if I, a Greek Orthodox, were married in the Catholic church, my marriage would not be recognized by the Orthodox church."

Joan said, "I have been through Catholic parochial and high schools, and I graduated from a Catholic college. I cannot believe that what you are saying is true."

"I ask you to invite the Roman Catholic theologian of your choice to a marvelous dinner at Danny's Restaurant, Baltimore's finest, and you will hear this truth from his very lips."

"You're on," Joan replied. She made several phone calls, and, the following Saturday evening, she and I picked up Father Flag. The dinner at Danny's was excellent, the discussion scintillating, and Father Flag said, "Joan, it is difficult to believe, but Harris is correct. Our Roman church accepts the sacraments of the Orthodox church as valid, but the Orthodox do not recognize Roman Catholic sacraments."

Joan was flabbergasted. We returned Father Flag to his parish house, and Joan said, "Okay, we will get married in the Greek Orthodox church."

I went with Joan to meet with the priest of the Greek Orthodox Annunciation Church in Baltimore. "Father, Joan and I would like to get married in the Orthodox church, and Joan's parents have agreed to attend, even though they are devout Roman Catholics. To accommodate them, I ask that you perform our wedding ceremony primarily in English, rather than primarily in Greek."

It was 1969, and the Greek priest replied, "Bud, I will be happy to marry Joan and you in the Orthodox Church, but the ceremony will be primarily in Greek."

"But, Father, Joan's parents are making a concession by agreeing to the wedding in our church, and I want to make it comprehensible to them, as well as to me and to the vast majority of my friends, hardly any of whom understand one word of Greek. I really want you to perform the ceremony primarily in English."

"Bud, I'm sorry. The ceremony must be primarily in Greek."

"Father, let's get the record straight. I, a member of the laity, am not here to serve you, the priest; rather, it's the other way around—you, the priest, are here to serve the laity. It's the sacrament which is sacred, not the language."

"Bud, if you want to get married in the Orthodox Church, you will do it in Greek."

I replied, "Well, Father, in that you are flat wrong." Joan and I left.

A week later, Joan and I attended services at St. George's Antiochian Orthodox church in Washington, D.C. At the conclusion of the liturgy, Joan and I approached the priest, and I explained our situation, ending with, "Father, would you marry us in English?"

"Of course. I can certainly understand, since Joan's family, you, and the majority of your friends do not understand Greek, that you would want to get married in English." Shortly thereafter, Joan and I were married at St. George's Orthodox Church—entirely in English.

Joan was invited to her first George-family shower. Not being Greek, Joan assumed that she should arrive at the time specified in the shower announcement. However, she found that she was the very first to arrive. Indeed, some time elapsed before the second guest arrived, who happened to be a distant cousin of mine named Lilly.

Lilly, who had not attended our wedding, was delighted to learn that Joan was my bride. Lilly's parents had come from the Island of Kythera, and she began telling Joan some family history. When Joan returned from the shower, she informed me that Lilly had told her that one of my ancestors was a Scot who had settled in Kythera. I was stunned. "Joan, I've warned you that Greeks tend to exaggerate."

"Lilly said that if you denied it, you should call your brother, Ted."

Confidently, I called Ted, and, in Joan's presence, said, "Ted, Lilly told Joan that we are descended from a Scotsman."

"Of course we are."

Shocked, I said, "Ted, I've been your brother for over three decades, and you've never told me that we were part Scottish."

"I thought you knew."

Joan and I lived in what had been my bachelor apartment for a year. Then Alex was born. Soon, everything became too crowded, with Alex's playpen, changing table, crib, etc., and we decided that we should find a house. My sister, Boo, was our real estate agent. The plan was that Boo and Joan would explore different houses, and, when Joan found one she liked, I would then look at the house. Joan loved the first house she visited with Boo. It was on Huntsman's Lane in Towson. I arranged to see it the next day. I visited the house with Joan, Boo and the seller's real estate agent. I toured the house, and it was impressive. Standing on the front lawn, I said to the seller's real estate agent: "You know, I grew up in an apartment, and this lawn seems very intimidating because it's so big. I have never mowed a lawn in my life."

The house sat at the bottom of a very steep hill, at the top of which stood another house. The steep hill was all grass. Continuing on with the agent, I said, "However, I would *never* buy that house at the top of the hill."

"Why don't you like the house at the top of the hill?"

"Look at that steep hill with all that grass. I would have to spend my life cutting grass on that steep hill."

The agent said, "See that telephone line at the top of the hill. That is the boundary line between the house on the hill and your property. This steep hillside is *your* property."

That did it for me! I told Joan that I was opposed to buying the house on Huntsman Lane. "Besides, this is the very first house you've looked at. You'll find another one."

Joan was disappointed, but we left.

For the next year, every house we looked at Joan compared unfavorably to the Huntsman's Lane house: "Oh, yes, this house is okay, but it doesn't have a butler's pantry like the house on Huntsman's Lane." "This is really nice, but it does not have a wet bar downstairs or a sunken dining room like the house on Huntsman's Lane."

Finally, I said, "Joan, you win. I'm going to knock on the door of the house on Huntsman's Lane, and I'm going to say to whoever comes to the door, 'Whatever you paid for this house, I'll pay double. I must have *this* house on Huntsman's Lane'."

Finally, Joan and I found our house. It was situated in a lovely wooded area, but it had only a small concrete pad at the rear of the house. Since Joan loved the sun and I loved the shade, we would often sit in our chaise lounges on the concrete pad, Joan in the sun, and I under a large umbrella. From time to time, I would have to get up from my lounge to move the umbrella so that I could continue my stay in the shade. As we were lying there one day, I said, "Joan, we ought to build a ledge out from the house. Then I wouldn't have to move the umbrella around as the sun shifts. You could be in the sun, and I could be under the ledge. Actually, we could screen in the area under the ledge to keep insects out."

Several days later, upon returning home from work, I found a white-haired gentleman in my home. I asked Joan who he was, and she answered, "The architect."

"What do we need an architect for?"

"To build the addition."

"What addition?"

"The addition to our house. He's going to draw up some plans for us to look at."

You can imagine my shock when, upon reviewing his plans, I noticed that the roof of our addition was to be all glass. I said to Joan, "I wanted the ledge so that I could have shade. Why would I put on a new addition with a glass roof?" Joan and I negotiated vigorously for the next several days. With twelve roof panels, we finally compromised on four glass and eight opaque panels.

The house backs up to a golf tee which is part of the east course of the Baltimore Country Club. Because the tee was quite visible from our house, Joan, who is an accomplished horticulturist, plunged into planting trees and shrubs all around the house. She was determined to screen the golf tee from our view.

One Saturday morning, as she arose from bed, she looked out of our bedroom window and saw a group of deer feasting on some of her newly planted azaleas. She threw on a bathrobe, rushed into the kitchen, grabbed a wooden spatula and a big pan, and raced out to the edge of the garden area, where she began pounding loudly on the pan with the spatula, trying to scare the deer from her azaleas. Suddenly, she felt eyes on her, and she looked at the nearby golf tee where four golfers (who could not see the deer) stared at her in disbelief. One of the golfers had been ready to tee off when Joan had begun her pounding.

What kind of a woman is Joan? One day, as she was driving her Jeep with me in the passenger seat, she said, "Harris, it's a good thing you're sitting there."

"Why is that?"

"Because I just saw you going into that house on the corner, and, if you weren't sitting right here, I would stop my Jeep and pound on the door to find out what you're doing in that house."

DAFI females have their formidable moments!

A Second Language Comes in Handy

The value of knowing more than one language first hit home many years ago. Needing a summer job while attending Duke, I applied at the Paul Jones Distillery headquarters and was hired to work in a warehouse located in Essex in southeastern Baltimore county. I had never been to Essex and didn't know how long it would take me to get to work from Towson. Having to check in by 8:00 a.m., I left Towson very early the first morning and found my car pulling up outside the warehouse at 6:40 a.m. I had over an hour to kill.

I spotted a small coffee shop that was open and went in. A short order cook was standing behind the counter, and a lady was tending to the cash register in front of the store. I ordered a coffee and a donut from the man. The donut I finished in five minutes. I still had over an hour to go. I paid the lady for a newspaper and read it in fifteen minutes. Deciding to do the crossword puzzle, I asked the man if I could borrow a pencil. He handed me a short pencil stub, and the lady called to him (in Greek)

Pro-sai-ksai na mee klepsee to mo-lee-vee sou ("Be careful that he doesn't steal your pencil.")

I gave no indication that I had understood what the lady had said. I took the pencil, returned to my booth and commenced working on the puzzle. The lady's eyes never left me. At 7:45 a.m., I folded my newspaper, got out of the booth, and handed the pencil stub to the lady, saying

Fgar-ees-toe yia to mo-lee-vee sou ("Thank you for your pencil.")

~ ~ ~ ~ ~

My Navy buddy, Chris Sakellis, and I were bachelors in a Jacksonville, Florida hotel lobby, waiting for an elevator. A curvaceous young lady joined us. Chris murmured to me,

Tee o-ray-o ko-ma-tee ("What a lovely piece.")

Glowering at Chris, the young lady interjected,

Alla o-hee yia ta don-tee-a sou ("But not for *your* teeth.")

~ ~ ~ ~ ~

Joanne Potter and I had been childhood friends in Towson, and we unexpectedly bumped into each other.

"Bud, I just met a new friend from Greece, Alex, who is a student at Hopkins medical school. He's really cute. I'd like to surprise him. How do you say, 'Hello, how are you?' in Greek?"

"*a-lecko, sa-ga-poe pa-ra poe-lee.* Let me write it phonetically for you."

I scribbled on a piece of paper. How surprised Alex must have been to hear Joanne say—in Greek—

"Alex, I love you very much."

~ ~ ~ ~ ~

Joan and I had signed up for a Thomas Tour of eastern Europe. The tour consisted of four days in Budapest, five days in Istanbul and eight days in Greece. The tour had booked excellent hotels in Budapest and Istanbul, and when the thirty Americans on our tour arrived at the hotel in Athens, we were delighted—a luxurious hotel, conveniently located, with a superb view of Athens. There was, however, one huge problem—the hotel was stiflingly hot and humid because, as our group had been informed, the air-conditioning system was broken. August in Athens without air-conditioning was unbearable.

Joan and I were waiting in the lobby for another couple when an elderly lady on our tour walked up to the front desk and asked a clerk why the air-conditioning was not working. The clerk responded, "I am very sorry, Madam, but, unfortunately, the hotel's air-conditioning system is broken."

"*Psef-tee*," whispered a second clerk behind the counter.

Knowing that "*psef-tee*" was the Greek word for "liar," I walked up to the desk, and, in the presence of the lady, announced that I knew now that the air-conditioning system was not broken. Further, unless the air-conditioning system was working in time for the tour's "welcoming dinner" that evening, I would make it my business to see that Thomas Tours terminated its contract with this hotel and used another hotel on all future tours. At that moment our friends arrived, and the four of us left the hotel. When, several hours later, we returned, it was a relief to find that the hotel was delightfully cool.

As Joan and I entered the dining room for our tour group dinner, we were greeted by a standing ovation.

~ ~ ~ ~ ~

My brother-in-law, John, during World War II, was a PT boat commander in the south Pacific, and another boat commander in his squadron, Dean Lewis, was also of Greek descent. One night on patrol, when radio silence had been ordered, Dean, just to bedevil the enemy, broke radio silence and asked over the radio (in Greek), "John, before the war, what was the most dangerous situation you ever faced?"—to which John replied (in Greek), "Dean, I was playing second base for St. Johns College in Annapolis, Maryland, and Charlie Keller, who later played for the Yankees, was batting for the University of Maryland. Keller hit the ball so hard that it skipped between my legs before I could get my glove from my knee to the ground. If that ball had hit me in the head, it would have killed me."

In 1944, the Japanese did not follow baseball, particularly in Greek.

The King of Kompost

An apartment dweller all of my life, I had had no experience mowing lawns, raking leaves, or taking care of gardens. My marriage to Joan brought me fully into domesticity. When we moved into our present house in 1972, I gained much experience fast. A large lawn surrounded the house which had been built in a wooded area. Joan quickly set about establishing woodland gardens all around the house.

One day, as I was unloading bags of compost which Joan had just purchased at a local garden store, I asked, "Is this compost the same kind of stuff as leaves, grass clippings, apple peels, and the like?"

"Yes, it is," Joan replied.

"Well, we don't need to buy this stuff any more. I can make it here on the property. We have plenty of leaves, we have grass clippings, and we have kitchen waste."

The first thing I did was buy a leaf shredder. I selected a spot for the compost pile in our back yard which was in the sun, and I began shredding leaves. It was good exercise for me to rake the leaves into piles and then bend over, pick up leaves and throw them into the shredder. I accumulated the shredded leaves in the compost pile. I researched composting at the library. Soon I was adding grass clippings, coffee grounds, weeds, eggshells, and dirt from the garden. I created a basin at the top of the pile to catch water, and, at least once each week, I would turn the pile over.

On Father's Day, Joan gave me a compost bin with three sections. I put sticks in the bottom of each section to help aerate the compost, and I began turning the pile over at least three times each week. The following Father's Day, Joan gave me a present of five hundred baby earthworms, which I sprinkled into each of the three bins. These worms aerated and fertilized the compost.

I then read that the very first grass clippings of the year were significantly higher in nitrogen than grass collected later in the season. As I was walking past the Towson courthouse in early April, I noticed that the courthouse lawn was being mowed for the first time that spring. I paused and saw the workmen stuffing grass clippings into huge green garbage bags. One of the workmen identified the supervisor for me, and I asked him, "What do you do with those bags filled with grass clippings?"

"We put them inside the Dempsey dumpster next to the courthouse on Pennsylvania Avenue," was his answer.

I asked, "Please do me a favor and leave three of the bags in front of the Dempsey dumpster? I will collect them this afternoon."

"Sure, I'll do that for you."

At 4:30 p.m., I stopped my car next to the dumpster and opened the trunk. With much effort, I picked up a large garbage bag and plopped it inside my trunk. As I was hoisting the second bag, I heard a voice call out, "Bud George, what on earth are you taking from the garbage dumpster to spirit away in the trunk of your car?"

I looked in the direction of the voice and saw a Baltimore County judge, Kenneth C. Proctor, standing on the sidewalk.

"Judge Proctor, these are the very first courthouse grass clippings of the spring. They're loaded with judicially-rich nitrogen which has emanated all winter from the courthouse. I am transporting that judicial richness to mix into my compost pile on Timonium Road. Many thanks."

Smoking

When Alex was born in 1970, Joan said to me, "You've got to stop smoking cigars. I've read an article that says that tobacco smoke is detrimental to a baby's health."

Prior to Alex's birth, I had smoked as many as ten cigars a day. It was purely a habit, but I enjoyed smoking cigars. Because of Alex, I gave them up, and, to my surprise, I found that it was not difficult. (It was so easy, in fact, that I did it several times.) However, as I walked sidewalks or entered elevators, I became much more acutely aware of the aroma of a good cigar. Indeed, once, on an elevator, when I wanted to get off on the fourth floor, I rode all the way to twelve, because that was the exit floor for the guy smoking an elegant cigar.

~ ~ ~ ~ ~

My case was to begin on a Tuesday, and, on the previous Sunday, I needed to spend hours finalizing preparations with my expert witness. The expert arrived, a cigar in his mouth and a box of cigars in his hand, and he said, "I can't work for hours without a cigar." He had exquisite taste, and the aroma of his cigar was intoxicating. He asked, "Why don't you join me? These are excellent cigars."

I hadn't smoked a cigar for perhaps five years. I thought for a moment... Joan is visiting her mother today. I will arrive home before she does. I took a cigar, lit it, and took a puff.

"This is one *great* smoke."

My expert witness and I worked on his questions and answers. He was the keystone of my case. Hours later—and after I had smoked at least four cigars (to the expert's six), the conference ended.

Joan had not yet returned home when I drove into my garage. Knowing that my clothes reeked of cigar smoke, I took them all off and sealed everything that I had been wearing tightly in a plastic garbage bag (for later delivery directly to the cleaners). I then took a shower, shampooed my hair, and put on a smoke-free set of clothes. I sat down to read the Sunday newspaper, awaiting Joan's return. I heard her car pull into our garage. Joan opened the door, stepped inside and was greeted excitedly by Scamp, our little schnauzer. Joan immediately proclaimed, "You've been smoking cigars."

I was flabbergasted.

"How ridiculous can you be? What makes you think I've been smoking cigars?"

Joan's answer revealed treachery in my household. "Scamp smells like cigar smoke."

I then remembered that, upon arriving home (and before taking off my clothes), Scamp had greeted me so enthusiastically that I had picked him up for a moment. Obviously, my clothes had rubbed against Scamp's fur, which had absorbed and retained the stench of cigar smoke.

~ ~ ~ ~ ~

I also enjoyed an occasional pipe smoke. Pipes become intensely personal to their owners.

I was handling a case for an extremely eccentric client. During a conference, I was smoking my pipe while he was smoking a cigarette. My secretary asked me to come into the reception room for a moment. I placed my pipe in the pipe tray on my desk, excused myself for a moment, and left the office. When I returned to my office, I was stunned to see my client puffing on my pipe.

"Hey, this is one good pipe," he said.

"It's yours!" I graciously replied.

Poseidon

According to Greek mythology, Kythera was the birthplace of Aphrodite, goddess of love. As a young bachelor, I contrived my own mythology: Kythera was one of three small islands off the coast of Greece. Dionysus, god of wine, was the god revered on one island, all of the inhabitants of which had enormous capacities for drinking. The second island worshipped Artemis, goddess of the hunt, and everyone on that island was an expert hunter. In Greek mythology according to Bud George, Aphrodite being the goddess of love, all Kytherians are great lovers!

Incidents have occurred during my life which convinced me that at least certain Greek gods—particularly Poseidon—still retain great power, even today. In 1969, when my siblings, their families and I visited Kythera for the first time, we were all staying at a motel on a beach fronting on the Ionian Sea. Having arisen late one morning, I put on my bathing suit and walked down to the beach, where my sisters and their spouses were ensconced in beach chairs under umbrellas. It was a bright sunny day with a few clouds scattered in the sky.

I greeted everyone with a *ka-lee mai-ra* ("good morning") and walked down to the water's edge where my five nieces and nephews (aged eight to fourteen) were frolicking in the calm blue waters. My eyes must have appeared to have been still somewhat befogged with sleep because, as soon as they saw me, they all began to chant, "Look at Uncle Bud, still half asleep. Wake up, Uncle Bud!"

Their mocking, shrill voices got to me, and, with a grand sweep of my arms, stretching skyward, I intoned, in a loud voice, "Poseidon, god of the sea, punish these children for making fun of your devotee, Uncle Bud."

Had I not been there, I would not have believed what next happened. Before another word was spoken, wind suddenly began blowing toward me from the sea. Clouds quickly materialized, turned dark, and waves began to crest higher around my small nieces and nephews. The wind blew even harder, and the waters became turbulent. The sun disappeared behind the darkened clouds—all within twenty seconds of my call upon Poseidon.

My sisters came down to the water's edge and began calling in their children. My mind raced back to my school days, remembering how many ancient Aegean sea battles had been won because of an abruptly erupting storm. Eight year old Nicholas was the last to emerge from the water. As he headed toward his mother, he gave me a resentful look and whined, "Why did you do that?"

I developed a healthy respect for Poseidon that day.

Fourteen years later, Joan and I took Alex (who was twelve) and Jenifer (who was seven) to Sanibel Island off the coast of Florida for spring break. Sanibel was noted for having innumerable beaches, upon each of which were collected thousands upon thousands of sea shells. Joan and I had worked hard to make this an enjoyable vacation for our children. We bowled with them, drove into their bumper cars, and played miniature golf and video games. Mostly, though, we went from beach to beach, sorting through and collecting sea shells. Joan and I wanted to ensure that Alex and Jenifer were having maximum fun on their spring vacation. On our last day on Sanibel, Jen and I were walking toward the last beach we would visit (Joan and Alex were walking ahead of us), and I asked Jen, "Jen, have you had a good time here on Sanibel?"

"No!" came Jen's surprise reply.

"Gosh, why not? We collected hundreds of shells, played miniature golf and spent every day—from morning till night—doing everything that Alex and you wanted to do. What haven't you liked about Sanibel?"

"Well, in all of the beaches we've gone to, we haven't seen a single starfish. I really wanted to see a starfish."

"All right, Jenifer, let's ask Poseidon, god of the sea, to have a starfish for you to see on this last beach."

In a few minutes, we walked up a wooden ramp leading over the dune to the beach. As we started down the ramp, I could not believe what I saw—the beach was littered with many starfish. Jenifer gleefully ran to the closest one, knelt down in the sand, carefully looked at the starfish.

"Jenifer, Poseidon has delivered."

Jen answered, "I know. He's really nice."

The four of us began walking along the beach. Jen excitedly ran from starfish to starfish. Her quest had ended happily, and I learned again not to sell Poseidon short.

Not long ago, my law club—the Dissenters—sponsored a day of fishing on the Chesapeake Bay. The usual wager was made: he who caught the largest fish would collect one dollar from each of his boat mates. During our first five hours of fishing, fish were caught, but they were all approximately the same size. No one fish was clearly the largest.

As time dragged on, I realized that our fishing excursion would soon end. I had been reluctant to call upon Poseidon, but time was getting short. I thought: Poseidon, you brought the storm to the Kytherian beach, you delivered a multitude of starfish on Sanibel's beach, and now I'm asking you to hook me the biggest fish of the day.

I caught nothing for the next forty-five minutes. (Poseidon, what I'm asking of you is not too trivial compared to delivering storms and a multitude of starfish. What good does it do me to be your devotee if you don't land me the largest fish today.) Again I waited, but my baited hook was ignored until—all of a sudden—I finally felt a tremendous tug on my line. I started reeling in, but it was a battle. It seemed as if I had hooked a whale. My buddies noticed me strenuously struggling. Al Brennan said, "That fish is working its way off your line." Chris Kahl and Lee Parks wagered as to whether my line would break.

I continued trying to reel in, but I was having a difficult time. The captain had been watching the contest, and, after five more minutes, he said, "I'm afraid that you have hooked a skate, and I'm going to have cut your line." My friends cackled with joy. (Poseidon, have you cruelly toyed with me? You let me catch the biggest fish, but, since I can't bring it onto the boat, I can't win the wager.) The captain, standing by my line, held a small knife in his hand and leaned over the side of the boat. Suddenly he exclaimed, "Hell, that's no skate. That's one big rockfish." He sheathed his knife and grabbed a large net. "Keep reeling and keep the head of your pole up," he instructed.

Twenty-one pound Jumbo turned out to be thirty-seven and a half inches long, the biggest fish caught that day (thanks again, Poseidon).

Family: A Small and Crazy World

In July 1942, my sister Mary married John and moved with him to Newport, Rhode Island where he was attending the U.S. Navy's officer candidate school. John and Mary lived in the second floor apartment of an old house in Newport. There being no air-conditioning, the windows had to be kept open at all times to let in whatever breeze there was in the hot summertime. Mary had never learned to cook.

Mary's first try at cooking was a Greek dish which was John's proclaimed favorite—meatballs with egg-lemon sauce. Mary struggled in the kitchen for several hours, trying her best to follow what for her were gibberish directions in a Greek cookbook. When John arrived home, he ascended the steps to the second floor, and Mary proudly announced that she had completed her first attempt at Greek egg-lemon meatballs. John said the meatballs smelled wonderful, and he was famished. John sat at the table which Mary had set for the two of them. Mary proudly spooned some meatballs on to John's plate and carefully ladled sauce on top. Mary did likewise on her own plate and sat down to eat. John forked the first meatball slathered in sauce and plunged it into his mouth. He said nothing.

"John, do you like the meatballs?"

"Yes, but they're not as good as my mother's."

Mary waited for a moment, rose slowly from her chair, walked to the stove, picked up the large pot of meatballs in egg-lemon sauce, took two strides to the window, and heaved the pot and its contents into the yard below. Greek meatballs in egg-lemon sauce were now splattered over a large portion of the side lawn at 42 John Street, Newport, Rhode Island.

John sat transfixed at the table, aghast at what he had seen.

John was married to Mary for over fifty years, and he never—even once—criticized her cooking again.

~ ~ ~ ~ ~

I picked up the ringing phone.

"Uncle Bud, do you know where my father is today?"

"Val, your father told me yesterday that he was going to go to Golden Ring Mall to meet his brother George, who was going to drop off his wife there at 9:00 a.m. Then your father was going to follow George to some golf course in Harford County."

"But I got a call fifteen minutes ago from Uncle George, telling me that my father never showed up to meet him. I went to Dad's house, and his car and golf clubs are gone."

"Well, Val, maybe your father had an errand that delayed him. I don't know where he could be, but let me know when you find him."

As I hung up the phone, I thought, ever since Mary had died, Val had been worried about her father. John was a burly Mediterranean-type, large in frame, swarthily handsome, and with once jet-black hair turned gray. He drove an enormous black Cadillac convertible, so luxuriously mammoth that pedestrians turned to look as it drove past. George had told him, "John, I'm dropping my wife off at Hecht Company at the Golden Ring Mall at 9:00 a.m., and I will be driving her gray SUV. You wait for me at the entrance of Hecht's, and, after I drop Peggy off, you follow me up to Willow Green Golf Course in Harford County, where our tee time is 10:30."

At 8:55, Saturday, John, his convertible's top down, idled his engine across from the entrance to Hecht's department store at the Golden Ring Mall. After several minutes, the gray SUV pulled up in front of Hecht's and stopped. A woman emerged, turned, waved to the driver and headed for Hecht's entrance. The SUV started forward. As an automobile was pulling out of a parking space to get behind the SUV, John stepped on the accelerator, screeching his tires to bring his caddy directly behind the SUV, which pulled out of the parking lot and started traveling west on the Baltimore Beltway. Obviously, George is going to go north on I-95 to get to Harford County, John thought. John's caddy kept pace with the SUV as it approached I-95, but John was perplexed when the SUV proceeded past the I-95 north exit and took the next exit heading south.

"Where are you going, George? Harford County is north," John said aloud, dutifully following the SUV south.

Joe Bolgiano, the driver of the SUV, had first noticed the black caddy convertible when it noisily lurched behind him in front of Hecht's, cutting in front of an approaching automobile. The Cadillac had followed him out of the Mall parking lot on to the Beltway, and now, strangely, it seemed to be following him off the Beltway. I'm imagining things, Joe thought.

I'll wait until George stops, and I'll jump out and ask him where he's headed, John said to himself. The SUV approached a stoplight which was yellow. This will be my opportunity, John thought. However, to John's amazement, the SUV suddenly sped through the yellow light, and John had no alternative but to gun his motor and go through what turned out to be a red light for John. What is the matter with George, John wondered? We're still heading away from Harford County.

My God, the tough-looking guy driving that caddy convertible went right through a red light just to keep on my tail. Joe was becoming concerned. Why is he following me? As he approached a strip shopping center, Joe signaled a right turn into the parking lot. John did likewise. Joe turned his SUV into the lot, with John following close behind. The parking lot being almost empty, Joe pressed the accelerator, leaving John a short distance behind. John sped to catch up with the SUV, which pulled out of the lot and signaled a left turn into what looked like a very narrow neighborhood street. John likewise signaled a left turn and began waving frantically at the SUV ahead of him, trying to get George's attention.

Joe's mind was racing. The guy's definitely chasing me. If he thinks I'm going to stop, he's crazy. I've got to shake him. Despite the left-turn signal, Joe continued straight until he came to a stop at a red stoplight at the next intersection. Totally confused, John pulled up behind the SUV. As John opened the door to get out of his convertible, he was flabbergasted when the SUV ignored the red light and suddenly bolted through the intersection. John slammed the door to the driver's seat but had to wait because a truck was approaching the intersection. Seconds later, the light turned green, and John sped through the intersection, looking frantically for the SUV, which was nowhere in sight.

What's the matter with George? Heading in the wrong direction, not letting me catch up with him, ignoring my hand waves. It was as if he was trying to lose me.

"Uncle Bud, have you heard anything from my father yet?"

"No, Val, I haven't."

"I called some of the emergency rooms in the hospitals, and he's not there. I know that it's too early to call the police for a missing person. I'm just beside myself with worry. I tried to call Uncle George again, but I can't get hold of him."

"Val, don't worry. I'm sure your dad will show up soon, but let me know when you locate him."

Having lost the SUV, John decided to proceed to the golf course where he was supposed to have met George. It was almost 10:00 a.m.

"Uncle Bud, I called a friend of mine on the police force. I think that maybe my father has been car-jacked. His swanky black Cadillac convertible could have attracted the attention of some hopheads or carjackers. He undoubtedly had the top down on such a beautiful day, and he might seem like easy pickings to unsavory characters."

"Val, I'm sure your dad will turn up soon."

John heard a honking horn behind him and looked in his rearview mirror. There was an SUV, and it was blinking its headlights. Dammit, there's George. John pulled over to the side of the road, and the SUV followed and stopped.

"John, I'm sorry I couldn't get to Hecht's at 9:00. Peggy was late, and I didn't get there until 0915. I looked everywhere but didn't see your caddy. Where have you been?"

"George, a gray SUV pulled up in front of Hecht's exactly at 9:00, a lady got out, and the SUV took off. I was sure it was you, and I followed it. But every time I got close, the SUV did something crazy to lose me. It went through red lights, gave fake turn signals and raced across shopping center parking lots."

"John, you were following the wrong SUV. Frankly, if I saw your husky Mediterranean frame following me in that huge black Cadillac convertible, no matter which way I turned or in what direction I headed, I would try to lose you too. Hey, I better let Val know that I've found you."

~ ~ ~ ~ ~

It was 1905, and, on Ellis Island, a small Greek woman, who spoke no English, approached the immigration official who spoke no Greek.

"What is your name?"

Somehow, the Greek woman understood, and she answered "Yannoula."

"Huh, that sounds like Beulah. Your name in English is Beulah Souris."

In the Greek tradition, the first daughter is named after the paternal grandmother, the second daughter after the maternal grandmother. Thus, the second daughter born to James and Tassea George was named Beulah George. Beulah adopted the nickname "Boo."

When Boo graduated from high school, there were basically only two professions open to women—schoolteacher or nurse. Since Boo was likely to faint at the sight of blood, she decided to become a schoolteacher. Boo was personable, attractive, and vivacious, and she plunged wholeheartedly and passionately into numerous activities, one of which was oil painting. Boo signed her paintings, B. George.

One day, I looked closely at Boo's paintings. "Boo, you have real talent, but I wish that you would sign your paintings Beulah instead of B. George. There may be many painters in the world named B. George, but you may be unique as Beulah." Boo thereafter signed her paintings Beulah.

Towson was having an art festival in the courthouse yard, and amateur artists had been invited to display their paintings. Excitedly, Boo called to inform me that her paintings would be on display that coming Saturday. I said that I would be sure to check out her collection. That Saturday, I wandered around the courthouse grounds, stopping to look at various paintings, and finally I came to some that I recognized. I noted that some were signed B. George and others Beulah. As I was standing there, a lawyer friend of mine, Richard Reid, sauntered up, and, after exchanging greetings, he too began looking at Boo's paintings.

"My God," he said, "These paintings are signed Beulah. I had a schoolteacher named Beulah, and I really disliked her."

I said nothing. Richard continued to look at Boo's other paintings. "Gosh, some of these pictures are signed B. George. I guess the artist's name is Beulah George. Hey, Bud, Beulah George is not related to you, is she?"

"Yes, Richard, she's my sister. Why did you dislike her as a schoolteacher?"

"In my senior year at Sparrows Point High School, she was my English teacher. Every day of the school year she pounded into our heads vocabulary, vocabulary, vocabulary. We had new words to learn every day. We got vocabulary tests every week. Vocabulary, vocabulary, your sister was obsessed with vocabulary. I had vocabulary words coming out of my ears. And, these vocabulary tests were all Beulah's own thing. The other English teacher at Sparrows Point did not have *any* special vocabulary tests or exercises in her class. Beulah's English class had to do all the things that the other class had to do *plus* accommodate Beulah's monomania to teach her students vocabulary."

"Well, I certainly am sorry that you didn't like my sister."

"But, Bud, that's only the first part of the story. The very next year, I entered Yale University, and suddenly, I fell madly in love with your sister. Richard Reid— from little Sparrows Point High School in the eastern corner of Baltimore County, Maryland—possessed the very best vocabulary in my entire freshman class at Yale, better than the vocabulary of graduates from Phillips Academy, Groton and the most elite preparatory schools in the country. It finally dawned on me how lucky I was to have had Beulah George as my teacher."

Boo ultimately decided to go into real estate. In fact, Boo was the realtor trying to find Joan and me our first house. One day, Boo took Joan to look at a house for sale in Greenspring Valley. Boo parked in front of the house, and, with Joan beside her, Boo knocked on the front door. A maid appeared, and Boo said, "We're here to see the house." The maid opened the door, Joan and Boo walked into the living room, paused and looked around. "How garishly decorated," Boo murmured to Joan.

Boo and Joan inspected the dining room, kitchen and master bedroom. They pulled open closet doors and frequently commented to each other about the many things that could be done to improve the look of the house. They went into a large family room, and each agreed that it was decorated in poor taste. However, with a few cosmetic changes, the family room could be made quite inviting. They explored the club basement, garage and a utility room filled with dirty laundry. As Boo and Joan prepared to leave, Boo asked the maid, "Do you happen to know why the owners are selling this house?"

The maid answered, "I didn't know that the owners were selling this house."

Boo asked, "Isn't this 3412 Fallstaff Road?"

"No, this is 3410 Fallstaff Road."

Joan and Boo sidled to the front door and bolted toward their automobile.

Alex

When Joan was around eight months pregnant with our first child, I decided to prepare myself for my upcoming visit to the fathers' room at the hospital. I filled a beach bag with items to pass time for an expectant father. I put in a deck of cards, a cigar holder, two different types of cigars, a pipe and pipe tobacco, and Ambrose Bierce's *The Devil's Dictionary.*

Joan and I had been invited to a dinner party at this time, and she was attracted by one salad dish—tomatoes, onions and cucumbers marinating in olive oil/vinegar. I reminded her that she sometimes had trouble digesting onions and cucumbers. Nevertheless, Joan ate a portion of the salad. At least it was not fattening.

The next afternoon—Sunday—Joan, I and my entire family had been invited to the 2:00 p.m. wedding of a close relative. As we were dressing for the wedding, Joan was uncharacteristically silent. Finally, I asked, "Joan, is everything all right?"

She gave me a guilty look, "You warned me to stay away from those onions and cucumbers, and I didn't listen. Now, I have excruciating stomach pains, and the doctor hasn't given me anything for that."

"Well, I'll call the doctor and pick up what he recommends at the pharmacy."

I called the doctor's emergency number and learned that he was at the hospital. "Joan, we'll stop by the hospital, and he can give you something there for your stomach pains. We'll be late for the wedding, but we'll do the best we can."

Forty-five minutes later, the doctor, after examining Joan, informed me, "Joan is not having stomach pains. She is having the baby!"

"What?" I was flabbergasted. My beach bag was back at our apartment, and I was totally unprepared for any wait in the fathers' room. I couldn't leave the hospital to get the beach bag because the baby might come at any moment. I couldn't even call my family because they were all at the wedding. I had no alternative but to sit and wait in the fathers' room.

I wondered what Joan was going through. I had seen movies—women screaming in pain, sometimes for days. On the other hand, I remembered what my county secretary had told me about having a baby: "It's as easy as opening the door and throwing out the cat." And she had had four children.

The number of men in the fathers' room varied. Sometimes the room was crowded; sometimes there were just a few of us. Our sole communication with the baby world was a telephone on the wall. From time to time, the phone would ring. A man would pick it up, listen for a moment, and then call out: "Whitney!," "Brown," "Flynn."

One of those waiting would scurry to the phone, listen for a moment, abruptly place the receiver on the hook, and dash out of the room.

At last, someone called, "George!"

"This is Harris George."

"Go to the delivery room door," said a loud voice.

"What was it, a boy or girl?"

"*Go to the delivery room door,*" and the dial tone sounded.

As I approached the delivery room door, I noticed that the man who had just left the fathers' room was standing in the corridor. The door opened. A nurse stood in the doorway, holding a baby wrapped in a blue blanket.

"Mr. Ross?" she asked.

"I am Mr. Ross," said the man.

"Mr. Ross, here is your handsome son."

Mr. Ross took the blue blanket into his arms, and the nurse and he walked down the corridor.

Alone, I now stood outside the delivery room door. Suddenly, the automatic door opened—and I felt a sharp, stabbing pain in my chest. Two nurses were standing in the doorway, and each was holding a baby wrapped in a pink blanket. I felt faint, and my heart was pounding.

Looking at me, one of the nurses asked, "Mr. Coppola?"

Rushing up the corridor, a man shouted, "I am Mr. Coppola."

The nurse smiled.

"Mr. Coppola, I am pleased to present you with your two daughters."

My heart continued to pound. Two minutes later, the door opened again, and a nurse handed me a bundle wrapped in blue—my favorite (and only) son, Alexander.

~ ~ ~ ~ ~

When Alex was six, I was preparing to defend a case involving breach of contract. The evening before the case began, I had brought my trial book and exhibits home to review. I had the exhibits in a pile on my desk, and I left the room for a few moments. Upon my return, I was horrified to see that Exhibit #1—the very contract upon which the suit was based—had been defaced during my absence. In the wide margins and in the spaces between paragraphs, the very heavy hand of a small child had drawn numerous blocks, circles and triangles.

I tried to erase Alex's handiwork. Of all the papers, I thought, Alex picked Exhibit #1. My erasing didn't help. Alex had put such heavy pressure on his pencil that Exhibit #1 still showed clearly the indentations of many blocks, circles and triangles.

I summoned Alex and scolded him for having disfigured my exhibit. "I will just have to apologize profusely to the judge and to other attorney for what you've done to this very important paper! You should be ashamed for what you've done."

Alex did not answer. He stood erect, with his eyes floorward.

Many months later, I walked to my study desk and noticed that an insignificant paper lying on the desk had boxes, circles and triangles written all over the margins and top of the page. This time, at the bottom was a childish scrawl—Alex did this.

~ ~ ~ ~ ~

On Christmas morning, our custom was that Joan and I would leave the bedroom area first to make certain that Santa was not still there. Then we would shout "The coast is clear." Alex and Jenifer would race into the living room to open all the presents that were around the Christmas tree. When Alex was eight and Jenifer three, Joan and I were relaxing in our chairs, watching the children gleefully ripping wrappings.

Alex looked up. "Gee, Dad, I'm sorry all of the presents I got you didn't arrive."

"Alex, what presents did you get me?"

"Cheeses, lots of cheeses!"

"Cheeses? How did you pay for lots of cheeses?"

"I just marked the box 'bill me later'."

~ ~ ~ ~ ~

When Alex was eighteen, I was to take him to Lewisburg, Pennsylvania, for his freshman year at Bucknell University. Joan had broken her leg only a week earlier, and she was not going to accompany us. As this was Alex's first departure from home for any extended period of time, there were hugs and kisses with his mom and his thirteen year-old sister, Jenifer. Finally, Alex and I left the house, got into my car and started off toward Pennsylvania. However, only five minutes later, I realized that I had forgotten something and had to return home. When we arrived, Joan and Jenifer were surprised, but not half as surprised as Alex was to find one of his clothes drawers emptied of his Gilman School sport shirts, all of which were now piled up on Jenifer's bed.

"Gosh, Jen," he said, "Couldn't you at least wait until the body was cold in the grave?"

Soon, we were on our way again, and, a little over two hours later, we arrived in Lewisburg, Pennsylvania. Alex and I checked into a motel since the next morning was the beginning of orientation week for incoming freshmen. Early the next morning, I leaped from bed, and, as I shaved, I began to whistle a cheery tune. After a while, Alex said, "Gee, Dad. You sound mighty cheerful. It's almost like you're happy to be getting rid of me at Bucknell."

"Alex, it's not that I'm happy to be rid of you at Bucknell. But, you're eighteen years old now, and the law says that you are an adult. You *are* an adult, and you will be responsible for yourself away at college. When you were living at home, and you said that you'd be home at midnight, I'm the dumb doodle who would sit up, waiting for you at 1:00 a.m., worried that you might have been in some accident, or to some party where rowdy behavior had brought the police. I'd have all sorts of worries till you got home.

"But, Alex, one thing I do *not* do is worry about something that worry can't help. You are now an adult, going to college in Pennsylvania, and you alone are responsible for your behavior and actions here. It won't do me any good to worry about you while you are here at Bucknell. I don't know any lawyers or judges here in Lewisburg, and you really are entirely on your own. However, I do have something for you to keep while you are at Bucknell."

I reached into a bag, pulled out a pennant from Towson State University, and handed it to Alex. "Alex, I suggest you hang this Towson State pennant on your dormitory room wall, just as a reminder. If you do not apply yourself, or if your social life at Bucknell makes your marks suffer, you will transfer to Towson State. You will then come home to live again under my roof, and, each day when I leave for my office, I will take you with me. You can walk to the Towson campus from my office, and, when you finish your classes, you can come to my office and do your homework in my conference room. You know what time I leave for the office in the morning, and you know what time I come home."

Alex did very well academically at Bucknell.

Jenifer

When Jenifer was three, she awakened early in the morning, eager to get to her first day of nursery school. Excitedly, she said, "Jenifer's going to school with Mommy and Alex."

Eight-year old Alex said, "Oh no, Mom and Alex are not going to school with Jenifer. She's going alone."

Jenifer suddenly started crying. Mom asked, "Jenifer, why are you crying?"

Tearfully, Jenifer explained, "I can't drive a car."

~ ~ ~ ~ ~

When Jenifer was small, I wanted her to develop healthy eating habits. "If you drink milk that is not skim milk, it's like drinking white paint." Sugar was identified as the "white destroyer." Whenever Jenifer had ice cream at home, I sprinkled wheat germ on top.

Jenifer seemed slightly confused when, at a young friend's house, she was given a bowl of ice cream. She asked, "Is it okay to eat ice cream without wheat germ?"

~ ~ ~ ~ ~

When Jen was nine, I came home from work one day to hear, "Dad, I've volunteered you as manager of my softball team. The first practice is tomorrow at 5:00."

The first day of practice was a startling revelation for me. Although Jenifer handled herself well catching and throwing the ball (having previously played ball with Alex and me), many of Jen's teammates had never swung a bat or thrown a softball. I arrived at the first practice early, and I picked up the necessary equipment—several bats and balls, bases and T-shirts. I soon learned that conducting a baseball practice with nine-year old girls, some of whom had never batted or thrown a ball before, could be hazardous. Some girls, when swinging a bat, would release their grip, sending the bat flying through the air. Many girls had difficulty throwing the ball straight.

I called a quick meeting with the parents/coaches. Bill and June, both dentists, had brought their daughter, Christine, and Frank had brought his twin daughters. June explained, "Some of the girls here are from single mom households. Many of them have never had a ball thrown to them or swung a bat."

"Well, before someone gets hurt, we've got to devise a way to learn to play this game without danger to the girls," Bill said.

June volunteered, "When Christine was small, we took her to an instructional camp, where the girls stood about four feet apart, tossing the ball underhanded to each other until they had caught five throws without dropping one. When they accomplished that, each girl would take one step backwards." I said, "Hey, that sounds great. Let's do it." In short order, the danger was minimized, and the girls began learning how to enjoy (and safely play) the game of softball.

Some of my happiest times were the next three years when I was managing Jenifer's team. Some of Jenifer's teammates were her friends from Bryn Mawr School. Sometimes, during practice, the girls would dawdle, and I would consistently call out, "Hustle, hustle, time is money. Don't dawdle, hustle." This became sort of a joke to Jenifer and her friends because, as they passed each other in Bryn Mawr's halls, their greetings were frequently, "Hustle, time is money," and the girls would burst into laughter. I was amazed at the ability and poise displayed by girls with no previous experience. Given the chance to play, with considerate and gentle instruction, some of these girls developed into good softball players. Most of all, we ensured that all girls, regardless of ability, played in all games and enjoyed being on a team together.

As Jenifer turned eleven, I was in my third year as manager of her team. One day, I had had a difficult case in court, and it did not end well. I arrived about ten minutes late to find that the game had already begun. Jenifer's team was on the field, and I could see that the opposing team had already loaded the bases. Bill said, "There are none out, and Sally unfortunately can't pitch the ball over the plate."

Still bristling from court, I watched Sally throw two more balls before I snapped, "Come on, Sally, get the ball over the plate." Bill came up to me, put his arm around my shoulder, and said, "Bud, Bud, she's only eleven years old. Take it easy." I realized immediately that Bill was right. I was taking my courtroom anger out on this eleven-year old girl who was doing the best she could. "Bill, you are absolutely right. I've got to get myself in a different frame of mind."

At the end of the season, I told Bill, June and Frank, "Coaches, I am burned out after three years. I am going to have to resign as manager of this team." June interjected immediately, "Bill will be the manager next year."

Bill, dismayed, looked at June. June continued, "Bill, you've been a coach for three years. Bud has done his job, and now it's time for you to do yours." Bill said, "Well, I'll be the manager on one condition—that Bud is one of my coaches." Everyone looked at me, and I said, "Of course."

Letters were sent out to all parents about the managerial shift. The next year, Jen's team was playing its first game. Pitcher Sally did not begin well. She threw eight straight balls. Bill snarled his first managerial remark, "Sally, get that ball over the plate!" I walked up to Bill, put my arm around his shoulder and said, "Bill, Bill, she's only twelve years old. Take it easy."

~ ~ ~ ~ ~

By this time, Jenifer enjoyed playing another game at Bryn Mawr. To her friends, she said that she loved Satan, and that Satan constituted a very important part of her life. Only her close friends knew that Satan was the name of her family's Great Dane.

~ ~ ~ ~ ~

A client wanted me to shorten a contract I had drafted for him. I replied, "When I write a contract calling for the other party to pay my client a sum of money, that contract must follow the 'Jenifer Rule'. My daughter Jenifer is ten years old, and the contract that I draw must be clear enough to be completely understood by a ten-year old girl. Otherwise, the contract might not be unambiguous enough for a judge to enforce."

About a year later, Joan, Jenifer, and I walked into a shopping mall on a busy Saturday afternoon. As we approached an escalator, I saw my client racing toward us. He ignored Joan and me, extended a handshake toward Jenifer, and said, "Miss Jenifer, of 'Jenifer Rule" fame, I presume."

~ ~ ~ ~ ~

In her junior year at Bryn Mawr School, Joan and I took Jen on tours of numerous colleges. Finally, we asked her where she would like to go. Jenifer answered, "Actually, I can't make up my mind between two schools."

"Which ones?"

"Well, I like Duke."

I said, "Well, I'm not surprised, Jenifer. I loved Duke, and I'm sure you will too."

"Jenifer, what is your other choice?", Joan asked.

"The Naval Academy."

Joan and I were shocked, and I said, "Jenifer, you've lived in this house for almost eighteen years, and you have never said the word 'Navy' one time."

Joan interjected, "Harris, it's all your fault. You've spent your whole life telling the world what a wonderful life you had as a naval officer. You also have your study decorated with pictures of the ships on which you served *and* that Navy poster, saying 'The Navy Wants You'." After some discussion, Joan and I convinced Jenifer to go to Duke, where she could take Navy ROTC and have a far more flexible social life than she would have at the Naval Academy.

Jenifer did not have an automobile while at Duke. Whenever she was home for holidays or summer vacation, she would drive her mother's car to get around. One day, as I drove my car into my garage after work, I noted that Joan's car was not there. I thought that perhaps Joan and Jenifer had gone shopping together. As I entered the house from the garage, I immediately encountered Jenifer.

"Hi, Jen. Where's Mom gone?"

"Mom's upstairs."

"Jen, where's Mom's Jeep?"

"Mom's upstairs."

Confused, I started ascending the stairs of our split level home. Joan was standing on the top level, looking down at me.

"Joan, where is your Jeep?"

"It's in the woods."

"In the woods? What woods?"

"In *our* woods."

"What is your Jeep doing in our woods?"

"Harris, just walk out onto the apron outside our garage and look into the woods. You'll see my Jeep. Jen rushed home, pulled my Jeep up in front of the garage door, left the driver's door open, and dashed into the house. Unfortunately, she didn't put the brake on fully. My Jeep rolled down the apron, jumped the railroad tie, and traveled backwards down the hill into our woods. Again unfortunately, the driver's door, which Jen had left open, hit a tree on the way down the hill and is lying on the hillside. Go take a look at it, but don't be upset."

Jenifer followed me through the garage and onto the apron, at the edge of which I saw Joan's Jeep facing toward me. I also saw the Jeep's door lying on the hillside.

"Dad, I hope you won't be angry. I was just very careless."

I turned toward Jenifer and gave her a big hug.

"Jen, who cares about the Jeep? I'm just glad that you are okay and didn't try to stop that Jeep."

Jenifer has been a much better driver ever since.

Retired Lawyers' Malady

Every retired lawyer of my acquaintance has developed the same serious malady—his wife's putting on her overcoat invariably precipitates an involuntary conditioned reflex, which causes the lawyer to ask three questions of his wife:

1. Where are you going?
2. When will you be back? and
3. What am I going to do until you get back?

So I wrote this book.